# FOUR MYSTERY DRAMAS

## THE PORTAL OF INITIATION
A Rosicrucian Mystery through Rudolf Steiner

## THE SOUL'S PROBATION
A Life Tableau in dramatic scenes as sequel to the
Portal of Initiation
Through Rudolf Steiner

## THE GUARDIAN OF THE THRESHOLD
Soul events in dramatic scenes by Rudolf Steiner

## THE SOUL'S AWAKENING
Soul and Spirit events in dramatic scenes by Rudolf Steiner

Translated by Ruth and Hans Pusch

## PUBLISHER'S NOTE

The collected dramas in this volume were first published as four separate books. They were published as a single volume in 1978 by their original publisher, with the page numbers unchanged. This facsimilie reprint of that edition is being produced in response to public demand for the collected mystery dramas of Rudolf Steiner.

This book is a translation of the German *Vier Mysteriendramen*, vol. 14 in the Collected Works of Rudolf Steiner. This authorized translation published by kind permission of the Rudolf Steiner Nachlassverwaltung, Dornach, Switzerland.

ISBN 10 : 0-88010-581-X
ISBN 13 : 978-0-88010-581-1

# THE PORTAL OF INITIATION

A Rosicrucian Mystery

*through*

## Rudolf Steiner

*translated by* Ruth and Hans Pusch

# INTRODUCTION
## to this new edition.

In theatre workshops it is a new custom to call the script of a play a 'score'. This translation of the four Mystery Dramas wants to be read aloud and listened to, in the way we listen to a musical score. It is meant not only for eyes looking at the paper, but for ears, and larynxes that are active.

The present edition has tried to preserve the vitality with which the thoughts behind the words are expressed, and the rhythmical flow of the lines, so characteristic of Rudolf Steiner's dramatic style. Many almost insurmountable obstacles arise for the translator through the freedom of sentence construction in the German text which leads often to ambiguity. Difficulties come also from Rudolf Steiner's creation of new words, words that are in harmony with the spirit of the German language. He thus gives the spoken word a mobility and transparency through which spirit realities can reveal themselves. The English language rarely allows this kind of spiritualization. But the speaker or the reader, reading aloud, can achieve much by the way he speaks the lines: he has to put them into motion, by having the last word of the sentence in mind already at the start. Such a mobility gives the listener the opportunity to grasp quickly and clearly the underlying thought. This penetration to the vividly moving thought is the best a translation can achieve.

The translation offered here is the result of work connected with the stage productions of the Mystery Drama Acting Group in New York City and Spring Valley, New York. The amateur group, composed of members of the Anthroposophical Society, can look back to over fifteen years of stage activity with annual performances. The translations were kept in a fluid state with the help of some of its language-gifted members. Seven names stand out as main contributors: Arvia Mackaye Ege, Lisa Monges, Ruth Hofrichter, Christy Barnes, Fred Heckel, Paul Allen, Norman Macbeth. A special tribute is due to the first translation by Mr Harry Collison and his friends.

A thorough revision of the text, preparatory to the final printing, became the task of Ruth and Hans Pusch, both intimately connected with the Drama Group. What can be enlivened and stimulated, during rehearsals, and developed by the individuals who grow gradually into their parts has had now to be rigidly fixed on the printed page.

If this translation serves as a 'score' for the spoken word and the listening ear, it may live up to the challenge contained in the words addressed by Benedictus to Capesius in the First Scene of THE SOUL'S PROBATION:

> 'I do not wish my words alone to say
> what they convey as covering of concepts.
> They turn the natural forces of the soul
> to the realities of spirit.'

Michaelmas 1972                                    Hans Pusch

4

## THOUGHTS ON THE SEAL

The design displays two different forms, seven times repeated: one is narrowly rounded, opening toward the centre; the other, a widely curved form which opens to the periphery, with slightly thickened ends; the opening of the small form has thinner ends. The dynamics here displayed give the impression of a rhythm between contracting and expanding, directed toward the inner and the outer. From the periphery a force can be felt pouring into the receptive gesture of the larger curve. The dominance of such a force from the circumference has its influence on the inner form, turning it toward a central space which is left free.

In moral terms: self-centredness has to give way to the impact exerted from without. In this dynamic direction from the outer to the inner, responding to an active receptiveness for the outer, we have a distinct characteristic of the genuine Rosicrucian attitude: open your inner eyes and ears to the world of spirit as it is revealed in Nature around you, and you will find an answer to the divine origin and nature of your own being.

To affirm this Rosicrucian approach, certain letters are added, in a dynamic sequence. An E starts on the left side within one of the large curves; then follow, parallel with the circumference, D- N- I.* With the next three letters the placement changes; they are directed towards the centre: C- M- P-. Then, with a final swing around to the centre, three letters occupy the free space: S- S- R-. It is the motion of a spiral going from outside into the centre. The letters stand for an ancient saying which has been the secret core of genuine Rosicrucianism. In its threefoldness it expresses the essence of the Trinity:

*Ex Deo Nascimur (out of God we are born)* –

*In Christo Morimur (in Christ we die)* –

*Per Spiritum Sanctum Reviviscimus (through the Holy Spirit we are reborn).*

That these letters are added in such a dynamic way to the seal of the PORTAL OF INITIATION connects the drama with the historic current of esoteric Christianity. It is in its spirit that the action moves and proceeds from scene to scene; in these three phases 'of the saying' the characters of the play find their own growth and transformation expressed.

* In the design, the J is the curved form of 'I'.

# CHARACTERS

*In the Prelude and Interlude*

SOPHIA
ESTELLA
TWO CHILDREN

*In the Mystery*

JOHANNES THOMASIUS
MARIA
BENEDICTUS
THEODOSIUS, whose archetype is revealed during the course of the play as the Spirit of Love.
ROMANUS, whose archetype is revealed during the course of the play as the Spirit of Action.
RETARDUS, active only as a spirit.
GAIRMAN, whose archetype is revealed during the course of the play as the Spirit of the Earth-brain.
HELENA, whose archetype is revealed during the course of the play as LUCIFER.
PHILIA, ASTRID, LUNA } friends of Maria, whose archetypes are revealed during the course of the play as the Spirits of Maria's soul-forces.
PROFESSOR CAPESIUS
DOCTOR STRADER
FELIX BALDE, who is revealed as the bearer of the Spirit of Nature.
FELICIA BALDE, his wife.

7

THE OTHER MARIA, whose archetype is revealed during the course of the play as the Soul of Love.

THEODORA, a seeress.

AHRIMAN, conceived to be active only as soul.

THE SPIRIT OF THE ELEMENTS, conceived to be active only as spirit.

A CHILD, whose archetype is revealed during the course of the play as that of a young soul.

# SYNOPSIS

Prelude: Two divergent views of modern life are exchanged between Estella and Sophia. Their dialogue sets the background of the exoteric world from which the events of the Mystery Drama detach themselves as the expression of an entirely new beginning in our cultural and spiritual life.

Scene One: We witness the meeting of sixteen individualities, inspired by a lecture just given by Benedictus in the house of Maria. Their conversation becomes decisive for the inner path of Johannes Thomasius, the young painter. This first meeting contains all the motives which will continue in supersensible pictures and happenings: the doubts and objections of the two scientists, Professor Capesius and Dr. Strader; the awe-inspiring seership of Theodora; Felix and Felicia Balde's mountain solitude; the Other Maria's curative forces; Theodosius' warmth of heart; Romanus' down-to-earth practicality; Gairman's wit; Helena's illusionary enthusiasm. The impact of their joys and sorrows is absorbed by Johannes and leads to his first inner experience in the next scene.

Scene Two: Johannes' soul reveals itself to him as a landscape of rocks and springs, out of which resound the ancient mystery words: 'O Man, Know Thou Thyself.'

Scene Three: A meditation room. A child receives a word of blessing from Benedictus. Johannes goes through a severe test in his inner development by witnessing a strange occurrence between Benedictus and Maria. As will become more and more apparent in the Mystery Drama, the spoken word itself takes on a new force: the mantric lines spoken by Benedictus will transform themselves for Johannes into the experiences of Scenes Four to Seven.

9

Scene Four: With full-awakened consciousness Johannes enters the Imaginative world on whose very threshold he encounters cosmic beings from above and below: Lucifer and Ahriman. The elemental world becomes manifest to him. The Spirit of the Elements has brought the souls of Capesius and Strader up to a sphere from which they can survey the surface of the earth. They appear here in their true nature, Capesius young and Strader old in character. Then the Other Maria appears to them, arising from the rocks and transforming their speeches into forces which spread out over the surface of the earth, nourishing its elemental beings.

Scene Five: Before the inner eye of Johannes, the hidden Mystery Place of the spirit leaders of humanity is revealed. In a subterranean rock temple the four Hierophants stand, representing the spirit forces of the East, South, West and North. Felix Balde and the Other Maria find their way into the temple, because 'the time is now at hand' to open its treasures to mankind; that is, to lift the truth of the temple's existence into the day-consciousness of modern man.

Scene Six: Felicia enters the elementary world at the request of the Spirit of the Elements. She tells a fairy tale for the first time in human evolution directly to the elemental beings, stimulating and provoking by it the 'Earth's Brain' in the character of Gairman.

Scene Seven: The Spirit World. This scene, in which Maria converses with the three soul forces has been treated in its cosmic aspect by Rudolf Steiner in his lectures on 'The Secrets of the Biblical Story of Creation', which followed the first performance of 'The Portal of Initiation' in Munich, August 1910. He refers also to the part which Theodora plays in the spirit world when her seership reveals past events: an early incarnation of Maria as an apostle of Christianity of the Hibernian Mysteries. At the end of the scene, Benedictus speaks again mantric words which in their essence lead to the Sun Temple, Scene Eleven.

Interlude: Estella tells of a performance which has a similar plot to the Mystery Drama, with the fundamental difference that it ends where the latter begins. Sophia's words about the creative capacity of the artist and the need of our time to lift it into full consciousness form a kind of prologue to Scene Eight.

Scene Eight: Johannes Thomasius has painted a portrait of Professor Capesius. He has acquired the capacity of conscious penetration into the spirit background of the individuality. Therefore the shock which Strader receives when he realizes the cognitive forces active in art.

Scene Nine: Johannes' soul is enhanced by the experience of new spiritual impulses in himself. He is able to identify himself with beings and events of his surrounding world, thus widening himself into his environment.

Scene Ten: Johannes goes through intensive trials and illusions arising from his enthusiasm which carries him into a luciferic sphere of self-enjoyment and self-reliance. The spirit presence of Benedictus awakens in him cognitive forces, revealing to him the seductive powers of Lucifer and Ahriman. Through this act of cognition he is able to hear his voice of conscience, re-establishing his inner balance.

Scene Eleven: Just in medieval times the true 'mysteries' led to the secret of resurrection, so here in the Sun Temple the deepest secrets of spirit guidance become manifest. The individualities who have begun the path to higher knowledge find their places, for the good of humanity, within the temple under the guidance of the spirit leaders in wisdom, love, and force of will. They form a spiritual community, based on diversity, by which the retarding tendencies are overcome.

As the inspiration for the play originates in Goethe's 'Tale of the Green Snake and the Beautiful Lily', at the end of 'Conversations of German Emigrants', a comparative list of the characters can be helpful for a deeper insight into the ensemble of the play.

| | |
|---|---|
| BENEDICTUS | — Golden King |
| JOHANNES | — Youth |
| MARIA | — Lily |
| PHILIA | |
| ASTRID | — Three Maidens of Lily |
| LUNA | |
| THEODOSIUS | — Silver King |
| THE OTHER MARIA | — Green Snake |
| ROMANUS | — Copper King |
| FELIX BALDE | — Man with the Lamp |
| FELICIA | — Woman with the Basket |
| RETARDUS | — Mixed King |
| CAPESIUS | |
| STRADER | — Two Will-o-the-wisps |
| THEODORA | — Hawk |
| SPIRIT OF ELEMENTS | — Ferryman |
| GAIRMAN | — Giant |
| CHILD | — Canary |

- - - - - - - - - - - - - - - -

# PRELUDE

*A room in Sophia's house; the main colour is a yellow red. Sophia, her two children, a boy and a girl; then Estella.*

THE CHILDREN sing (*Sophia accompanying them on the piano*)
    The light of the sun is flooding
    The realms of space;
    The song of birds resounds
    Through fields of air;
    The tender plants spring forth
    From Mother Earth
    And human souls rise up
    With grateful hearts
    To all the spirits of the world.

SOPHIA      Now go to your room, children, and think about the words we have been practising.

    (*Sophia leads the Children to the door. Estella enters.*)

ESTELLA      I am so happy to see you, Sophia dear. I hope I'm not intruding.

SOPHIA      Not at all, Estella. I'm glad you've come.
    (*She invites Estella to sit down and takes a seat.*)

ESTELLA      Have you good news from your husband?

13

| | |
|---|---|
| SOPHIA | Quite good, he writes that he's finding the conference of psychologists most interesting, although the way some of the great problems are approached is not very intriguing. With his training in observing people, he is especially aware of one thing: how a kind of spiritual short-sightedness prevents modern psychologists from looking clearly at the essential riddles. |
| ESTELLA | Doesn't he intend to speak about something important himself? |
| SOPHIA | Yes, on a subject that seems to him, and also to me, very important. However, he hardly expects any results from it in view of the biased attitude of his listeners. |
| ESTELLA | Sophia, a special wish brings me here. Couldn't we spend the evening together? Tonight is the performance of 'The Uprooted'. Nothing would please me more than going to the play with you. |
| SOPHIA | But you've forgotten, dear. Just tonight my Society is giving the performance we've been preparing so long. |
| ESTELLA | O yes – that slipped my mind. I should have liked so much to spend the evening with you, my dearest friend. I was rejoicing with all my heart at the thought of having you beside me to look into the real depths of our present-day life. But your world of ideas – which is so alien to me – will destroy even the last remnant of our friendship, that has bound us together since our schooldays. |

| | |
|---|---|
| SOPHIA | You've said that so often; and yet, again and again you've had to admit that our opinions need not raise any barriers between our feelings for each other. They are still the same as they were in our younger years together. |
| ESTELLA | It's true. I have often said so. And yet it constantly makes me bitter to see with every year how your feelings become more and more estranged from everything in life that seems to me worthwhile. |
| SOPHIA | Dear Estella, we could mean much more to each other just by a mutual respect for the differences in our dispositions and the directions they've taken. |
| ESTELLA | Cold reasoning often tells me you are right. But oh, something in me rebels against the way you look at life. |
| SOPHIA | Honestly, if you would only admit to yourself that you're really asking me to deny the very core of my nature. |
| ESTELLA | Yes, I'd admit even that, if it were not for one thing. I can well imagine that people who think differently can very well come together with complete sympathy. But actually the direction of your ideas makes you assume a certain superiority. Other people can exchange their views and realize that they do indeed differ in their standpoints, which still are equally justified. Your view, however, claims to be more profound than all the rest, which it looks on simply as products of a lower level of human development. |

| | |
|---|---|
| SOPHIA | You should know from what we have discussed so often that no one who shares my views evaluates a person according to his opinions or his knowledge. |
| ESTELLA | That sounds very well, but it doesn't rid me of a certain suspicion. I cannot close my eyes to the fact that a view of the world which ascribes to itself unlimited depths must lead to a certain superficiality. Just think of those of your friends who try to impress with the mere pretence of profundity! You are much too dear a friend for me to point out to you those fellow-thinkers who swear by your ideas and display their spiritual arrogance in the worst possible way. At the same time, the empty triteness of their minds shows through every word and action. And I won't remind you how callous and unfeeling some of your adherents have been towards their fellow-men. At least your greatness of soul could never keep you from the duties our daily life demands of anyone who in the best sense of the word can be called good. |
| SOPHIA | But you can also say that we make every effort not to overestimate an individual, merely because he has been allowed to serve our particular view of life. |
| ESTELLA | And now you are going to desert me tonight – just when we can experience true art speaking out about life! This shows me that when it comes to appreciating art – even in you – your world view pro- |

duces a definite superficiality, if you'll forgive my saying so.

SOPHIA        Where do you find this superficiality in us?

ESTELLA       I can say, at this special moment, that I have now become aware of what genuine art is. I think I understand how it lays hold of the very essence of our lives. And I shudder at the thought of what you prefer, Sophia, to this interest in art that is involved with life itself. Your kind of drama seems to me nothing more than an old-fashioned, didactic-allegorical kind of presentation; instead of living people, you display puppet-like types, indulging in symbolical events.

SOPHIA        Estella dear, you don't want to understand that a wealth of life can be found exactly where you see nothing but a web of abstract thoughts. And that there may be people who call your 'Living reality' actually poverty-stricken if it is not measured by the source it springs from. This may sound harsh but our friendship calls for unvarnished honesty. The spirit means to you – as to so many others – only the instrument of knowledge. You are conscious only of the thought-aspect of spirit. You have no conception of the living, creative spirit that forms human beings with the same elemental power as the germinating forces in Nature form a seed. Like so many others, what you call unsophisticated and original in art, for instance, to me denies the spirit ... But our attitude towards the world unites fully conscious inner activity with the power of spontaneity. We consciously absorb whatever is unsophisticated and do not rob it of its refreshing richness and originality.

ESTELLA        All that is far removed from everything that daily pleads with us for compassion and active concern.

SOPHIA        For you it's enough to have merely reflective thoughts about an individual human being: that he is the result of the conditions around him. You don't want to see that thought can dive down into the creative spirit to touch the very source of existence – and then emerges to reveal itself as the actual creative, germinating force. As little as the forces of the seed have to *teach* the plant to grow but rather unfold within it as a living entity – so little do our ideas teach. They pour themselves into our being, life-enkindling, life-bestowing.

ESTELLA        You know me long enough to be aware of how I freed myself from a way of living and from thoughts which only follow the dictation of tradition and conventional opinions. I've tried to understand why so many people seem to suffer undeservedly. I've made an effort to get to know the heights and depths of existence. I've also asked the help of science, as far as it's been accessible to me, and obtained helpful answers.

SOPHIA        And it is to Spirit-oriented ideas that *I* owe everything that gives life its meaning. I owe to them not only courage but also insight and strength. They give me the hope that I can make of my children human beings who are not merely capable and useful in external life, in the conventional sense, but who are able to sustain an inner tranquillity and contentment in themselves . . . Let me say one more thing: I'm quite certain that the dreams you share with so many others can only materialize if men succeed in connecting what they call reality and life with those deeper experiences which you've often termed fantastic, wild imaginings.

ESTELLA     To me it is clear that only in art can we experience the true, the higher reality. I seem to feel the pulse-beat of our time when I allow such art to challenge me.

SOPHIA     It may seem strange to you when I confess that I find much that to you appears genuine art to be only fruitless criticism of life. For no hunger is stilled, no tears are dried, no source of moral degradation is uncovered, when merely the outer appearance of hunger or tear-stained faces or degraded characters are shown on the stage. *How* this is usually done is unspeakably distant from the real depths of life and the true relationships between living beings.

ESTELLA     I understand what you are trying to say, but it only shows too clearly that you prefer to indulge in fantasy rather than face the truths of life. We really go in two different directions in this. So I'll have to be resigned to do without my friend tonight. (*She rises.*) I must go. I think we should still remain the same good friends.

SOPHIA        We should indeed.

              (*During the last words Sophia leads Estella to the
              door.*)
              *Curtain*

*Footnote:*
  The original, extremely long, single speeches have been divided and somewhat
rearranged by the translators in order to come closer to the conversational style
of the modern stage. This has been done only for the Prelude. Nothing has
been omitted, except in the title of the play which Estella describes: 'The Dis-
inherited from Body and Soul', here rendered as 'The Uprooted'. A first version
of the Prelude will be found in the Appendix.

# SCENE ONE

*A room, rose red in tone; on the right, as seen from the audience, the door to
a lecture hall. The various persons enter gradually one after another from this
hall and linger for a time in the room. Here they discuss some of the things
which have been aroused in them by a lecture to which they have just listened.
Maria and Johannes enter first, then others join them. The lecture ended
some time earlier, and the following is the continuation of conversations already begun in the hall.*

MARIA       It grieves me so, my friend,
to see you lamed in spirit and in soul, –
and I must see the loving bond,
uniting us ten years, as fruitless, too.
Now this momentous hour, wherein
we have been privileged to hear so much
that rays forth light into dark depths of soul
has brought you only pain.
With many a word our speaker uttered
I felt within my heart
how deeply wounding it must be for you.

– – – – – – – – – – – – – – – –

When formerly I looked into your eyes,
they flashed back joy at all they saw.
And then your soul held fast
in pictures full of beauty
what sunlight and bright air,

21

revealing riddles of existence
by flooding earthly objects,
can paint in fleeting moments.
Your hand was still unskilled;
in glowing sturdy color
you could not yet embody
what hovered full of life before your soul.
Yet nonetheless there lived in both our hearts
the glowing faith that surely
a future day would add
the art and cunning of the hand
to joy of soul, immersed
so deeply in the stream of life.
What searching spirit forces can reveal
about the wondrous nature of the universe
would pour forth happiness
from your creative work
into the hearts of men:
or so we thought and hoped.
A future blessing in the guise
of highest beauty, springing from your art: thus
I painted for myself your spirit's goal.
But now the forces of your inmost being seem
to be extinguished;
creative joy is dead;
your arm that wielded once the brush
with youthful strength
seems almost paralyzed.

JOHANNES    Alas! It is so.
I feel all former fire
has disappeared out of my soul.
With dullness only does my eye

behold the glancing beauty
that sunlight pours out over everything.
My heart stays nearly numb
when changing moods of air
are wafting all around me.
My hand will not be moved
to force into a lasting present
what fleetingly
from grounds primeval
the elemental powers may conjure.
Creative, joyous urge
no more wells up
and darkness shrouds
the ways of life for me.

MARIA I must deplore so deeply
that this should come to you
from everything that is for me the highest:
the stream of heavenly life.
O friend, within this changing play
we call existence,
a spirit life, eternal, hides itself.
And in this life each soul can weave and move.
I feel myself in spirit forces
that work as though in ocean depths;
I see the life of men
as rippling wavelets on the surface of the sea.
I feel myself at one with that deep sense of life
for which men strive unceasingly,
and which appears to me
as simply our own being's revelation.
I've seen how often this was closely joined
to someone's inmost core:

it raised him to the greatest height
to which the human heart aspires.
Yet as this lives in me,
it shows itself as evil fruit
as soon as I allow myself
to come in touch
with any other human being.
This fate of mine reveals itself
in all I sought to give to you,
who came to me in love, –
for at my side you wished
to tread courageously the path
that was to lead to noble work.
And what has come of this?
All that reveals itself to me
as purest life in its own inmost truth
has brought your spirit only death.

JOHANNES     Yes, that is so.
What bears your soul aloft
to light-filled heights of heaven
hurls me down –
when feeling it with you –
into dark gulfs of death.
In friendship's radiant dawn
you led me onward to the revelation
that pours forth light into those realms of dark
which every night, unconsciously,
the human soul must enter;
where wanders, too,
the erring human being when
death's blackness seems to scoff
at all life's truest meaning.

Then you affirmed for me
the earnest truth of life's return.
At that time I was able to imagine
that, gradually maturing, I'd become
a genuine spirit-man.
It seemed self-evident
that keenness of my eye
and the creative certainty as artist
would only bloom for me
out of your fire's noble force.
I let it work upon me then, this fire!
But oh, it robbed me of the interplay
of my soul forces.
Remorselessly it pressed out of my heart
all faith I had in world and life.
And now I've come so far,
I even lack the clarity to know
if I should doubt or should believe
the revelations from the spirit world.
I have not even power
to love what heralds within you
the beauty of the spirit.

MARIA     For years now I have had to recognize
that my own way to live the spirit-self
becomes its opposite
when mingling with the ways of others.
Yet I must also see
how rich with blessing
this power of the spirit is,
when it can reach the human soul by other paths.

*(Enter Philia, Astrid and Luna)*

This power speaks in words,
and in these words lies strength
to lead men's way of thinking
to cosmic heights,
creating there a mood of joy
where dreariness has been.
And it can change frivolity of mind
to worthy, earnest feeling; it gives
to men a sense of certainty.
And I – I am completely seized
by just this spirit power
but must perceive
the pain and desolation
it bears with it,
when pouring forth out of my heart
into the hearts of others.

PHILIA   It was as if a symphony

(*Enter Professor Capesius and Dr. Strader*)

of feelings and opinions
had sounded in the circle
uniting us just now.
Harmonious tones were there
but also many a harsher dissonance.

MARIA   When many people join in conversation,
their words present themselves before the soul
as if among them stood, mysteriously,
the Archetype of Man.
It shows itself diversified in many souls,
just as pure light, the One,
reveals itself within the rainbow's arch
in many-colored hues.

CAPESIUS     So one has now
in many years of earnest search
explored the changing character of different epochs,
examined, too, what was alive in those great
    spirits
who set before men's souls the goals of life
and wished to bring to light
the groundwork of reality.
One could believe to have enkindled
the lofty powers of thought in his own soul
and stirred up many questions about destiny.
One could assume he felt
the firm support of judgment in the mind,
whenever new experience
pressed questions on the soul.
But now this so-called firm support
begins to sway beneath me when – amazed –
I hear today, as I have heard before,
the kind of thought that's furthered here.
And it will break completely under me
when I consider how far-reaching
its *consequences* are in life.
Quite frequently it has been my concern
to bring what I have gleaned
from mysteries of the past into such words
that listening hearts might be both held and
    moved.
And I was glad if I could really warm
the smallest corner of my hearers' inner being.
Indeed I seem to have achieved some good;
of failure I can not complain.
But all this work of mine bears out the view
which men of action love to emphasize:

that thoughts are only shadows, nothing more nor
    less,
within the realm of life's reality.
They can indeed enkindle
creative forces for our life;
to shape them does not lie within thought's
    power.
So I have long resigned myself
to these few modest words:
where only thought's pale shadows work,
all life is paralyzed
and all that goes with life.
More potent than the wisest words,
enriched with art,
will prove in life to be the gifts of Nature,
the talents,
and also destiny itself.
Tradition, like a mountain weight,
and mindless prejudice
will always crush
the power of the best of words.
Yet what is here revealed
gives much for men like me to think about.
Such an effect is easy to explain
where fervour of cult-frenzy, pouring over souls,
makes fools of men.
But nothing of this kind is present here.
Alone through reason is the soul approached.
And yet you can create with words
true strength for living
and touch the deepest in the heart.
Besides, this curious Something
can even penetrate the sphere of will;

although to those like me, who follow older
    paths,
this Something must appear as only shadowy
    thought.
I am quite unequipped
to disavow such things;
I simply cannot let them work on me.
So strangely does this all begin to speak, –
yet not as if it were for me
to ward off such experience:
it almost seems
as if this Something
could not within itself
endure me as I am.

STRADER        I do agree quite fully
with those last words of yours.
And I would emphasize more strongly even
that all effects upon the soul
which we observe arising from ideas
can not in any sense decide
their value in the realm of knowledge.
The question whether it is truth or error
that's living in our thinking
must face the single verdict of pure reason.
And nobody can seriously deny
that what here offers answers
to solve life's greatest mysteries
in words of only seeming clarity
is quite unfit for such a scrutiny.
It speaks alluringly to human minds
and only tempts the credulous human heart.
It claims to open doors into those realms

before which, modest and perplexed,
with stern deliberation, science stands.
Those truly faithful to this science
ought to acknowledge that no one
can know from whence are gushing
the sources of our thought
or where life's first foundations lie.
Though this admission will be hard
for him who all too eagerly
would know what lies beyond all knowledge,
yet every glance imposes on the thinker's mind
most forcefully the limits of this knowledge,
should he be looking at the world outside
or turning his attention inward.
If we deny our reason
and what experience has proved,
our steps will sink in nothingness.
And who can fail to see how little
our modern forms of thought
will seriously accommodate
what here is claimed as novel revelation?
Not much indeed is needed
to show how utterly this revelation lacks
what gives to thought its firm support
and lends the sense of certainty.
It may well warm the heart, this strange, new
    revelation;
the thinker sees in it mere wishful dreams.

PHILIA      Such words will always come
from knowledge that has been achieved
through dry, prosaic reason.
But this is not enough to satisfy the soul

that needs to find belief in its own being.
It will forever listen to the words
which speak to it of spirit
and strive to understand
what formerly it dimly sensed.
To speak of the unknowable
may well allure the thinker
but never human hearts.

STRADER      I realize how much there lies
in that objection; it's aimed
at simple reasoners,
who only spin out threads of thought
and ask what will result from this or that
on which they have already formed opinions.
It can't, however, be applied to me.
No outer cause has made me
devote myself to thought.
As child I lived within a pious circle,
beholding rites that overwhelmed my senses
with pictures of the heavenly realms
so skilfully displayed
to comfort simple folk.
And in my boyish soul
I felt at times pure bliss
when I looked up in rapture
toward highest worlds of spirit.
To pray was then my heart's necessity.
I had my schooling in a cloister,
and so my teachers were the monks;
the greatest longing in myself
was to become a monk –
this was my parents' warmest wish as well.

Just as I was to be ordained a priest,
a stroke of fate removed me from the cloister.
And for this accident I must be grateful,
for long since had my soul
been robbed of its untroubled peace,
until chance rescued it.
I had been meeting many things
that have no place within a cloister;
I came on natural science in some books
that were forbidden me
and learned from them of modern research.
Adjusting was laborious;
I had to search out many paths.
So what I found as truth was certainly
not won by clever thought alone.
In many heated battles I have torn
from out my spirit
what brought me peace and blessing as a child.
I understand the heart
with longings for the heights. But, for myself,
because I recognized that what
all spiritual teaching brought was dream,
I had to find the solid ground
that only facts and science can impart.

LUNA    We each must understand in our own way
the meaning and the goals of life.
I surely lack ability
to prove through modern science
what I receive as spiritual teaching here.
However, I feel clearly in my heart
that but for it my soul would surely die,
just as my limbs would die deprived of blood.

Dear Doctor Strader, you have much to say
opposing us.
And what you have described
about your inner struggles
lends weight to all your words, –
with even those
who cannot follow all you say.
But I must often ask myself
why it should be that common sense
can find the words of spirit
so plain and natural
and takes them warmly to itself
but feels a shivering of cold
when it seeks nourishment of soul
in words like those you have just spoken?

THEODORA (*who has entered earlier*)

Although I feel at home
here in this circle,
the words which I must hear
seem very strange to me.

CAPESIUS     And why this strangeness?

THEODORA     I cannot speak of it myself.
Maria, you explain.

(*Exit Theodora*)

MARIA     Our friend has many times described
a strange experience that befell her.
She felt one day as though transformed
and nowhere could she find an understanding.

All felt estranged by her peculiar nature,
until she found our circle here.
Not that we claim to understand
what is unique in her,
but through our kind of thinking we become
quite willing to accept unusual things.
We value every sort
of human being here.
In our friend's life had come a certain moment
when everything that had to do
with her own life appeared to her to vanish;
the past was all as if extinguished in her soul.
And since this transformation first took place,
this state of mind repeatedly returns.
It lasts but a brief time, and otherwise
she is like other people.
But when she falls into this state,
she lacks almost completely
the gift of memory;
the power also of her sight is gone;
what lies around her she can feel, –
she does not see it.
Her eyes begin to shine
with a peculiar light,
and pictures then appear to her
which first were dreamlike,
but now they are so clear
that only as the prophecy of times to come
they can be understood.
This we have often seen.

CAPESIUS    That is exactly
what pleases me

so little in this circle:
that superstition is mixed up
with logic and with reason.
It has been always so
for those who take such paths.

MARIA      If you can still say this,
you do not know
how we regard these things.

STRADER    As for myself,
I must acknowledge,
to hear about such actual revelations
is preferable to all these doubtful spirit teachings.
For though I lack
the answer to the riddle of such dreams,
I see them nonetheless as facts.
I take it there would be no chance
for us to be a witness
to this strange state of mind?

MARIA      Perhaps, – for here she comes again.
It almost seems
as if this wonder wants
to show itself.

THEODORA  I am impelled to speak.
Before my spirit stands a Form in shining light,
and from it words sound forth to me.
I feel myself in future times,
and human beings I perceive
who are not yet alive.
They also see the Form;

they also hear the words,
and thus they sound:
You have lived long in faith;
you have been comforted by hope.
So now be comforted with sight;
receive new life through Me.
I lived once in the souls
who sought Me in themselves
through words My messengers proclaimed
and through the strength of their devotion.
You have beheld in the senses' light,
have had to put your faith in spirit realms.
Now you have won
a drop of spirit vision, –
O feel it deeply in your souls.

— — — — — — — — — — — — — —

A human being
emerges from the radiant light.
It speaks to me:
You shall proclaim to all
who have the will to hear,
that you have seen
what men shall soon experience.
The Christ once lived upon the earth,
and from this life it follows
that He encompasses as Soul
men's growth on earth.
He is united with the spiritual part of earth.
But human beings could not yet behold Him
as He reveals Himself in such a form of
    being,
because they lacked the eyes of spirit
which later shall be theirs.

But now the time draws near
when with new power of sight
the men on earth shall be endowed.
What once the senses could behold,
when Christ lived on the earth,
will be perceived by souls of men
when soon the time shall be fulfilled.

(*Exit Theodora*)

MARIA It is the first time
that she has come before so many people.
She only has been moved before
when two or three were present.

CAPESIUS It seems indeed most strange
that she should feel impelled, as though
commanded or required, to make this revelation.

MARIA That may seem so.
And yet we know quite well her nature.
If at this moment it was her wish
to send her inner voice into your souls,
the only reason must have been
that this same voice's source
wished thus to speak to you.

CAPESIUS It's come to our attention
that of this future gift
of which she spoke, half dreaming,
much mention has been made quite recently
by him who is the one, we're told,
inspiring all this circle.

Is it not possible
the content of her words could spring from him
and that the manner only be from her?

MARIA        Were this in truth the case,
we would not give it weight.
The fact remains, however, after careful proof:
until she came into our circle,
our friend knew nothing of our leader's teaching,
and none of us had heard of her before.

CAPESIUS     We have to do then simply with a fact
such as occurs at times, conflicting
with all the laws of nature,
and which we must regard as illness.
To judge life's riddles clearly
can healthy thought alone accomplish
and what springs forth from wide-awake mentality.

STRADER     And yet we have a fact before us!
It certainly must be important
what was just said to us.
We might be forced –
if we discard all other theories –
to take transference of ideas
through psychic power in earnest.

ASTRID       Oh! If you could only step on to the ground
your thought so anxiously avoids!
The false belief, that lets
the revelations of such natures seem
peculiar, strange, or even ill,
would surely melt away, as snow in sunlight.

It is significant but is not strange.
For small appears to me this wonder
when I behold the thousand wonders
that every day surround me.

CAPESIUS        It is indeed one thing
to recognize what's everywhere revealed,
but quite another what is shown us here.

STRADER        To speak of spirit
is only needed
when things are placed before us
which do not lie within the scope
laid down with such precision
by natural science.

ASTRID        The gleaming rays of sunlight
that glisten in the morning dew,

(*Felix Balde enters*)

the spring that gushes from the rocks,
the thunder rolling in the clouds, –
they speak to us a spirit language.
I've sought to understand it.
The might and meaning of this speech
is only faintly mirrored in
your scientific research.
I've felt my soul rejoice
when such speech made its way into my heart
as human word and spirit science
alone can grant to me.

FELIX BALDE    That was a right good word.

MARIA
I must express to you
how much my heart rejoices
to see for the first time among us here

(*Felicia Balde enters*)

a man I've heard so much about.
It stimulates the wish
to see him now more often here.

FELIX BALDE
I'm unaccustomed
to mingle with so many people,
and not just unaccustomed.

FELICIA BALDE
Ah yes, it is the way with him!
It keeps us quite in loneliness.
Year in, year out, we hear
scarce more than what we speak ourselves.
And were it not for this good man,

(*she indicates Capesius*)

who sometimes comes up to our cottage,
we'd hardly know
that other people were alive.
And if the man
who spoke now yonder in the hall
and with his good and noble words
has stirred us all so deeply,
were not to meet my Felix
going about his work,
you would know nothing
about us long-lost people.

MARIA
So the professor often visits you?

| | |
|---|---|
| CAPESIUS | Assuredly, and I must truly say |
| | I owe to this good lady |
| | my deepest gratitude. |
| | She gives me of her gifts so richly, |
| | as no one else can do. |
| | |
| MARIA | And of what nature are her gifts? |
| | |
| CAPESIUS | I must allude, |
| | if I'm to tell about it, |
| | to something which in truth |
| | seems far more wonderful to me |
| | than much that I have heard of here, |
| | because it speaks more to my heart. |
| | I scarcely should be able in another place |
| | to bring the words across my lips |
| | which here I find so easy. |
| | I feel my soul, at times, |
| | as though entirely empty and exhausted; |
| | it is as if the very fountainhead |
| | of knowledge had run dry within me, |
| | as if I could not find one word |
| | that seems worthwhile to speak or to be heard. |
| | And when I feel such barrenness of spirit, |
| | then I escape and go where these good people |
| | have their refreshing, quiet solitude. |
| | And there Felicia tells me many a tale, |
| | in pictures fabulous, |
| | of beings dwelling in the land of dreams |
| | and in the realm of magic fairy tales, |
| | who live a motley life. |
| | The tone in which she tells of them |
| | recalls the bards of ancient times. |

I do not ask the sources of her words,
but this one thing I clearly know:
that new life wells and flows into my soul
dispelling its paralysis.

MARIA        That such great things are said
about Felicia's art, –
this blends harmoniously,
in every way,
with all that Benedictus said
about the hidden fount of wisdom in his friend.

FELIX BALDE    The one who spoke just now,

*(Benedictus appears in the doorway)*

as if his spirit dwelt
in cosmic spaces and eternities,
has truly little reason to say much
about a simple man like me.

BENEDICTUS    My friend, you are mistaken.
Of untold value is for me each word of yours.

FELIX BALDE    It was but meddling,
the wish to chat,
when you at times gave me the honor
of walking at your side along our mountain paths.
I only dared to speak
because you hid
how much you know yourself.
But now our time is up and we must go.
We have a right long way
to reach our quiet home.

FELICIA BALDE  It was a real refreshment
to be for once among some people.
It will not happen soon again.
There is no other life will do
for Felix but his mountains.

(*Exit Felix and Felicia*)

BENEDICTUS  Felicia indeed is right;
he will not come so soon again.
It's taken much to bring him here this time.
And yet the reason does not lie
with him, that no one knows of him.

CAPESIUS  I took him only for some odd stick
and found him talkative
the many times
I spent with him.
But his eccentric speech
remains obscure to me,
wherewith he brings to light
the things he claims to know.
He speaks of sun-born beings
that dwell within the stones,
of moon-dark demons
who constantly disturb their work,
about the sense of number in the plants.
A listener will not for long
find any meaning whatsoever in his words.

BENEDICTUS  But one can also feel
as if strong powers of Nature sought within his
    words
to manifest themselves in their own being's truth.

(*Exit Benedictus*)

STRADER
Already I can feel
that painful days
are coming in my life.
For since the time
when in my cloister's loneliness
I made my first acquaintance with that knowledge
which struck relentlessly my deepest soul,
has nothing moved me more
than the encounter with the seeress.

CAPESIUS
What should disturb you here so greatly
I cannot see.
I am afraid, dear friend,
that if you lose your certainty of mind in this,
you soon will find the gloom of doubt
descending upon everything around you.

STRADER
The fear of just this doubt
torments me frequently.
From my experience
I have no knowledge otherwise
about this gift of seership.
But oftentimes when unsolved riddles torture me,
there rises ghostlike to my spirit vision
a frightful, dream-born being out of spirit
        darkness.
It lies upon my soul like lead
and, terrifying, clutches at my heart.
It speaks through me:
You must compel me
with your stunted weapons of dull thought,

or you are nothing but
a fleeting phantom of your own delusion.

THEODOSIUS (*who has entered earlier*)

This is the fate of those
who only can approach the world through
    thinking.
The spirit's voice, however, dwells within us.
We have no power to penetrate the veil
spread out before the senses,
and thought can bring us knowledge merely of
    the things
that disappear in course of time.
The spirit, the eternal,
is only found within the inner depths of man.

STRADER

The fruit of pious faith
is able to bring peace to souls
who can, sufficient in themselves,
seek out such ways.
But strength of real knowledge
will never thrive upon this path.

THEODOSIUS

And yet there are no other ways

(*Enter Romanus and Gairman*)

to quicken in the hearts of men
true knowledge of the spirit,
though pride can tempt one to distort

(*Enter Helena*)

to images of phantasy
the genuine feelings of the soul;
and it will paint alluring visions

where only faith should be, in simple beauty.
Of everything said here in such an animated way,
as knowledge brought from higher worlds,
one thing alone
has value for the honest heart and mind:
that only in the spirit world itself
the soul can feel at home.


THE OTHER MARIA (*who has entered with Theodosius*)

What is contained within such words
may satisfy a man,
as long as he feels moved
to merely *speak* of things.
But in the midst of life with all its striving,
its search for happiness, its misery,
a different food is needed
to hand to human souls.
An inner urge has guided me
to dedicate the rest of my whole life
to those whose destiny
has brought them suffering and need.
And it was oftener my task
to ease the pain within their souls
than suffering of body.
On many paths I felt indeed
the weakness of my will
and constantly I had to win
fresh strength from the abundance flowing here
out of the fountain of the spirit.
The warm and magic power of words,
that here I listen to,
streams down into my hands

and flows through them
like balsam, when they touch the sorrow-laden;
and it transforms itself upon my lips
to strengthening words which carry comfort
to pain-racked hearts.
I do not ask the source of these words' power;
I look upon their truth
when, full of life, they give me life.
So every day I see more clearly
that they derive their strength not from my will
in all its weakness, –
but daily they create myself for me anew.

CAPESIUS          But surely there are many
who – though they lack this revelation –
do untold good?

MARIA          Indeed such people can be found
in many places.
But it is something else our friend would like to
          say,
and when you learn about her life,
you will speak differently.
When unused forces
can flourish in the bloom of youth,
love springs abundantly
out of the heart's good soil.
Our friend, however, had exhausted
her life's strong forces through excessive work,
and all her courage
was taken from her
by bitter weight of destiny.
She sacrificed her strength

in bringing up her children carefully;
her courage ebbed when early death
took her beloved husband from her.
In such a state, fate seemed to have in store
a weary remnant only of her life.
But powers of destiny then brought her
into our circle and the teaching of the spirit,
wherein her own life forces blossomed
a second time.
With her new aims in life,
fresh courage streamed into her heart.
In her the spirit has, in truth,
from the decaying seed, created
the new-born man.
And if, with such creative forces,
the spirit shows it can be fruitful,
this seems to justify
the way the spirit is revealed.

And now, let this be said without impertinence, –
that is, if pride does not lie hidden in these words,
if in the heart there live high moral purposes,
if we are sure our teaching
is not our own achievement –
that only spirit
explains itself within us –
with this in mind, it can be said
that in your way of thought, there weave
dim shadows only
of the real sources of man's being.
The spirit which ensouls us
unites itself in inward warmth with everything

that in the depths of life
spins human destiny.

Throughout the years since I have been allowed
to serve this active work,
I've met with far more wounded hearts
and far more longing souls
than many would imagine.
I prize the lofty flight of your ideas
and your proud certainty of knowledge.
I like to think that at your feet
a throng of eager hearers sit,
and that for many souls
there flows from out your work
uplifting clarity of thought.
And yet it seems to me such certainty
dwells in this thinking only
as long as it remains apart, within itself.

The kind of thought I follow
sends into deep realities
the fruitage of its words,
because in deep realities
it will implant its roots.
Far distant from your thinking lies
the script upon the spirit heavens,
with forceful symbols heralding
the new-grown shoot
upon the tree of man.
Though clear and sure may seem
your thinking, that lives on in the old way,
it can supply the tree's dry bark

but does not reach
into the living power of its heart.

ROMANUS    I cannot find the bridge
that leads across
from mere ideas to actual deeds.

CAPESIUS    One overvalues here the power of ideas,
but on the other hand you fail to grasp
the course of real life. Indeed it is ideas
that are the seeds of every human act.

ROMANUS    If this good person has achieved so much,
the impulse lies
in her warm heart.
When work is done, men surely need
refreshment and renewal from ideas.
But only training of the will,
combined with skill and strength
in all the genuine work of life,
will further human progress.
When whirr of wheels
is humming in my ears,
and when contented human hands
are labouring at machines,
it's then I feel the powers of life at work.

GAIRMAN    I've often lightly said in passing
that I am fond of joking
and only find in it some spirit, –
that for my brain it nonetheless
remains a pleasant means
to occupy the time

between the hours of work and those of pleasure.
But this remark has now become to me
    distasteful.
An unseen power has laid hold of me,
and I have learned to feel
what is much stronger in our human nature
than the thin house of cards our wit sets up.

CAPESIUS    And nowhere else but here have you been able
            to find such spiritual power?

GAIRMAN     The life which I have led
            has brought me varied spirit values;
            I had no wish
            to pick their fruits.
            And yet this kind of thought
            has drawn me to itself,
            despite how little I myself have done.

CAPESIUS    We have enjoyed enriching hours here
            and must be grateful to the hostess of this house.

            (*Everyone, except Maria and Johannes, go out.*)

JOHANNES    Stay here a little longer.
            I am afraid – O so afraid!

MARIA       What is it? Tell me.

JOHANNES    First came our leader's words,
            and then what all these people said –
            now I feel shattered to the core.

| MARIA | How could these words
affect you so intensely? |
|---|---|
| JOHANNES | Each word became for me
at every moment
a frightful sign
of my own nothingness. |
| MARIA | It was indeed significant
to hear poured out in a short time
so much about life's battles
and human character
in all this interplay of words.
And yet it is the nature
of the life we lead
to wake the human spirit to expression.
What otherwise is brought to light in course
of time
is here revealed within an hour or two. |
| JOHANNES | ... A mirrored image of the whole of life,
that showed me clearly to myself.
What is revealed to us out of the spirit
has led me to perceive how many men,
who think themselves a whole, in fact
bear in themselves one single facet only.
In order to unite within myself
all these divergent sides,
I started boldly on the path taught here --
and it has made of me a nothing.
What all these people lack
I know quite well;
I also know, |

they stand in life
and I in empty nothingness.
Whole lifetimes were summed up
in brief and weighty speeches.
And my life, too,
as picture rose within me.
The days of childhood first were painted there
with happy wealth of life.
My youth was painted there
with the proud hopes
awakened in my parents' hearts
by their son's talents.
The dreams of mastering an art
which were my very life in those glad days, –
they all rose warningly
from spirit depths.
And those dreams rose, as well,
wherein you saw me
transmuting into form and color
what lives for you in spirit.

– – – – – – – – – – – – – – –

Then flames I saw leap forth,
that turned the youthful artist's dreams and hopes
to ashen nothingness.
Out of this barren void
another picture formed itself:
it was a gentle human being,
who once had linked her destiny
with mine, in faithful love.
She wished to hold me, years ago,
when I was called
to go home to my mother's funeral.
I wrenched myself away, –

for mighty was the force
that drew me to your circle
and to the goals
put forward here.
No sense of guilt
remained in me from that past time,
when I destroyed a bond
which for the other had meant life itself.
And when the message came to me
that her life slowly ebbed away
and finally succumbed,
it never touched me till today.
Just now our leader in that room
expressed with earnest words
how we may injure, even ruin –
if our own striving is not right –
the destiny of those
bound to us in love.
O awful sounded back to me
these words out of the picture,
resounding forth from every side
like an excruciating echo: –
You are her murderer . . .
And thus the forceful, earnest speech we heard
has been the motive for the others
to look into themselves.
In me, however, it has quickened
the consciousness of deepest guilt.
Through it I can perceive
how wrongly I have striven.

MARIA         In this grave moment, O my friend,
              you enter gloomy realms.

And there no one can help you – only he
in whom we put our trust.

(*Helena returns; Maria is called away.*)

HELENA  I feel compelled to stay
a little while with you, –
your eyes have looked
unhappy now for weeks.
How is it that the glorious, shining light
can bring such gloom into your soul,
when you with all your strength
are striving for the truth?

JOHANNES  And has this light
brought only joy to you?

HELENA  Not simply joy
as I knew formerly, –
but joy
that springs up, bursting into life,
within the words
through which the spirit
proclaims itself.

JOHANNES  And yet I say to you:
what works creatively
can also crush.

HELENA  An error must be creeping then
with craftiness into your soul,
if this is possible.
For if anxiety

instead of blissful freedom
and sorrowful despair
instead of joy of spirit
flow from the sources of the truth for you,
then seek out all the faults
that block your way.
How often have we learned
that health is the true fruitage of our teaching,
and from it living forces bloom.
How should it cause the opposite in you?
I see these fruits in many people
who gather trustingly around me here.
Old ways of life become
strange and still stranger to the soul;
new well-springs open for the heart,
which then renews itself.
To see into the depths of being
does not create desires
which can torment.

(*Exit Helena*)

JOHANNES    It took me many years to understand
that what our senses show is an illusion,
unless the knowledge of the spirit
can join with it as true companion.
But that the words of highest wisdom
are only an illusion of the soul in *you*,
a single moment has revealed.

*Curtain*

# SCENE TWO

*A place in the open; rocks and springs. The whole surroundings are to be thought of as within the soul of Johannes Thomasius. What follows is the content of his meditation.*

(*From the springs and rocks resounds:*)
*O man, know thou thyself.*

JOHANNES   For many years these words
of weighty meaning I have heard.
They sound to me from air and water;
they echo up from depths of earth.
And just as in the acorn secretly
the structure of the mighty oak is pressed,
within the power of these words
there is contained
all that my thought can comprehend
about the nature of the elements,
of souls as well as spirits,
of time and of eternity.
The world and my own nature
are living in the words:
O man, know thou thyself!

(*From the springs and rocks resounds:*)
*O man, know thou thyself.*

JOHANNES      And now! – within me
it is becoming terribly alive.
Around me darkness weaves,
within me blackness yawns;
out of the world of darkness it resounds,
out of soul-blackness it rings forth: –
O man, know thou thyself!

(*There sounds from springs and rocks:*)
O *man, know thou thyself.*


JOHANNES      And now it robs me of myself.
I change with every hour of the day.
I melt into the night.
The earth I follow in her cosmic course.
I rumble in the thunder,
I flash within the lightning,
I am. – But oh, I feel
already separated from my being.
I see my body's shell.
It is an alien being outside myself;
it is remote from me.
There hovers nearer now another body
and with its mouth I have to speak:
'He brought me bitter sorrow;
I gave him all my trust.
He left me in my grief alone.
He robbed me of the warmth of life
and thrust me deep into cold earth.'
She, whom I left, unhappy one,
I was now she herself,
and I must suffer her despair.
Self-knowledge lent me strength

to pour myself into another self.
O cruel words!
Your light is quenched by its own power.
O man, know thou thyself!

*(There sounds from springs and rocks:)*
*O man, know thou thyself.*

JOHANNES    You guide me back again
into the spheres of my own being.
Yet how do I behold myself!
My human form is lost;
as raging dragon I must see myself,
begot of lust and greed.
I clearly sense
how an illusion's cloud
has hid from me till now
my own appalling form.
The fierceness of my being will devour me.
And running like consuming fire
through all my veins I feel those words,
which hitherto with elemental power
revealed to me the truth of suns and earths.
They live within my pulse,
they beat within my heart,
and even in my thought itself I feel
those unfamiliar worlds flare up as wild desires.
This is the fruitage of the words:
O man, know thou thyself.
*(There sounds from springs and rocks:)*
*O man, know thou thyself.*

JOHANNES    There from the dark abyss,
what being gloats on me?

I feel the chains
that hold me fettered fast to you.
Prometheus was not chained so fast
upon the cliffs of Caucasus
as I am chained to you.
Who are you, horrifying being?

(*There sounds from springs and rocks:*)
*O man, know thou thyself.*

JOHANNES    oh, now I recognize you.
It is myself.
So knowledge chains to you, pernicious monster,

(*Maria enters, but is not noticed
by Johannes for the time being*)

myself, pernicious monster.
I sought to flee from you.
The worlds wherein my folly fled,
in order to be free from my own self,
have dazzled and have blinded me.
And blind I am once more within the blinded
    soul.
O man, know thou thyself!

(*There sounds from springs and rocks:*)
*O man, know thou thyself.*

JOHANNES (*as if coming to himself, sees Maria. The
meditation passes over into inner reality.*)
Maria, you are here!

MARIA    I've looked for you, my friend,
although I know

how dear to you is solitude,
now that so many people's views
have flooded through your soul.
And I know, too, that at this time
my presence cannot help my friend.
An urge that is obscure
is driving me to you this very moment
when words of Benedictus have called up,
instead of light, such bitter grief
out of your spirit depths.

JOHANNES     How dear to me is solitude!
How often have I sought it out,
to find in it myself,
whenever pain and joy of men have driven me
into the labyrinths of thought.
Maria, that is past.
What Benedictus' words at first
drew forth out of my soul,
and what I then lived through
from everything those people said,
seems little to me now
if I compare it to the storm
which solitude has brought
into my heavy brooding.
O this solitude!
It drove me into cosmic spaces;
it tore me from myself.
Within that being to whom I brought such grief
I rose again but as another,
and had to bear the pain
which I myself had caused.
The fierce, dark solitude

61

then gave me back myself
but only to appal me
at the abyss of my own being.
_ _ _ _ _ _ _ _ _ _ _ _ _ _ _ _
For me, man's final refuge,
for me, my solitude is lost.


MARIA        I must repeat my words to you:
no one but Benedictus can now help you.
The firm support we lack,
we both must have from him.
For know, I also can no longer bear
the riddle of my life,
unless some sign from him
can make the answer clear to me.
The lofty wisdom, pointing out
that only semblance and illusion
are spread out over all our life
as long as human thinking grasps alone its surface,
I've often held it up before my mind.
And every time it says:
you must be clear that an illusion
is shrouding you, though often it may seem
    the truth:
that evil fruit could come from your desire
to wake that light in others
which lives in you yourself.
My soul's best part can see
that heavy feelings of oppression
in you, my friend,
from living at my side
are too a portion of the thorny path
that leads you to the light of truth.

You must live through each terror
to which illusion can give birth
before the truth reveals itself to you:
thus speaks your star.
Yet through this starry word is also clear to me
that we must wander on the spirit paths together.
But when I seek these paths,
there spreads itself before my gaze, dark night.
And blacker still becomes this night
through much which I must meet
as fruit of my own being.
We both must look for clarity in that light,
which for the eye can vanish
but never be extinguished.

JOHANNES    Maria, are you then aware
through what my soul has fought its way?
A heavy load indeed
has fallen upon you, dear friend.
Yet foreign to your being is that power
which has so wholly shattered me.
You can ascend to brightest heights of truth;
you can direct your steady gaze
at men's confusion.
In light, in darkness,
you will affirm yourself.
But every moment can
deprive me of myself.
I had to plunge into those people
who through their words revealed themselves
    just now.
I followed one into the cloister's loneliness,
I heard within the other's soul

Felicia's tales.
I was each one,
but for myself I died.
I'd have to have the faith
that beings spring from nothingness,
if I should cherish any hope
that from the nothingness in me
a human being ever could be born.
They force me out of fear into the darkness,
and hunt me through the darkness into fear,
these words imbued with wisdom:
O man, know thou thyself!

(*From the springs and rocks resounds:*)
*O man, know thou thyself.*

*Curtain*

# SCENE THREE

*A room for meditation.*
*Benedictus, Johannes, Maria and a Child.*

MARIA
I'm bringing you the child.
He needs a guiding word from you.

BENEDICTUS
My child, from now on you shall come
to me each evening to hear the words
that then should dwell with you
before you enter the soul realm of sleep.
Will you do this?

CHILD
I'll do it gladly.

BENEDICTUS
This evening fill your heart,
till sleep enfolds you,
with strength from these few words:
'The heavenly powers of light are carrying me
into the spirit's house.'

*(The Child is taken out by Maria,*
*who then returns.)*

MARIA
And now that this child's destiny
shall in the future flow
within the shadow of your paternal care,
I too may ask your guiding counsel,

for I've become his mother
through powers of destiny,
if not by blood.
You showed me how
to bring him up
from that first day
when I discovered him,
left by his unknown mother at my door.
And all your rules
I followed for his guidance
worked wonders on my foster child.
For every force could come to light
that in his body and his soul lay hidden.
It soon was clear that your advice
sprang from the realm
which sheltered this child's soul
before it built its body's sheath.
We saw it hopefully unfold
and shine more brightly each new day.
You know how hard it was for me at first
to gain the child's affection.
He grew up in my care,
yet nothing more than habit
first joined his soul with mine.
He looked to me, perceiving only
that I gave him all he needed
for the well-being of his body and his soul.
Then came the time when in his heart
love was enkindled
for me, the foster mother.
An outer cause brought forth this change.
The seeress came into our circle.
The child became attached to her

and learned, enchanted by the way she spoke,
one or the other charming word.
Then came a moment when exaltation
laid hold of our strange friend;
our child could see
the glimmering light within her eyes.
He felt his young soul shaken to the core
and, frightened, rushed to me.
From this time on
the child has been devoted
to me in warmest love.
Yet since he now received his care from me
not just through natural impulse
but with awakened feeling, –
since his young heart stirs warmly
whenever he looks lovingly at me, –
the treasures of your wisdom
have lost their fruitfulness.
And withered now is much
that had already ripened in the child.
I saw revealed within his being
what for my friend has proved so terrible.
I'm ever more a dark enigma to myself.
Do not deny my asking this grave question:
why do I ruin friend and child
when lovingly I try to do for them
the work that spirit guidance
lets me perceive within my heart as good?
You've shown to me the lofty truth:
illusion's veil is covering the surface of our life.
Yet I must have clear knowledge,
if I must bear this destiny
which is so cruel and which works such evil.

**BENEDICTUS**  There forms itself within this circle
a knot out of the threads
which karma spins in world becoming.
O friend, your sorrows
are part of such a knot of destiny in which
the deeds of gods entwine themselves with
     human life.
When on the pilgrimage of soul
I had attained that stage
which granted me the honour
of serving with my counsel in the spirit spheres,
there came to me a higher being
which should descend into the realm of earth
to take up its abode within a human body.
Man's destiny is now demanding this
at such a turning point of time.
A great step forward in the evolution
is only possible when gods
unite themselves with man's own lot.
For spirit eyes, which should awake
in human souls, can only be evolved
when first a god has laid the seed
within a human being.
The task was now assigned to me
to find that human being
who might be worthy to accept within his soul
the seed-force of the god.
I had to link a deed of heaven
unto a human destiny.
My spirit's eye made search –
it fell on you.
Your course of life had fitted you
as mediator for new healing forces.

In many lives you had acquired
an openness for the nobility
alive in human hearts.
The precious quality of beauty,
the highest claim of virtue,
you carried in your gentle soul
as spirit heritage.
What your eternal ego
brought down into this life through birth
matured to ripened fruit
in your first youthful years.
You did not scale too soon
the lofty spirit heights.
The longing for the spiritual world
did not arise in you
till you had fully grasped
the senses' innocent delights.
Your soul encountered love and anger while
    as yet
your thought was far away
from all desire for spirit.
To drink the joy of Nature in her beauty
and pick the fruits of art
was all you wished to find as riches in your life.
And you could gaily laugh
as only a small child can laugh
who has as yet no knowledge
of life's grey shadow side.
You learned to fathom human happiness,
and mourn men's pain, in times
when not an inkling had yet dawned
of questioning the root of joy and sorrow.
The soul who shows such character

encounters earthly life
as the ripe fruit sprung from many lives.
Its childlike nature is its blossom, not
its root of being.
It was this soul alone that I could choose
as mediator for that spirit
who should attain to active power
within our human world.
So comprehend now that your being
must change into its opposite
when pouring forth from you to other beings.
The spirit in you works
in everything that can grow ripe in man
as fruit for realms eternal.
And therefore much it must destroy
that only has its place within the realm of time.
Its sacrifice in death, however,
is seed of immortality.
What flourishes for higher life
must bloom from death of lower being.

MARIA:  So this is how it stands with me.
You give me light,
but light that robs me of the power of sight
and tears me from myself.
Am I then nothing but a spirit's mediator
and not my own true being?
No more will I endure
this form of mine,
which is a mask and not the truth.

JOHANNES  Dear friend, what is it?
Your gaze has lost its light.

Your body's turned into a pillar.
I take your hand –
and it is cold as death.


BENEDICTUS    My son, you've had to meet with many trials;
but now you stand before the hardest one.
You see her body's covering.
And yet before my gaze
her *self* soars into spirit spheres.


JOHANNES    O see, her lips begin to move.
She speaks . . .


MARIA    You gave me clarity,
yes, clarity, that shrouded me
in darkness on all sides.
I curse your clarity,
and you I curse
who made of me
a tool of those wild arts
through which you seek to misguide men. –
Not for one moment have I ever doubted
how high you stand in spirit.
Yet now one single instant has sufficed
to tear all faith in you out of my heart.
And I must recognize that they are hell-born
    beings,
the spirits whom you serve.
I had to mislead others
because you misled me!
I'll flee from you in regions
wherein no word of yours can penetrate,

and yet be near enough
so that my curses can still reach you!
The fire of my blood
you've torn away from me
and given to your own false god
what must be mine.
The fire of this blood,
O may it burn you!
I had to trust
in lying and deceit,
and to accomplish this
you had at first to make of me
a phantom form.
I've often had to see
how deeds and thoughts of mine
were changed into their opposite.
So now let all
that once was love for you
be changed into wild hatred's fire.
I'll hunt through all the worlds
to find that fire
that can consume you.
I cur . . . ah . . .

JOHANNES    Who is it that is speaking here?
I do not see my friend, –
I see a gruesome being!

BENEDICTUS    Maria's soul is hovering in the heights;
she's left behind her here with us
her mortal semblance only.
And where a human body
is left without a spirit,

there's room which then
the enemy of good seeks out
to step into the realm of visibility.
He finds a body's covering
and through it he can speak.
Just such an adversary spoke
who strives now to destroy the work
I must fulfil
for many human beings' future,
for you as well, my son.
For could I take these curses,
just spoken by Maria's vacant shell,
as other than the tempter's guile,
you should not follow me.
The enemy of good was at my side;
and you, my son, have seen
plunge down into the darkness
the temporal part of her
to whom your whole love radiates.
Because so often spirits
have spoken to you through her lips,
world karma has not spared you
from hearing through them also
the prince of hell.
Now you can seek her finally
and learn to know her being's core.
For she shall be the image of that higher man
to whom you shall aspire to raise yourself.
Her soul is soaring forth to spirit heights
where men can find their being's primal form
that in itself is rooted.
You now shall follow her to spirit realms
and see her in the Temple of the Sun.

There forms itself
within this circle
a knot out of the threads
which karma spins in world becoming.
My son, you have stood firm so far;
you will progress still further.
I see your star in its full radiance.
There is no place in sense existence
for battles such as men must fight
who strive for consecration.
What sense existence hides as riddles
which can be solved by intellect,
what human hearts receive from such existence, –
no matter if it comes from love or hate
or whether it bursts forth with frightful power –
this for the spirit seeker must become
a field on which he, uninvolved,
directs his vision from without.
For forces must unfold themselves for him
which are not found upon this field itself.
You had to wrest your way through trials of soul
which only come to those
well armed to meet those powers
belonging to the spirit worlds.
And had those powers not found you ready
to tread the path of knowledge,
they would have had to lame your feeling
before you were allowed to know
what now has been revealed to you.
The beings who can gaze at world-foundations
lead men who strive into the heights
at first up to that summit

where can be shown
if strength is theirs
for conscious spirit sight.
Those who possess such forces
can be released out of the world of sense.
The others still must wait.
You have sustained your Self, my son,
when powers of the heights have shaken you
and spirit forces shrouded you in dread.
Your Self has strongly battled its way through,
when doubts were wrestling in your breast
and sought to give you over to dark depths.
You have been my true pupil only
since that portentous hour
when you, despairing,
felt that yourself was lost,
and yet the strength in you still held you firm.
I was allowed to grant from wisdom's treasures
what gave you strength
to hold yourself,
though you believed no longer in yourself.
So was the wisdom which you conquered
more truthful than the faith
bestowed on you.
You are now found mature.
You now may be released.
Your friend has led the way.
In spirit you will find her.
I can still further give you the direction:
call forth the fiery power of your soul
with words which, uttered through my mouth,
give you the key to spirit heights.

75

They will accompany you
when nothing longer guides you
which eyes of sense can still behold.
With your whole heart now willingly receive them:
 *Light's weaving essence radiates*
 *through far-flung spaces*
 *to fill the world with life.*
 *Love's blessing pours its warmth*
 *through time's long ages*
 *to call forth revelation of all worlds.*
 *And messengers of spirit join*
 *light's weaving essence*
 *with revelation of the soul.*
 *And when with both the human being*
 *can join his own true self,*
 *he is alive in spirit heights.*
O spirits who can be perceived by man,
quicken with life the soul of this our son.
Let shine in him
what can illumine
his soul with spirit light.
Let sound in him
what can awaken
his self to joyous spirit growth.


SPIRIT VOICE (*behind the scene*):
 Thoughts now guide him
 to depths of world-beginnings;
 what as shadows he has thought,
 what as phantoms he has felt
 soars out, beyond the world of forms, –
 world, of whose fullness
 men, when thinking,

dream in shadows;
world, from whose fullness
men, when seeing,
live within phantoms.

*Curtain*

# SCENE FOUR

*A landscape whose unique nature is to represent the soul world. Lucifer and Ahriman appear first. Johannes is visible at one side, in deep meditation. What follows is experienced by him in meditation.*

LUCIFER       O man, know yourself.
                 O man, experience me.
                 You've wrenched yourself away
                 from spirit guidance,
                 and you have fled
                 into free earthly realms.
                 You've sought your own true being
                 in earth's confusion;
                 to find yourself
                 proved your reward
                 and proved your fate.
                 Me you have found.
                 Spirits desired
                 to cast a veil before the senses:
                 I tore the veil apart.
                 Spirits desired
                 to follow only their own will in you:
                 I gave you your own will.
                 O man, know yourself.
                 O man, experience me.

AHRIMAN    O man, know me.
O man, experience yourself.
You have escaped
from spirit darkness,
and you have found
the light of earth.
So suck the power of truth
from my solidity.
I harden stable ground.
Spirits desired
to rob you of the senses' beauty.
I activate this beauty
in solid light.
I lead you onward
into essential truth.
O man, know me.
O man, experience yourself.


LUCIFER    There was no time
when you did not experience me.
I've followed you through many lives.
And I could fill you
with strength of selfhood,
self-being's joy.


AHRIMAN    There was no time
when you did not perceive me.
Your body's eyes have looked on me
through all earth evolution.
I could shine out for you
with pride of beauty,
with bliss of revelation.

JOHANNES (*to himself, in meditation*)
>This is the sign about which Benedictus spoke.
>Two powers stand before the world of soul.
>The one dwells in us as the tempter;
>the other dulls the gaze
>when it is turned toward outward things.
>The one assumed the woman's form
>who brought before my eyes the soul's delusion.
>The other can be found in everything.

>(*Exit Lucifer and Ahriman*
>THE *Spirit of the Elements appears with*
>*Capesius and Strader, whom he has brought out of*
>*subterranean depths to the surface of the earth. It is*
>*to be imagined that, as souls, they look out over the*
>*earth's surface.*)

SPIRIT OF THE ELEMENTS
>So here is now the place
>which you so ardently desired.
>It cost me care enough and trouble
>to satisfy your wish.
>The spirits and the elements
>arose in raging storm,
>when I was forced to enter
>their kingdom with your beings.
>Your kind of thought resisted
>the ruling of my power.

CAPESIUS (*grown young*)
>Mysterious being,
>who are you,
>who's brought me through the spheres of spirits
>into this pleasant realm?

SPIRIT OF THE ELEMENTS

        The human soul beholds me only
        when services I render him are over.
        Yet he obeys my powers
        throughout all course of time.

CAPESIUS

        I am but little moved
        to ask about the spirit
        who led me here.
        I feel the forces of my life
        grow warm in this new realm.
        This light expands my breast.
        I sense the whole world's might
        within the beating of my pulse.
        Anticipation of all I shall achieve
        is rising in my heart.
        I will transform to words
        this kingdom's revelation,
        invigorating me so gloriously.
        And human souls shall blossom
        to life imbued with beauty,
        when I can bring to them
        enthusiasm from the springs
        which here flow forth to me.

        (*Lightning and thunder from the heights and depths.*)

STRADER (*grown old*)

        Why are the depths so shaken;
        why do the heights resound,
        when dreams of hopeful beauty
        well forth from this young soul?

        (*Lightning and thunder.*)

SPIRIT OF THE ELEMENTS

To human dreamers as yourselves
such words of hope ring proudly.
But in the depths of worlds,
illusions of wrong thinking
forever wake such echoes.
You hear it only at those times
which bring you near to me.
You think that you are building
at truth's exalted temples,
but your work's consequences
unfetter powers of storm
within primeval depths.
Thus spirits must break worlds apart,
should temporal deeds of yours not bring
destruction, even death
to the eternities.

STRADER

For the eternities, then, error and illusion
would be what seems the truth
to man's best search for knowledge!

(*Lightning and thunder.*)

SPIRIT OF THE ELEMENTS

Yes, error and illusion, –
as long as man's mind searches
in a realm estranged from spirit.

STRADER

You may well call my friend a dreamer,
who in the joy of youth
paints his own goals courageously
with so much noble fire.
In my old heart, however,

your words fade out and die,
in spite of storm and thunder
which are their mighty helpers.
I wrenched myself out of the cloister's peace
to self-esteem of research.
Throughout long years now I have stood
amid the storms of life.
And men believe
what I entrust to them
out of my deepest sense of truth.

(*Lightning and thunder.*)

SPIRIT OF THE ELEMENTS

Then it behooves you to acknowledge
that no man can know
from whence are gushing the sources of his
    thought
or where life's first foundations lie.

STRADER

O these words, they are the same
which in my youthful days of hope
resounded terribly
within my soul,
when all support of human thought,
believed so firm, began to sway.

(*Lightning and thunder.*)

SPIRIT OF THE ELEMENTS

You must compel me
with your stunted weapons of dull thought,
or you are nothing but
a fleeting phantom of your own delusion

STRADER        Once more such terrifying words.
These too resounded
out of my inmost core,
when once a seeress made me feel
the threatening sting of doubt
and so destroyed for me
the circle of firm thought.
But that is quite behind me.
I will defy your power,
you ancient one, who so deceivingly
displays the image of my being
within the mask of Nature's ruler.
Yet, otherwise than you suppose,
shall reason overcome you.
For if it has attained
its proudest peak in man,
it will then be the master
and not the slave of Nature.

(*Lightning and thunder.*)

SPIRIT OF THE ELEMENTS

The world is ordered so
that work performed
demands return of service.
I have bestowed on you your selfhood.
You owe me my reward.

CAPESIUS      I will create out of my soul
the spirit counterpart of things.
When Nature, to ideals transfigured,
arises within human works,
she is repaid enough
in being truly mirrored.

84

And if you feel yourself akin
to the great Mother of all worlds
and have your origin in depths
where primal powers rule,
then let my will,
that lives for lofty ends
within my head and breast,
reward you for your deed.
For it has lifted me
from clouded feeling to proud thought.

(*Lightning and thunder.*)

SPIRIT OF THE ELEMENTS

You can behold
how little your bold words are worth
within my realm.
For they unfetter storms
and rouse the elements in wrath
to rage against all order.

CAPESIUS

Then you may seek reward
wherever you can find it.
On genuine spirit heights
man's impulses of soul
must give themselves the measurement
and order of their own.
For he cannot create
when others wish to utilize
the work that he brings into being.
The bird's song pouring from its throat
is in itself enough.
And so it is reward for man

when he, creating,
finds bliss in his activity.

(*Lightning and thunder.*)

SPIRIT OF THE ELEMENTS
It will not do
that you refuse me payment.
If you yourselves cannot accomplish it,
then tell the woman
who has endowed your souls with power
that she must pay for you.

(THE *Spirit of the Elements disappears.*)

CAPESIUS        He's vanished.
Now whither shall we turn?
To find in these new worlds
the right direction
is first of all our task.

STRADER         To follow the best way that we can find,
with confidence, and use our caution,
should lead us to our goal.

CAPESIUS        It seems to me
we'd best be silent as to goal.
We shall attain it
if we obey courageously
the impulse of our inner selves.
To me this impulse says:
let truth become your guide,
unfolding sturdy forces
and shaping them to noble form

in all you undertake;
then must your steps
lead rightly to the goal.

STRADER

And yet from those first steps of ours,
awareness of the rightful goals
should not be absent, if they are
to be of benefit to men
and give them happiness.
The man who serves none but himself
need follow only his heart's urge,
but he who wishes to help others
must know for sure
just what his life requires.

(THE *other Maria, also in soul form, becomes
visible.*)

But look, – what a mysterious being!
It is as if the rock itself
had given birth to it.
From out what world foundations
do such beings come?

THE OTHER MARIA

I wrest my way through rocky depths
and seek to clothe the rocks' own will
with human words;
I sense the being of the earth
and wish to think the earth's own thoughts
within the human head;
I drink in air of purest life
and bring the powers of air
transformed to human feeling.

STRADER      You cannot help us then.
             What must remain in Nature's realm
             is far from human striving.

CAPESIUS     I love your language, woman,
             and gladly would translate your kind of speech
             into my own.

THE OTHER MARIA
             So strange to me
             are your proud words.
             The way you speak
             I cannot understand.
             But if I let your words
             resound out of my being differently,
             they spread out over all the things
             that fill the spheres about me
             and answer then their riddles.

CAPESIUS     If what you say is true,
             then change for us our questions
             about right values in men's lives
             into your speech, so that
             an answer comes to us from Nature.
             We are incapable ourselves
             of asking the great Mother in a way
             that she can hear our words.

THE OTHER MARIA
             You see in me the humbler sister only
             of that high spirit being
             who dwells within the realm
             from which you have just come.

She has assigned to me this sphere
that I may show her mirrored image
to human senses here.

CAPESIUS Have we then fled from that domain
in which our longing could be satisfied?

THE OTHER MARIA

If you do not discover
the pathway back,
it never will go well with you.

CAPESIUS And which way is the right way then?

THE OTHER MARIA

There are two ways.
When power in me reaches to its height,
all beings of my realm
begin to radiate in most majestic beauty,
and sparkling light then gleams
from rock and water;
on every side is glowing
the richest wealth of color,
and gaiety of creatures floods the air
with cheerful sounds.
If you will give your souls
to all the pure delights of my existence,
you will soar forth on spirit wings
toward primal origins of worlds.

STRADER That is no way for us.
In our speech it is called fantastic.
We want to stay upon the ground,
not fly into the cloudy heights.

THE OTHER MARIA
                    And if you wish to go
                    the other way,
                    you must renounce
                    your haughty spirit.
                    Forget what reason must dictate.
                    Let Nature's mood first conquer you.
                    In manhood's breast let childhood's soul,
                    untouched by shadow-images of thought,
                    hold sway, naively true.
                    Then will you come, though not through knowing,
                    but surely, to the springs of life.

                    (THE *Other Maria disappears.*)

CAPESIUS            So after all, we are thrown back upon ourselves.
                    And we have merely learned:
                    our task would be to work
                    and to await in patience
                    the fruits that ripen from our deeds.


JOHANNES (*as if out of his meditation. Here as in the following scenes
                    he sits at one side and does not himself take part in the
                    action.*)
                    In realms of soul I find again
                    the human beings who are known to me.
                    The man who spoke about Felicia's fairy tales:
                    I could behold him here
                    as in his younger years;
                    and also he who as a youth
                    had chosen to become a monk:
                    here as an old man he appeared to me.
                    And with them was the Spirit of the Elements.

                    *Curtain*

# SCENE FIVE

*A Subterranean Rock Temple, the hidden Mystery Place of the Hierophants.*

BENEDICTUS (*in the East*)
As you have been my true companions
in realms of everlasting life,
so I have come to you
today, to ask the help
I need, to weave
the threads of destiny for one
who must receive from us the light.
Through many trials and sorrows he has passed
and has in bitter pain of soul
prepared for consecration
which now shall bring him knowledge.
My task is thus fulfilled
as spirit-messenger, to bring
the treasures of this temple
to earthly human beings.
It lies with you, my brothers, now
to carry out my work.
I have revealed to him the light
which guided him
to his first spirit vision.
That the vision
may turn to truth

your work must join with mine.
My word springs forth from me alone.
Through you the cosmic spirits sound.

THEODOSIUS (*in the South*)
The power of love speaks thus,
uniting worlds
and filling beings with reality.
Let warmth now flow into his heart;
and he shall realize
how he draws near the cosmic spirit
by giving up the vain
illusion of his self-bound life.
You have at last set free
his sight from sleep of sense;
now warmth shall stir and wake the spirit
out of his inner being.
You have drawn forth the self
out of his body's sheath;
now love shall make his soul grow firm,
that it become a mirror
wherein must be perceived
what happens in the spirit world.
And love will give him power
to feel himself as spirit,
and so create for him the ear
that hears the words of spirit beings.

ROMANUS (*in the West*)
My words are also not
the revelation of my being;
through me the world-will speaks.
And as you have so strengthened

the one entrusted to your care
with power to live in spirit,
so shall this power lead him
through bounds of space and ends of time.
Into those spheres he now shall pass
where spirits act, creative.
They will reveal themselves to him,
demanding of him deeds.
And he will do them willingly.
The cosmic builders' goals
shall quicken him with life;
divine primordial sources
bespirit him;
world-ruling powers
grant strength to him;
the mights of spheres
illumine him;
and lords of worlds
befire him.

RETARDUS (*in the North*)

You have been forced since earth's beginning
to suffer me within your midst.
Today too in your council
my word must have a hearing.
Till you can carry out
all you've so finely spoken,
will take as yet some little time!
So far the earth herself
has given us no sign
to indicate her longing
for new initiates.
As long as yet no mortals

have come into this place,
who, uninitiate,
can set the spirit free
from sense reality,
so long am I permitted
to curb your eagerness.
They first must bring us tidings
that new-won revelation
seems needful to the earth.
Till then I hold your spirit light
imprisoned here within this temple,
that it may not bring harm
instead of healing
to human souls still unprepared.
I give to man
that part of my own being
which makes the senses' truth
appear to him the highest,
as long as spirit wisdom
can blind his inner eye.
So faith may still continue
to lead him toward the spirit,
and all his goals of action
can likewise still be guided
by blind desires and passions
that grope their way through darkness.

ROMANUS We have been forced since earth's beginning
to suffer you within our midst.
But now the time has run its course
which was allotted to your work.
In me the world-will feels
that human beings are approaching

*(Felix Balde appears in his earthly form, the
Other Maria in soul form out of the rock.)*

who, uninitiate, can free the spirit
from sense appearance.
You are no longer granted
the power to hinder us.
Out of their own free will
they now approach our temple
to bring you word
that, joined with us,
they wish to help the working of the spirit.
Till now they felt themselves
not yet prepared for this,
but clung to the belief
that visionary power
must stand apart from reason.
They now have clearly seen
where men are led today by reason,
which set apart from wakeful seeing
goes erring in the depths of worlds.
And they will speak to you
of fruits, which through your power
must ripen in the souls of men.

RETARDUS    You two who still unconsciously
have forwarded my work,
you shall still further help me.
If you will keep aloof from what
belongs alone within my realm,
so shall the place, reserved
for you to work, remain
as you have had it in the past.

| | |
|---|---|
| FELIX BALDE | A power, speaking to my spirit |
| | out of the depths of earth, |
| | has bidden me come hither |
| | into the place of consecration, |
| | for it would tell through me |
| | of all its sorrow, all its needs. |
| | |
| BENEDICTUS | My friend, so let us hear |
| | what you have learned within your inmost soul |
| | about the bitter sorrow |
| | in depths of earth. |
| | |
| FELIX BALDE | The light that shines in men |
| | and is the fruit of knowledge |
| | has to become the nourishment |
| | for powers who in earthly darkness |
| | do service to the cosmic course. |
| | But now for long they have been forced |
| | to lack such sustenance. |
| | For what evolves today |
| | within the brains of men |
| | can serve the surface of the earth, |
| | but does not penetrate the depths. |
| | A fine new superstition like a spook |
| | haunts clever human heads: |
| | they turn their gaze toward world beginnings |
| | and like to fancy nothing |
| | but ghostly spectres in the spheres of spirit, |
| | thought out from sense illusion. |
| | The merchant would believe his customer |
| | had lost his mind who said to him: |
| | the mist that rises in the valley |
| | can be condensed to current coin, |

and with it you shall now be paid.
No merchant would accept
such money out of mist.
Yet if he thirst
to solve life's highest riddles,
he willingly accepts
whole cosmic structures made of nebulae,
if science hands them him
to pay his spirit needs.
A teacher who found out
that untaught scoundrels wished,
without examinations,
to rise to heights of knowledge
would threaten them with just disgrace.
Yet science does not doubt at all
that all untutored, void of spirit,
the antediluvian animal
could of itself become a man.

THEODOSIUS    Why do you not reveal to men
the sources of your light
which shines from out your soul
with such resplendent ray?

FELIX BALDE    I'm called a recluse and a dreamer
by those of kind intentions.
The others think of me
as just a blockhead
who all untaught by them
pursues his own poor nonsense.

RETARDUS    You show us how untaught you are
by speaking in such naive terms.

You do not know that men of science
possess sufficient shrewdness
to argue about world beginnings
as you have done.
And if they do not do so,
they know the reason why.

FELIX BALDE     I know quite well
that they indeed are shrewd enough
to understand such an objection
but certainly not shrewd enough
as to believe in it.

THEODOSIUS     What must be done
to give forthwith the powers of earth
what they so sorely need?

FELIX BALDE     As long on earth
those men alone find hearing
who are unwilling to recall
their own true spirit source,
so long the lords of metal ores
will hunger in the depths of earth.

THE OTHER MARIA

I gather, brother Felix, from your words
that you believe the time has ended now
in which we served existence on the earth,
still uninitiate through wisdom's light,
seeking to quicken spirit there and love,
out of our own life sources.
In you the spirits of the earth have risen,
creating light for you apart from science.

In me has love held sway, the love
which of itself develops in the life of man.
In union with the brothers who perform the rites
within the temple, let us further work
to bring forth fruits in human souls.

BENEDICTUS    If you unite with us
the work of consecration must succeed.
The wisdom I have given to my son
in him will blossom into power.

THEODOSIUS:    If you unite with us
the joy of sacrifice will grow,
and love will then weave through with warmth
the spirit seeker's life of soul.

ROMANUS    If you unite with us
the spirit fruits will ripen,
and deeds will quicken, which through spirit
    action
grow forth from soul discipleship.

RETARDUS    If they unite with you,
what will become of me?
My deeds will then prove fruitless
for pupils of the spirit path.

BENEDICTUS    You will transform yourself to other life
for you have done your work.

THEODOSIUS    You will live on in sacrifice
if you will sacrifice yourself.

ROMANUS    You will bear fruit in human deeds
           if I can cultivate the fruit.

JOHANNES (*as in the previous scene, out of meditation*)
           Here stood before the eye of soul
           the brothers in the temple.
           In figure they resemble men
           well known to me in sense appearance.
           In spirit, only Benedictus was the same.
           The one upon his left
           bears likeness to that man
           who only through his feelings
           wished to approach the spirit.
           The third resembles him
           who only recognizes powers of life
           in mechanisms and external work.
           The fourth one is unknown to me.
           The woman who upon her husband's death
           turned to the spirit's light:
           I saw her in her deepest being.
           And Felix Balde came
           just as he is in life.

           *Curtain falls slowly.*

## SCENE SIX

*The same setting as in Scene Four.* THE *Spirit of the Elements is standing in the same place.*

FELICIA BALDE  You've had me summoned.
What do you wish from me?

SPIRIT OF THE ELEMENTS
Two men I've given to the earth.
Through you the spirit power
of both these men was quickened.
They found within your words
enlivening forces for their souls,
when arid thought had lamed them.
What you have given them
has put you also in my debt.
Their spirit is too weak
to pay me for the service
which I have rendered them.

FELICIA BALDE  For years one of the men
had visited our cottage
to gather there the strength
that kindled fire in his words;
then later on he brought the other with him.

And so the two devoured
the fruits whose value then
was still unknown to me.
Yet little good
did I receive from them as thanks.
They gave to our good son
their kind of knowledge.
It was, of course, well meant
and yet through it our child
was stricken with soul death.
He'd grown and lived within the light
which Father Felix gathers
from what the spirits speak out of the springs,
the rocks, and mountains.
And joined with this was everything
that's grown within my soul
since my first childhood years.
But in the dismal shadow of dark science
our son's true feeling for the spirit died.
The happy child
became a man
with barren soul
and empty heart.
And yet you now demand
that I should pay
their debt to you!

Spirit of the Elements

It must be so.
Since you have served
the earthly part in them,
the spirit now demands through me
that you complete the work.

FELICIA BALDE It's not my custom
to refuse what I should do.
But tell me first of all
if harm will come to me
out of this deed of love.

SPIRIT OF THE ELEMENTS
What you first did for them on earth
despoiled your child of his soul strength.
What you now give their spirit
is lost to you for your own self;
and loss of vital powers
will show itself in you
as ugliness of body.

FELICIA BALDE They robbed my child
of all the forces of his soul,
and I should walk around
a monster in the sight of men,
that for them fruits may ripen
which bring but little good?

SPIRIT OF THE ELEMENTS
Yet you will work for mankind's good
and your own happiness as well.
The mother's beauty and the child's life
will blossom in a higher form for you
when one day in the souls of men
new spirit powers spring to life.

FELICIA BALDE What shall I do?

SPIRIT OF THE ELEMENTS
You often have inspired human beings:

so now inspire the spirits of the rocks.
You must bring forth out of yourself
one of your fairy tales
and at this time entrust it to those beings
who serve me in my work.

FELICIA BALDE So be it . . . Once upon a time
there was a Being
that flew from East to West,
following the journey of the sun.
It flew on, over lands and over seas;
and from the heights it watched
the busy life of men.
It saw how men love one another,
and how in hate they persecute each other.
Not anything could hinder
this Being in its flight;
for hate and love create
always the same a thousandfold.
But over one house on its way
the Being had to pause.
Within, there was a tired man
who pondered over human love
and pondered, too, on human hate.
His pondering had carved
deep furrows on his brow,
had turned his hair quite white.
In its concern for him,
the Being lost its guide, the sun,
and stayed at this man's side.
It was still in his room
at evening when the sun went down;
and when the sun returned,

the Being was once more
caught upward by the spirit of the sun.
Again it saw the many people
in love, in hate,
continue on their earthly course.
And when it came a second time
above the house, still following the sun,
its gaze fell there
upon a dead old man.

GAIRMAN (*from behind a cliff, invisible*)
Once upon a time there was a man
who tramped from East to West;
the urge for knowledge lured him on
to travel over lands and seas,
and by his rules of wisdom
he watched the busy life of men.
He saw how men love one another
and how in hate they persecute each other.
At every single instant
he saw himself at all his wisdom's end.
For how it is that hate and love
forever rule the earthly world
could not be brought into a law.
He noted many thousand cases,
yet lacked a comprehensive whole.
This dry researcher
encountered on his way
a Being of the Light,
upon whom life weighed heavily,
for it was in a constant battle
with a dark shadow-form.
'Well, who are you?'

inquired the dry researcher.
'Oh, I am Love,'
one being answered.
'In me behold dark Hate,'
so spoke the other.
The man, however, could
no longer hear these beings' words.
As deaf researcher, he tramped on
from East to West, this man.

FELICIA BALDE  And who are you
who thus distorts
each word of mine
in such uncalled-for manner?
It sounds like mockery,
and I am not the sort that likes to mock.

GAIRMAN (*appears*)
I am the Spirit of the Earth-brain.
A dwarf-like copy of me
is all that lives in men.
Full many a thing is thought therein
which is but mockery of itself
when I reveal it in the size
which it takes on within my brain.

FELICIA BALDE  So therefore you mock me as well!

GAIRMAN  I must right often ply
this kind of trade,
but mostly no one hears me.
I've seized this chance
for once at least to be upon the spot
where I am heard.

JOHANNES (*out of his meditation*)
> This was the man who said
> that spirit light had entered
> as of its own accord into his brain.
> And like her husband Felix
> Felicia came
> just as she is in life.

*Curtain*

## SCENE SEVEN

*The realm of spirit. Maria, Philia, Astrid, Luna, the Child; Johannes, first at a distance, then coming nearer; Theodora and lastly, Benedictus.*

MARIA

You, my sisters, at this hour
be once again my helpers,
as you have often been before, –
that I may make world-ether
resound within itself.
It shall ring out in harmony
and, ringing, permeate
a soul with knowledge.
I can behold the signs
that lead us to our task.
So shall your work
unite itself with mine.
Johannes, in his striving,
shall through creative deeds of ours
be raised to true existence.
The brothers in the temple
held council
how they could lead him
out of the depths to light-filled heights.
And they expect of us
that we arouse within his soul

the strength for soaring flight.
And so, my Philia, breathe in
clear essence of the light
from wide-flung spaces;
be filled with tones, enticing,
from souls' creative power,
that you can hand to me
the gifts you gather
from spirit grounds.
Then I can weave them
into the stirring dances of the spheres.
And you, too, Astrid,
beloved mirror-image of my spirit,
create the power of darkness
in streaming light,
that colours may shine forth.
Bring harmony to tonal being
so that world-substance, weaving,
can live and sound.
I can entrust then spirit feeling
to seeking human senses.
And you, O sturdy Luna,
you are as firm within
as is the living heart
that grows within the tree;
join with your sisters' gifts
the image of your own uniqueness,
that certainty of knowledge
be granted to the seeker.

PHILIA      I will imbue myself
with clearest essence of the light
from worldwide spaces.

I will breathe in sound-substance,
life-bestowing,
from far ethereal regions,
that you, beloved sister, with your work
may reach your goal.

ASTRID          And I will weave
into the radiant light
the clouding darkness.
I will condense
the life of sound,
that glistening it may ring
and ringing it may glisten,
that you, beloved sister,
may guide the rays of soul.

LUNA            I will enwarm soul-substance
and will make firm life-ether.
They shall condense themselves,
they shall perceive themselves,
and in themselves residing
guard their creative forces,
that you, beloved sister,
within the seeking soul
may quicken certainty of knowledge.

MARIA           From Philia's horizons
shall stream forth joyfulness.
The undines' power
of ever-changefulness shall rouse
a sensitivity of soul,
that the awakened one
can then experience

the world's delight,
the world's despair.
From Astrid's weaving
shall spring forth love's desire.
The airy life of sylphs
shall stir up in the soul
the urge for sacrifice,
that he, the consecrated one,
revive and quicken
those who are sorrow-laden,
those who are joy-entreating.
From Luna's strength
shall stream forth firmness;
the power of fire-beings
can actively create
soul-certainty,
so that the knowing one
can find himself
in soul-life-weaving,
in world-life-breathing.

PHILIA I will entreat the spirits of the worlds
that they, with light of being,
enchant soul feeling,
that they, with tone of words,
charm spirit hearing,
that he whom we must waken
may rise
upon soul paths
to heavenly heights.

ASTRID I will guide streams of love,
that fill the world with warmth,

into the heart
of him, the consecrated one,
that he can bring
the grace of heaven
to earthly work
and mood of consecration
to sons of men.

LUNA        I will from primal powers
beseech both strength and courage,
and will imbed them deep
within the seeker's heart,
that confidence
in his own self
may be with him
throughout his life.
He shall then feel himself
secure within himself.
And he shall pluck
each moment's ripened fruit,
to draw from them their seeds
for all eternity.

MARIA        With you, my sisters,
united for this earnest work,
I shall succeed
in what I long to do.
There penetrates the cry
of him, who's been so sorely tested,
into our world of light.

(*Johannes appears*)

JOHANNES      Maria, it is you. My suffering then

has brought abundant fruit.
It has now freed me from the phantom being
that I had formed from out myself
and that has held me prisoner.
I could attain to you on paths of soul
and this I owe to pain.

MARIA      What was the way that brought you here?

JOHANNES    I felt myself released from bonds of sense.
My gaze was freed from all the limits
imposed upon it by the moment.
I could see other things
within our human life
than what a single instant
can show within the narrowest circle.
Capesius, whom my senses' sight
has brought before me aged in years,
the spirit showed to me as young –
when, full of hopeful dreams,
the youth set out upon life's journey
that was to bring him constantly
a faithful throng of hearers.
And Strader, who is still
quite young in earthly life
and hardly has outgrown the cloister,
I saw as he might be
if he should follow out his aims
as he's conceived them until now.
And only those who are already filled
with spirit as they are on earth
appeared unchanged in spirit realms.
Both Felix and Felicia had kept

their earthly forms,
when I beheld them with my spirit eyes.
And then the Brothers in the Temple
showed me their favor
in speaking of the gifts that will be mine
if once I can attain
to lofty heights of knowledge.
And much more have I seen
with my new spirit vision
which in their narrow way
the senses first had shown me.
The light of true discernment
shone forth in my new world.
But whether it was dream that dawned in me
or spirit's true reality,
I could not yet distinguish.
And whether spirit sight had come in touch
with other things
or whether I had merely widened
myself into a world,
I could not tell.
Then you yourself appeared,
not as you are at present,
nor as the past has seen you;
no, I beheld you
as eternally you stand in spirit.
Not earthly was your being, –
I clearly recognized
the spirit in your soul.
It did not act as does a human being
within a sentient body;
it acted as a spirit
who gives existence to those deeds

that have their roots within eternity.
And only now that I can stand
before you in the spirit,
does full light shine for me.
In you my sense perception
had grasped so firmly true reality
that I am certain here
in spirit land as well;
it is no phantom form before me;
it is the very truth of being,
in which I there encountered you,
in which I now may meet you here.

THEODORA       I am impelled to speak.
Out of your brow, Maria,
springs forth a shining light.
The shine now shapes itself:
it takes on human form.
It is a man imbued with spirit,
and other human beings gather round him.
I look into long vanished times.
The holy man, whose form
ascended from your head,
lets stream from out his eyes
the purest calm of soul,
and tenderness gleams forth
out of his noble features.
Before him I perceive a woman
who listens with devotion to the words
which issue from his lips.
I hear the words, and so they sound:
'You have looked up in reverence
unto your gods.

I love these gods as you love them yourselves.
They have poured strength into your thoughts;
they planted courage in your hearts.
Yet of these gifts they bring,
a higher Spirit is the source.'
— — — — — — — — — — — — — — — —
I can behold how what he says
awakens fury in these people.
I hear their shouts: 'O kill him!
for he will rob us of the gifts
the gods have brought us.'
But still the man speaks calmly on.
He tells about the God
descending to the earth as Man
who thus has conquered death.
He speaks of Christ.
And as he goes on speaking,
their souls grow gentler;
one heathen heart alone resists
and swears a vengeance on the man.
I recognize this heart:
it beats again within that child
who nestles at your side.
To him there speaks the messenger of Christ:
'Your destiny does not allow
that you come near me in this life.
Yet I shall wait in patience;
your path will lead you to me in the end.'
The woman standing there before him
falls at his feet.
She feels herself transformed.
A soul is praying to the Son of Man;
a heart is given in love to the messenger of God.

*(Johannes falls to his knees before Maria.)*

MARIA          Johannes, what is dawning in you
you must awaken to full consciousness.
Remembrance at this moment freed itself
from fetters of the senses.
You were aware of me
and you have felt yourself
as we were joined in earlier life on earth.
The woman whom the seeress spoke about
was you yourself.
You lay thus at my feet
when long ago as messenger of Christ
I journeyed to your tribe.
What in Hibernia's holy places
was once disclosed to me about the God
who dwelt within a human being
and was the victor over powers of death,
I was allowed to bring to peoples
in whom were still alive
those souls who offered mighty Odin
their joyful sacrifice
and had to think of Baldur,
the radiant one, with sorrow.
When first your earthly eyes
beheld me in this present life, the power
which grew within you
with the message that I brought,
that power drew you to me.
Because it worked so strongly,
yet was unconscious in us both,
it had to weave into our lives
the suffering that we struggled through.

But in the suffering itself there lay the power
to lead us into spirit realms
where we now truly know each other.
Your pain increased to overflowing
through presence of so many people.
With them you are united through strength of
    destiny,
and so the revelation of their beings
could shake your heart so deeply.
Karma has gathered them about you now
to wake in you a power
that helped your life progress.
This power has so shaken you
that you were liberated from the body
and could ascend to spirit worlds.
Since you stand closest to my soul
and have kept faith to me through all your pain,
it therefore is my lot
to bring to its completion
the consecration, blessing you with spirit light.
The brothers who do service in the temple
have wakened you to spirit sight,
yet you can only know
this vision to be true
if in the spirit lands you find again
someone with whom in worlds of sense
you are already bound in deepest being.
In order that this one may meet you here,
the brothers sent me on before you.
It was the hardest of your trials
when I was summoned here.
I asked our leader, Benedictus,
to solve for me

the riddle of my life,
which seemed to me so cruel.
And blissfulness streamed forth out of his words
when he revealed his mission and my own.
He told me of the Spirit to whose service
the power within me should be dedicated.
And at his words
the purest spirit light within an instant
had flooded all my soul and had transformed
all sorrow into blissful joy.
And one thought only filled my soul:
he gave me light, –
yes, light that granted me the power of sight.
In this thought lived the will
to give myself completely to the spirit
and thus prepare the sacrificial deed
that might then bring me near to him.
This thought had greatest power.
It gave wings to my soul and carried me
into this realm where you have found me.
And at the moment when I felt myself
set free from senses of the body,
I could direct my spirit gaze toward you:
I had before me not Johannes only, –
I saw the woman who had followed me
in ancient times and who had joined her fate
so closely then with mine.
Thus spirit truth was given me through you,
who in the sense world are already
so closely linked with me in deepest being.
I had attained to certainty of spirit
and was empowered to give it on to you.
To Benedictus sending forth a ray

of highest love, I went before you, –
and he has given you the strength
to follow me in spirit spheres.

(*Benedictus appears*)


BENEDICTUS      You here have found yourselves
in regions of the spirit,
and so I may
once more be at your side.
I could confer on you the force
that urged you onward to these heights,
yet I myself could not
accompany you.
Thus wills the law
which I must follow.
You had first through yourselves
to gain the eye of spirit,
which makes me visible
here too for you.
The path of spirit pilgrimage
for you has just begun.
You will face sense existence
with fresh, strong forces
and, with the spirit now
unlocked to you,
you can serve human progress.
You have been joined by destiny
together to unfold the powers
which are to serve the good in active work.
And while you journey on the path of soul,
wisdom itself will teach you
that highest goals can be achieved

when souls will give each other spirit certainty,
will join themselves in faithfulness
for healing of the world.
The spirit's guidance has united you in knowledge;
so now unite yourselves for spirit work.
The rulers of this realm bestow on you,
through me, these words of strength:

*Light's weaving essence radiates*
*from man to man*
*to fill the world with truth.*
*Love's blessing gives its warmth*
*to souls through souls*
*to work and weave the bliss of all the worlds.*
*And messengers of spirit join*
*men's works of blessing*
*with purposes of worlds.*
*And when the man who finds himself in man*
*can join one with the other*
*the light of spirit radiates through warmth of soul.*

*Curtain*

# INTERLUDE

*It is assumed that the preceding scenes were the performance which Sophia has attended and that she is visited again on the following day by her friend Estella. The following takes place in the same room as the Prelude.*

SOPHIA      Do forgive me, Estella, for letting you wait. I was busy with the children.

ESTELLA     I had to come back. I'm so fond of you that I always long to share with you everything that stirs me deeply.

SOPHIA      You will always find me with ready interest in everything that affects you.

ESTELLA     The play, 'The Uprooted', moved me so very much. It may seem odd to you, but there were moments when all the human suffering I have ever known or observed seemed to take shape before me. With great artistic power the play presents not only the outward misfortunes of people but with astonishing insight a profound suffering of soul.

SOPHIA      It is difficult to form an accurate idea of a play or of any work of art by simply hearing about it. But I'd be glad if you would tell me what it was that moved you so much.

| | |
|---|---|
| ESTELLA | The dramatic construction was wonderful. The playwright shows how a young painter loses all his creative joy when he begins to grow uncertain in his love for a woman. She had given him the incentive to develop his talents. In her, through the purest enthusiasm for his art, a selfless love had sprung up, and, thanks to this, he was able to develop all his capacities. One might say, he bloomed in the sunlight of his benefactor. As he was often in her company, his feelings of gratitude gradually grew into a passionate love. This caused him to neglect, more and more, a poor girl who had been faithfully devoted to him. His indifference made her realize she had lost the heart of the man she loved, and she finally died of grief. When he heard of her death, the news did not seriously disturb him, because by now his feelings belonged only to his benefactor. Yet he gradually had to come to the conclusion that her friendly feelings would never change into passionate love. This drove all creative joy out of his soul and his inner life became ever more desolate. Now the young woman he had forsaken began to haunt his memory. And what had once been a man of promise became a desolate ruin of one. Without a single ray of hope, he ended in utter despair. – All this is enacted with the most vivid dramatic intensity. |
| SOPHIA | I can see how powerfully this play would affect you. I remember, even when you were a child, you used to suffer when you saw the fate of unhappy people driven by misfortune into bitterness and misery. |

ESTELLA    You misunderstand me, Sophia dear. I can easily distinguish between a dramatic work of art and reality. We must not judge art by the same feelings as those aroused in us by similar events in real life; we must judge it for what it actually is. What stirred me so deeply was nothing but the perfection of the artistic handling of a serious problem. I recognized again, quite clearly, that art can only reach to such heights by being faithful to the whole of life. The moment it departs from this, it becomes untrue.

SOPHIA    I understand you perfectly when you say that. I've always admired writers who could represent what you call the faithfulness to life; and it seems to me that particularly nowadays many have achieved a mastery in this. But it is just these great artistic achievements that have aroused in me a certain uneasiness. For a long time I couldn't explain it. Then one day a light dawned on me that provided the answer.

ESTELLA    And now you are going to tell me that your world-view has led you away from your former appreciation of realistic art.

SOPHIA    Let's not talk about my world-view today. For you know quite well that I felt like this long before I had the slightest knowledge of what you call my world-view. And I don't feel this only about so-called realistic art, but other schools, too, make a similar impression. This happens when I become aware of what I would call the untruthfulness, in a deeper sense, of various works of art.

124

| | |
|---|---|
| ESTELLA | I really don't follow you there. |
| SOPHIA | Just consider, Estella, – when you have perceived the complete reality of life, there comes into your heart a feeling of a certain poverty in works of art. For, of course, the greatest artist is only a bungler, compared with the perfection of Nature. The most finished artistic representation can never give me, at least, what I can get from the revelation of a landscape or a human face. |
| ESTELLA | But that is in the nature of things and can't be altered. |
| SOPHIA | It could be altered if people would only be clear on one point. They should realize that it is senseless to imitate with human forces what higher powers have already spread out before us as consummate works of art. Yet it is those same powers that have implanted in man the urge to continue the work of creation. Man can actually give to the world what those powers have not yet set before the senses. It is where the powers of creation have left the world of matter unfinished that man can apply his creative striving. Why should he then imitate Nature's perfection imperfectly, when he can transform what is unfinished in her into completion? Imagine this idea changed into an elemental feeling and you will understand why so much that you call art makes me feel uncomfortable. It is distressing to look at an imperfect representation of sense reality when even the most imperfect rendering of what lies hidden from external observation may prove to be a revelation. |

125

| ESTELLA | You are talking about something that nowhere exists. A genuine artist will never try to make a mere copy of Nature. |
| SOPHIA | That is just why so many works of art are unsatisfying. A creative person is led by the creative activity itself beyond Nature, – but he does not yet know the appearance of anything that lies beyond his sense perception. |
| ESTELLA | There is no possible way for us to understand each other on this point. It is very sad to me to see that in the most important human problems my dearest friend takes such a different path from my own. I hope our friendship will see better times. |
| SOPHIA | In this we should be able to accept whatever life has in store for us. |
| ESTELLA | Goodbye, Sophia dear. |
| SOPHIA | Goodbye, my Estella. |

*Curtain*

# SCENE EIGHT

*The same room as in Scene One.*

*Johannes (Standing at an easel, near which Capesius and*
*Maria are sitting)*

Those seem to be the final strokes;
I now can call the picture finished.
To study in particular
your being through my art
has been a special joy indeed.

CAPESIUS   This picture truly is for me a wonder,
and yet a greater one
is its creator.
The change which has occurred in you
is unlike anything
which men like me
have until now held possible.
One only can believe in such a change
because the evidence compels it.
I saw you first three years ago,
when I was privileged
to come in contact with the group
in which you've risen to such heights.
You were a greatly troubled man just then,
one saw with every glance into your face.

I had just listened to a lecture in your circle
and was then moved to utter words
I wrung with difficulty from my soul.
I spoke out of a mood in which
one otherwise thinks of oneself alone.
My gaze, however, rested constantly
upon the sorrow-laden artist,
who sat there in the corner, mute.
And yet his silent brooding
was of a quite extraordinary nature.
One could quite well believe
he did not hear a single word
of what was spoken round about him.
It seemed as if the sorrow which consumed him
possessed a life all of its own.
It was as if the man was not the listener
but more as if his grief itself had hearing.
Perhaps it would not be too much to say
that he was utterly obsessed by sorrow.
Soon after this I met you once again,
and you already seemed quite changed, –
for happiness shone from your eyes,
strength emanated from your being,
and noble fire sounded from your words.
At that time you expressed to me a wish
which seemed most singular to me.
You wanted to become my pupil.
And in reality these past three years
you have immersed yourself with zeal
in all I have to say on world events.
And as we got to know each other well,
I felt the riddle of your power as artist.
Each of your pictures was for me a fresh surprise.

*(During these words Strader has entered)*

In former days my thoughts had little inclination
to rise to worlds beyond our human senses.
Not that I doubted them, –
but to approach them as a scholar
then seemed presumptuous to me.
And now I must acknowledge
that you have changed my point of view.
I've heard you say repeatedly,
you owe your powers in art
entirely to that gift
of consciously perceiving other worlds, –
that you can put
into your paintings nothing
but what you've first beheld in spirit.
I see how in your work the spirit
can actively reveal itself.

STRADER
I've never understood you less.
In every artist, spirit surely
has livingly expressed itself.
What then distinguishes
Thomasius from other masters?

CAPESIUS
I have not ever doubted
that spirit shows itself at work in man;
yet in most cases
he is unconscious of its nature.
He works out of this spirit,
but does not understand it.
Thomasius creates, however, in the world of sense
what he can consciously perceive in spirit,

and he has many times confessed to me
no other way of work is possible for him.

STRADER      Thomasius is for me a marvel.
             And I confess quite frankly
             that in this picture here
             Capesius, whom I thought I knew,
             is for the first time revealed to me.
             I thought I knew him well.
             The portrait shows me clearly
             how little I have really known of him.

MARIA        Dear Strader, how can you admire
             so much the greatness of the work
             and yet deny the wellspring of such greatness?

STRADER      What has the admiration
             I give the artist
             to do with my believing in his spirit sight?

MARIA:       One can pay tribute to the work
             without believing in its source.
             Yet in this case there would be nothing to admire,
             had not the artist trod the path
             that's led him to the spirit.

STRADER      We should not say
             that to immerse ourselves in spirit means
             to penetrate it with cognition.
             A spirit power creates within the artist
             as it creates within the tree or stone.
             The tree however cannot know itself.
             One who observes it can alone do this.

The artist lives within his work
and not in spiritual experience.
But when I let my eyes
rest on your picture,
I can forget what is alluring to the thinker.
My friend's soul power shines
out of these eyes, though they are merely painted.
The scholar's thoughtfulness
lives on this brow;
the innate warmness of his words
streams from each colour tone
with which your brush
has solved this riddle.
O all these colours, – they are only surface,
and yet they're not.
It is as if they're only visible
to make themselves invisible to me.
These forms,
emerging as the colours' interplay,
speak of the spirit's weaving.
Indeed they speak of much
which they themselves are not.
Where can it be of what they speak?
It cannot be upon the canvas,
for there are only colours stripped of spirit.
Then is it in Capesius?
But why can I not see it in him?
Thomasius, what you have painted
itself destroys itself
the moment that the eye would grasp it.
I cannot understand
whereto this picture's driving me.
What is it urging me to grasp it?

What should I look for?
The canvas, – I would like to break it through
to find what I should look for.
And where do I take hold of what this picture
rays out into my soul?
I have to have it!
Oh, I am a man bereft of reason.
It seems that ghosts are tricking me, –
a ghost that is invisible, –
and in my weakness
I cannot yet discover it.
Thomasius, you are painting ghosts, –
into your pictures you have conjured them.
They lure us on to seek them
but will not let themselves be found.
O cruel are your pictures!

CAPESIUS        My friend, in this brief moment
you have completely lost the thinker's calm.
Consider only, if a ghost
should speak out of this picture,
I must myself be ghostly.

STRADER         Forgive me, friend,
it was but weakness. . . .

CAPESIUS        Believe but good
of such a moment.
You had quite lost yourself,
it seemed. The fact was, you were raised
above yourself.
What happened was for you,
as often it has been for me:

however strongly we may feel ourselves
equipped at such a time with all our thinking,
we have but proven to ourselves
that we are taken hold of by a power
which cannot have its origin
in reason or sense knowledge.
Who has endowed this picture with such power?
I'd like to call what I myself
experience through it a symbol.
It teaches me to know my soul
in ways that were not possible before.
And this self-knowledge is convincing.
Johannes Thomasius has probed my being
because he has the power
to penetrate through sense illusion
to spirit self, with his
unusual spiritual vision.
Now I perceive that ancient word of wisdom
'Know thou thyself' in a new light.
To learn to know our being,
we first must find that power in ourselves
that as true spirit
is able to conceal itself from us.

MARIA    To find ourselves, we must unfold that power first
that penetrates into our inmost being.
The word of wisdom says in truth:
Evolve yourself, in order to behold yourself.

STRADER    If one were to acknowledge that Thomasius
through the unfolding of his spirit,
has for himself won knowledge of the being
that dwells invisibly in you,

one then would have to say
that knowledge differs at each stage of life.

CAPESIUS    That is exactly what I would affirm.

STRADER     If this were so
then all our thinking is in vain,
and knowledge is illusion.
I would then have to lose myself at every instant.
– – – – – – – – – – – – – – – –
O let me be alone.

(*Exit Strader*)

CAPESIUS    I will go with him.

(*Exit Capesius*)

MARIA       Capesius is closer far to spirit knowledge
than he himself is yet aware,
and Strader suffers deeply.
His spirit cannot find
what ardently his soul is longing for.

JOHANNES    The inner being of both men
appeared before my spirit's eye
when first I was allowed
to step into the realm of soul.
I saw Capesius as a young man,
and Strader in those years
which still lie far ahead of him.
Capesius revealed a youthful promise
which hid much that his life
in realms of sense will not let ripen.

And it was this that drew me to his being.
I could in his soul first behold,
within the kernel of a human being,
capacities of this life that declared
themselves the sequel of a former life on earth.
I saw the battles he has struggled through
and which have built for him,
out of another life, his present-day existence.
I could not yet bring to my inner eye
his former life as well, yet nonetheless
I could see much in his uniqueness
that cannot be derived out of the present.
Thus in his portrait I could bring to view
what still holds sway within his depths of soul.
My brush was guided
by forces which Capesius unfolded
from former lives on earth.
And if I've thus unveiled for him his inmost self,
my picture has then rendered
the service which I had in mind.
As work of art I do not rate it highly.

MARIA It will work further in that soul, for whom
it pointed out the path into the spirit realm.

*(The curtain falls while Maria and Johannes
are still in the room.)*

# SCENE NINE

*Translator's Note:*
The 'erlebe dich' that sounds as a soul-echo from rocks and springs, is literally translated as 'experience yourself', but this expression does not quite do justice to the etheric quality of the scene. The impact of these words on Johannes is an ever-increasing awareness of the forces which fill and enliven his whole being.

The translators would have preferred the phrase: '*unseal* your being', because of its apocalyptic connotation denoting Johannes' vision of his higher self. But the rendering here offered, 'unfold your being', is a more active and familiar one and carries with it a gesture which implies an over-emphasis of self, the luciferic aberration to which Johannes is drawn in the following scene. The words themselves preserve, too, the significant sound-sequence L – B of the original.

# SCENE NINE

*The same place as in Scene Two.*
> (*From rocks and springs resounds:*)
> O man, unfold your being.

JOHANNES     O man, unfold your being!
For three years now I've sought
for power of soul, with wings of
       courage,
to give these words their truth.
Through them a man who frees himself can
       conquer,
and conquering himself, can find his freedom.
O man, unfold your being!
(*From rocks and springs resounds:*)
O man, unfold your being.
This power of soul is rising from within me
but only gently touching spirit hearing.
It harbours in itself the hope
that, growing, it will lead the human spirit
from narrowness far out to distant worlds,
just as the tiny acorn
mysteriously can expand
into the giant body of the noble oak.
The spirit in itself can bring to life
what weaves in air and water,
what has condensed to earth beneath.

For man can grasp
what has been taking hold of life
within the elements, in souls and spirits,
in time and in eternity.
The whole world-being lives within my soul,
when in the spirit there has taken root
the power that gives these words their truth:
O man, unfold your being!
(*From rocks and springs resounds:*)
*O man, unfold your being.*
I feel them sounding in my soul,
rousing themselves to give me strength.
There lives in me the light,
there speaks around me brightness,
there germinates in me the light of soul,
there works in me world-radiance.
O man, unfold your being!
(*From rocks and springs resounds:*)
*O man, unfold your being.*
I find myself secure on every side,
wherever these words' power follows me.
It will illuminate for me the senses' darkness
and will uphold me in the spirit heights.
It will enfill me with soul-substance
throughout all course of time.
The essence of the world I feel in me
and I must find myself in every world.
I see the being of my soul enlivened
through power that is my own.
I rest within myself.
I gaze on rocks and springs;
they speak the very language of my soul.
I find myself again within that being

to whom I brought such bitter grief,
and out of her I call out to myself:
'Oh, you must find me once again
and ease my suffering.'
The spirit's light will give me strength
to live the other self within myself.
O words of hope,
you stream forth power to me from all the worlds:
O man, unfold your being.
(*From rocks and springs resounds:*)
*O man, unfold your being.*
You let me feel my weakness
and place me close to lofty aims of gods,
and blissfully I feel
such lofty aims' creative might
within my frail earth form.
Out of myself shall be revealed the purpose
for which the seed lies hidden in me.
And to the world I'll give myself
by living out my very being.
I want to feel these words' full power,
although they sound so gently.
They shall become for me a quickening fire
in my soul forces
and on my spirit paths.
I feel now how my thinking penetrates
deep hidden grounds of worlds
and how its radiant light illumines them.
Such is the germinating power of these words:
O man, unfold your being.
(*From rocks and springs resounds:*)
*O man, unfold your being.*
From light-filled heights a Being shines on me,

and wings I feel
that lift me up to him.
I too will free myself, as every being does
who overcomes himself.
(*From rocks and springs resounds:*)
*O man, unfold your being.*
I see that Being.
I shall become like him in future times.
The spirit will then free itself in me
through you, exalted goal of man.
I will now follow you.

(*Maria enters*)
My eye of soul has been awakened
by spirit beings who have welcomed me.
And as I gaze into the worlds of spirit,
I feel within myself that power:
O man, unfold your being.
(*From rocks and springs resounds:*)
*O man, unfold your being.*
Maria, you are here?

MARIA        My soul has led me here.
             I could behold your star:
             it shines in its full power.

JOHANNES     I can unfold that power from within me.

MARIA        So closely are we linked
             that your soul's life
             lets its light shine into my soul.

JOHANNES     Maria, you are then aware

of what has just revealed itself?
For me, man's core of confidence,
for me, the certainty of being has been won.
I feel indeed the power of the words
which everywhere can guide me:
O man, unfold your being!
(*From rocks and springs resounds*:)
*O man, unfold your being.*

*Curtain*

# SCENE TEN

*A Room for Meditation*

THEODOSIUS   Within yourself you can unfold all worlds.
Bring me, as cosmic might of love, to life
    within you.
A being who by me is inwardly made radiant
feels his own strength of life enhanced
when happiness-bestowing, he serves others.
And so I weave the joy of growth into the
    universe.
There is no realm of life without my power;
there is no being who can live without me.

JOHANNES   Before my soul's eye you appear,
bringer of happiness to worlds.
Creative joy impels my spirit
when I see you as fruit of self-unfolding.
You stood before my spirit-gaze within the
    temple,
though then I could not yet be sure
if dream or truth appeared to me.
But lifted is the veil
that kept the light of spirit hid from me.
I know now you are real.
I will reveal your being in my deeds;
through you they shall work healing.

And Benedictus I must thank, –
through wisdom he has given me the strength
to guide my spirit vision to the world.

THEODOSIUS    Feel me in depths of soul
and bring my strength to all the worlds.
In deeds of love you shall partake of blessedness.

JOHANNES    I feel your presence give me warming light.
I feel creative power arising in me.

*(Theodosius disappears.)*

He has gone.
But he will come again
and give me strength out of the springs of love.
His light can vanish only for a time;
then it lives on within my being.
I may rely now on myself,
unfolding for myself the essence of love's spirit
    beings.
Through him I feel myself uplifted.
He shall reveal himself through me.

*(He grows uncertain, which gradually comes to
expression in his gestures.)*

And yet how strange I feel. . . .
It seems a being is approaching me in spirit.
Since I have been found worthy
of spirit vision,
I have this feeling always
when evil forces would lay hold of me.
And yet whatever comes,
I have the strength to set myself against it.

I can unfold myself within my Self;
these words give strength that is invincible.
Most strongly now I feel the opposition.
So it must be the fiercest adversary. . . .
Yet let him come, he'll find me armed.

— — — — — — — — — — — — — — — — —

The enemy of good, you must be he.
Through your strong power you can be felt.
1 know it is your purpose to destroy
whatever frees itself from your dominion.
I will make strong in me that power
in which you cannot have a single part.

(*Benedictus appears.*)

O . . . Benedictus,
you, the source of my new life.
It is not possible . . . no . . .
it cannot be . . . it dare not be yourself.
It must be a deception.
O come to life, good forces of my soul
and shatter the illusion
desiring to ensnare me.

BENEDICTUS     Ask of your soul if it can feel
what through these years my presence meant
    to you.
The fruit of wisdom grew through me,
and only by its help can you progress
and banish error in the spirit realm.
Experience me within yourself.
But if you would go further,
you must set foot upon the path
that leads you to my temple.

144

My wisdom shall still shine on you
but must flow forth from out the place
wherein I work, united with my brothers.
I gave to you the strength of truth.
If it enkindles its fiery might in you,
then you will find the way.

(*Exit Benedictus.*)

JOHANNES      O he has left me.
And whether I've dispelled illusion . . .
or a reality has left me . . .
how can I tell?
_ _ _ _ _ _ _ _ _ _ _ _ _ _ _ _

And yet I feel myself grown stronger.
It was not an illusion, but he himself.
O Benedictus, I experience you within me.
You've given me the power
which living on within
will sever truth from error in myself.
And yet . . . I just succumbed to strong illusion.
I felt with horror your approach
and could regard you as deception
although you stood before me.

THEODOSIUS (*reappears*)
You'll free yourself from all illusion
if you will fill yourself with forces that are mine.
Though Benedictus could accompany you to me,
*your* wisdom must now lead you on.
If you experience only
what he has placed in you,
you cannot then unfold yourself.

In freedom strive into the light-filled heights.
Receive my strength now for this striving.

(*Exit Theodosius.*)

JOHANNES
Your words sound glorious!
I must within myself bring them to life.
From all illusion they will set me free
when fully they pervade my being.
----------------
So work on further in my soul's foundations,
sublime, majestic words.
You must have had your origin in the temple,
since Benedictus' brother uttered you.
I feel you rising from my inmost being.
----------------
These words will sound out of myself
and so be comprehensible to me.
You spirit, living in myself,
arise from your concealment
and show yourself in your true being.
I feel already your approach.
You must appear to me!

(*Lucifer and Ahriman appear.*)

LUCIFER
O man, know me.
O man, sense yourself.
You've wrenched yourself away
from spirit guidance,
and you have fled
into free earthly realms.
You've sought your own true being
in earth confusion,

to find yourself
proved your reward.
Use this reward.
Affirm yourself
in spirit daring.
You will find alien being
in the wide regions of the heights.
It will confine you
to human fate.
It will oppress you.
O man, sense yourself.
O man, know me.

AHRIMAN      O man, know yourself.
O man, sense me.
You have escaped
from spirit darkness,
and you have found
the light of earth.
So suck the power of truth
from my solidity.
I harden solid ground.
You can, however, lose it.
By vacillating you disperse
the power of being.
And you can squander
in lofty light
the strength of spirits.
You can disintegrate.
O man, sense me.
O man, know yourself.

(*They disappear.*)

JOHANNES     O what is this? From me came Lucifer
and following him Ahriman!
Do I live through still more illusion?
By Benedictus' brother were those powers
summoned who in men's souls
create illusion only.

VOICE OF SPIRIT FROM THE HEIGHTS
    Thoughts now guide you
to depths of world-beginnings;
what to soul illusion impelled you,
what in error has sustained you,
appears to you in spirit light;
light of whose fullness
men, when seeing,
in truth are thinking;
light from whose fullness
men, when striving,
in love are living.

*Curtain*

## SCENE ELEVEN:

*The Sun Temple*

*The hidden Mystery Place of the Hierophants at the surface of the earth.*
RETARDUS (*in front of him stand Capesius and Strader*):

You've brought me into sore distress.
The tasks that I have given you
you have mismanaged badly.
I summon you before my judgment seat.
*Capesius*, I gave to you a lofty spirit nature,
so that ideas of human aspiration
became the pleasing content of your speech
and should have had the power to convince.
I guided your activity to circles
wherein you met Johannes and Maria.
You should have driven out their inclination
towards spirit vision through the power
your words might have upon them.
Instead of this, you gave yourself entirely
to the influence that came from them.
I opened for you, *Strader*,
the path to scientific certainty.
Your strength of thought should have destroyed
the magic power of spirit vision.
But you lack certainty of feeling.
The power of thinking slipped away from you
just when the chance of victory was there.

(*to both*)        My destiny is closely linked with what you do.

Through you are lost forever for my kingdom
Maria and Johannes, both seekers after truth.
Their souls I must hand over to the Brothers.

CAPESIUS    I never could convey your message rightly.
You gave me power to present the life of men.
I described what in one age or in another
had inspired human beings;
and yet I was not able
to paint the past with words that had the strength
to wholly fill the souls who heard them.

STRADER    The weakness into which I had to fall
is but the image of your own.
You could confer upon me knowledge,
but not the power to silence all the longing
which strives within man's heart for truth.
I always had to feel
quite other forces stir within me.

RETARDUS    You see the outcome of your weakness.
The Brothers now are coming with those souls
through whom they are to conquer me.
Johannes and Maria obey the Brothers' leadership.
(*Enter Benedictus with Lucifer and Ahriman; behind
them Johannes and Maria with Philia, Astrid and
Luna; then Theodosius and Romanus with The Other
Maria, Felix and Felicia Balde; finally Theodora.*)

BENEDICTUS (*to Lucifer*)
Johannes' and Maria's souls
have room no longer for blind forces;
they are upraised to spirit being.

LUCIFER           I must indeed release their souls.
The wisdom they have won
gives them the power to perceive me.
I only hold dominion over souls
as long as they can not behold me.
But still my might remains,
allotted me in world-becoming.
And though I may not tempt their souls,
yet in the spirit shall my power
let ripen for them fruits of greatest beauty.

BENEDICTUS (*to Ahriman*)
Johannes' and Maria's souls
have conquered error's darkness in themselves.
Their eyes of spirit they have opened.

AHRIMAN          I must renounce their spirit.
They turn now to the light.
And yet it will not be denied me
still further to delight their souls
with shine of semblance.
They will not any longer
believe it to be truth,
but they will have the power to see
*how* semblance manifests the truth.

THEODOSIUS (*to The Other Maria*)
Your destiny was closely linked
unto your higher sister's life.
I could bestow on her the light of love,
but could not give the warmth of love
as long as you continued to allow
the best part in your nature to arise

from darkness of your feeling only
and did not strive to see it clearly
with the full light of wisdom.
The influence of the temple does not reach
to motives rooted in blind instincts
however much of good they wish to do.

THE OTHER MARIA

I must admit that noble purposes
work blessing only in the light –
and turn now to the temple.
My feeling shall in future
not rob the light of love of its effect.

THEODOSIUS  You grant me through your insight power
to give Maria's soul-light to the world.
It always had to lose its strength
on souls who bear your former nature
and do not wish that love be joined with light.

JOHANNES (*to The Other Maria*)

I see in you the kind of soul
that also in myself has governed me.
I could not find the way
to reach your higher sister
as long as warmth of love remained
aloof from light of love in me.
The sacrifice you bring the temple
shall here be re-enacted in my soul.
In me the warmth of love shall sacrifice
itself unto the light of love.

MARIA  Johannes, you have won in spirit realms

knowledge now through me;
to spirit knowledge you will add
the soul's true being,
when you can find your inmost soul
as you found mine.


PHILIA       From out all world-becoming shall
the joy of soul reveal itself to you.


ASTRID       With all your being you will now
be able to illuminate the warmth of soul.


LUNA       You may then dare to live yourself as Self
when light can shine within your soul.


ROMANUS (*to Felix Balde*)
       You've stood aloof a long time from the temple.
You wished to recognize illumination only
when your own soul itself revealed the light.
Men of your nature rob me of the power
to give my light to earthly souls.
They only wish to draw out of dark depths
whatever they should give to life.


FELIX BALDE       It was men's very folly that from dark depths
has shown to me the light
and let me find my way into the temple.


ROMANUS       That you have found your way
can render me the power
to illuminate the will
of both Johannes and Maria,
that it shall not obey blind powers

but out of cosmic aims
shall give itself direction.


MARIA           Johannes, you have now beheld
yourself in spirit through myself;
you will as spirit experience your being
when cosmic light beholds itself in you.


JOHANNES (*to Felix Balde*)
I see in you, my brother Felix,
that impulse of the soul that in my spirit
has held my will in bondage.
You've willed to find the way into the temple.
Within my spirit I shall lead
the power of will the way
into the temple of the soul.


RETARDUS      Johannes' and Maria's souls
now wrest themselves out of my realm.
How shall they find henceforth
what springs from out my power?
As long as in themselves
the grounds of knowledge were still lacking,
they were delighted with my gifts.
I see myself compelled now to
relinquish both of them.


FELICIA BALDE That men can kindle in themselves
the fire for thought without your help,
I've shown you clearly.
There streams from me a knowledge
that's able to bear fruit.


154

| | |
|---|---|
| JOHANNES | This knowledge shall unite now with the light<br>that from the temple's boundless source<br>shines forth into the souls of men. |
| | |
| RETARDUS | Capesius, my son,<br>you are now lost.<br>You have withdrawn yourself from me<br>before the temple's light can shine for you. |
| | |
| BENEDICTUS | He has begun the path.<br>He feels the light<br>and he will win the power<br>to fathom in his soul what until now<br>Felicia has created for him. |
| | |
| STRADER | It seems that I alone am lost.<br>I cannot banish doubt itself,<br>and I shall surely never find again<br>the path that leads me to the temple. |
| | |
| THEODORA | Out of your heart<br>soars up a glowing light.<br>A human image<br>shapes itself from it,<br>and words I hear<br>this human image speaking.<br>And so they sound:<br>'I have now conquered for myself<br>the power to reach the light.'<br>My friend, trust in yourself!<br>For you yourself will speak these words<br>when once your time shall be fulfilled. |

(*The curtain falls*)

# APPENDIX

SKETCH* *for a* PRELUDE *to* THE PORTAL OF INITIATION *by Rudolf Steiner (replaced by the* SOPHIA-ESTELLA SCENES.)

*Wife and Husband*

WIFE        Goodbye, dear, I'm off to the performance our Society is putting on tonight.

HUSBAND    There you go again, leaving me alone, and it is always that Society of yours that takes you away from the children and me.

WIFE        You've often said you were resigned to it by now.

HUSBAND    Every time, though, I realize again that you are getting further and further away from everything that makes life worthwhile for me.

WIFE        O, you've spoken quite differently about that too at times.

HUSBAND    If two people love each other, one always has to be ready to give up something.

WIFE        It isn't possible for me to give all this up, and so,

* See: Entwürfe, Fragmente und Paralipomena zu den vier Mysteriendramen, Bibliographie 44.

wouldn't it be easier for you to let me go my own way?

HUSBAND     I can't figure out why you want to go and see a kind of marionette show about what you've been listening to in dozens of lectures.

WIFE        You know anything that is vitally important becomes interesting when it is presented in a new way.

HUSBAND     It may be 'vital' and 'interesting', but it has not much to do with real life.

WIFE        Let me tell you for the twentieth time that the jibe about 'real life' is downright foolish. Don't you see that I would never have had the courage to bring up our children for 'real life' if I'd only listened to all the dogmas you men stick to in our present time? You've admitted yourself that my courage and, what's more, my strength and insight came from a flexible way of thinking rooted in spirit realities. And you do admit its effect, but you won't take it seriously.

HUSBAND     Well, you see I am not altogether blind. Only you should realize that these ideas are unthinkable in connection with my work.

WIFE        Yes, but I've never urged you to go with me.

HUSBAND     It would not have done a bit of good, in any case. Even if curiosity had driven me to it, the idea of being ridiculous would have kept me back.

| | |
|---|---|
| WIFE | Now please, dear. Is it only feminine logic to say that those who poke fun at something which is obviously worthwhile make themselves ridiculous? |
| HUSBAND | I only know that the best minds of our time are fairly unanimous in their judgment. Public opinion finds this kind of hocus-pocus pitiful, if not actually dangerous. |
| WIFE | Public opinion is swiftly swayed, even when it's miles away from real knowing. |
| HUSBAND | Let's not get into that. Personally I can't afford to oppose public opinion without risking my position. |
| WIFE | I'm sorry about that. |
| HUSBAND | Just now I've been reading again how vague and illogical are all the things you people are saying. |
| WIFE | Your writer has probably gone into it about as deeply as others I've read. |
| HUSBAND | That may be. But it's something else to look at the ideas themselves. And even worse when you blow these up into a theatrical production. That goes against all the standards of good taste. What do you expect to get out of such a performance? Why, it can't be anything better than symbolic figures dressed up like straw dolls in spiderwebs of thought, – – – allegories as feeble signs of deep wisdom. It riles me that you don't see these things as I do. And how often have I begged you to let me take you to one of those relaxing shows that are true to life. |

| WIFE | You know I've gone quite often with you. I've always tried to accept the kind of nothingness that you like because, as you say, here at least something is happening! And really I discovered that the ordinary stage seems to reflect everyday life, that is unfortunately so empty! Why should I be intrigued by uninteresting characters on the stage who are manipulated like sleepwalkers? I am bored even by the new drama which pretends to be bursting with vitality. It is either without content – rightly so, because it mirrors truthfully our present time – or else it is a strong criticism of life, and, as such, pretty futile. For no hunger is going to be satisfied, no tears are going to be dried by showing starving characters or tear-drenched faces on the stage. |
|---|---|
| HUSBAND | But isn't it the triumph of modern art that it no longer tries to rise into idealistic dream-spheres but actually reflects the struggles of our daily life? |
| WIFE | You are talking now just like a theatre critic. I notice that you have the habit of reading their columns. |
| HUSBAND | Well, anyway, there's not much good said there about your hobby-horse. |
| WIFE | I'm glad of that. For if spiritual ideas would get to the point of pervading the daily papers, they would have to be squeezed into witty trivialities to please everybody. |
| HUSBAND | My dear, it's time for your performance. – I'm off, |

too. I didn't tell you that there's a gala opening tonight at one of the big theatres of an extraordinary new problem drama.

WIFE     I honestly hope you'll enjoy it. And when we come back here in a few hours, we will find each other again. I am sure our affection is not going to change. Goodbye now!

# THE SOUL'S PROBATION

A LIFE TABLEAU IN DRAMATIC SCENES
AS SEQUEL TO

# .THE PORTAL OF INITIATION

*through*

RUDOLF STEINER

*translated by*

RUTH AND HANS PUSCH

STEINER BOOK CENTRE, INC.

NORTH VANCOUVER, CANADA

*First edition in English*
*in this translation*
*1973*
*Second Printing 1973*

*Translated from* DIE PRÜFUNG DER SEELE
*published in Switzerland by*
*Verlag Rudolf Steiner*

*This edition is published by permission*
*of Rudolf Steiner Nachlassverwaltung,*
*Dornach, Switzerland.*

## THOUGHTS ON THE SEAL

The pentagram in the centre reminds us of the figure of a man standing in space: his legs placed firmly on the ground; his arms stretched out to the right and left; his head aiming skyward. This picture represents man in harmonious balance between heaven and earth, and in full control of his body.

Moving to the periphery, we find repeated patterns of outspread wings, influenced, as it were, by forces coming from the circumference, directed toward the centre. The middle part of the seal shows forms which respond to them by opening themselves like a blossom or chalice. The two forms, without touching each other, come close together like in- and out-going spirals. The designs around the periphery and those in the middle can be seen as a five times repeated double-form. Recognized as such, an astonishing relationship to the pentagram in the centre becomes evident.

One can make the experiment of cutting out a thin-lined copy of the pentagram and of laying it, with its 'feet' toward the centre, over one of the double-forms. It is now obvious that the straight lines

3

and angles appear exactly metamorphosed into curves and wings. The free space between the in- and out-going spirals falls directly there where the points of the two arms end. A mere description cannot give the picture as it presents itself in such an experiment, but one can also try to set one's imagination in motion and let the mind achieve the transformation of one form into the other.

We know that the law of metamorphosis is fundamental to an understanding of reincarnation. The changes from one life to another are only explainable if one can apply this law to the physical, psychic and mental differences. Nothing remains the same, but undergoes a vital 'sea-change'. This form-design helps to make our mind flexible enough to follow the process of metamorphosis, based on the pentagram, representing the human figure.

It is this central form which plays an important part in the experience of transformation, because it remains the solid basis from which one starts out and to which one returns. And the return is necessary, in order to keep a balance. The swinging, winging, curving, spiraling forms can tempt us to lose ourselves in them.

If we apply the dynamics of the seal to the play itself, the essence of the dramatic action becomes evident. 'The Soul's Probation' deals with a retrospect into the former incarnation in medieval times, consciously experienced by Maria, Johannes and Capesius – with different results, however. Capesius is so intrigued by the periphery and its cosmic dimensions that he cannot find his way back into his present body (his pentagram). Johannes lives on, unable to discard or erase the past for the sake of strength in the present. This conflict throws him into the arms of Lucifer. Maria alone remains soundly united with her pentagram, clearly aware of the law of metamorphosis. By virtue of her integrity, her 'star' nature, she defeats Ahriman.

Thus the seal can offer exercises in the metamorphoses of forms, and at the same time prepare a deeper understanding of the central dramatic events of the play itself.

Hans Pusch

4

# CHARACTERS, BEINGS AND EVENTS

The spirit and soul experiences of the characters in The Soul's Probation are a continuation of those in The Portal of Initiation.

Professor Capesius
Benedictus, Hierophant of the Sun Temple
_ _ _ _ _ _ _ _ _ _ _ _ _ _ _ _

Philia ⎫
Astrid ⎬ the spiritual beings who form the connection of the
Luna ⎭ human soul forces with the cosmos

The Other Philia, the spiritual being who impedes the connection of the soul forces with the cosmos
The Voice of Conscience

These are not allegorical, but are realities for spirit cognition.
_ _ _ _ _ _ _ _ _ _ _ _ _ _

Maria
Johannes Thomasius
Strader
Felix Balde
Felicia, his wife
The Double of Johannes Thomasius
Lucifer
Ahriman

Six Peasants and Six Peasant Women
Simon, the Jew, a former incarnation of Strader
Thomas, a former incarnation of Johannes Thomasius
A Monk, a former incarnation of Maria
The Grand Master, leader of a mystic Order

First Preceptor, a former incarnation of Capesius
Second Preceptor
First Master of Ceremonies
Second Master of Ceremonies
The Spirit of Benedictus
Joseph Kean, a former incarnation of Felix Balde
Dame Kean, a former incarnation of Felicia Balde
Bertha, their daughter, a former incarnation of The Other Maria
  (The Portal of Initiation)
Celia, Kean's foster daughter, a former incarnation of Theodora
  (The Portal of Initiation)

Theodosius ⎱
Romanus  ⎰ Hierophants of the Sun Temple

---

The events of Scenes Six through Nine are the content of Capesius' spirit retrospect into his former life. This same retrospect is experienced also by Maria and Johannes Thomasius, but not by Strader, whose former incarnation is seen only by Capesius, Maria and Johannes.

The pictures of the retrospect into the fourteenth century are conceived as results of imaginative cognition. They are to be taken as idealized representations of life events, not necessarily as history.

The way in which these lives are repeated (from happenings in the fourteenth century into the present day) should not be generalized. This kind of repetition can occur only at a turning point of time. Therefore, also, the conflicts as they are presented here as consequences from a former life are *only* possible for such a turning point of time.

6

# SYNOPSIS

It is evident that in THE SOUL'S PROBATION the central event is the retrospect into the former incarnations of medieval times. The four scenes before the retrospect (Scenes Two to Five) and the four scenes after it (Scenes Ten to Thirteen) are closely related to the central scenes, which describe the happenings in the Middle Ages.

Scene One stands by itself; it is concerned only with Capesius and his first break-through into spirit reality. It is a Faustian experience, that reminds us of the long monologue at the beginning of Goethe's FAUST, when the Spirit of the Earth confronts Faust. Mantric words in a book by Benedictus lead Capesius to the perceiving of his own soul forces outside himself. Instead of the usual third force at the side of Astrid and Luna, 'another' Philia appears. She is characterized by Rudolf Steiner as 'the spiritual being who impedes the connection of the soul forces with the cosmos.' She may be seen as an offspring of Retardus. Benedictus himself finds encouraging and strength-bestowing words for Capesius, hinting at the tests and trials lying in store for him. The scene ends in a mood of expectancy for the things to come. It is the overture to the whole play.

Scenes Two to Five bring, each in its own way, the idea of karma and reincarnation into the sphere of reality. In Scene Two Maria gathers into her Spirit Self, with Benedictus' help, the forces of the soul which will enable her to look back into the life preceding her present one. In Scenes Three and Five Johannes has to undergo a shock-experience, induced by Maria's firm advice that their separation has become inevitable for his own independent development. This shock loosens Johannes' etheric body, so that he can perceive first his soul forces and then, in a dramatic moment, his Double, in

7

connection with Lucifer and Ahriman. This loosening results also in a conscious experience of his former incarnation as Thomas, the miner. In Scenes Four and Five Capesius meets, in a conversation with Strader, the idea of reincarnation in a most unexpected way, and this is the beginning of his own insight. Strader has been able to realize the truth of repeated earth lives as logical consequence of modern scientific thinking. But for Strader himself this means only resignation and self-denial, because the working of karma cannot be brought into his consciousness. Capesius is deeply disturbed and puzzled by this encounter and feels compelled to seek a kind of refuge at the home of the Baldes. Here, surrounded by a landscape of mountains and forest, he converses with Felix and Felicia. But he has difficulties to follow Felix's trend of thought, whereas Felicia opens up for him, as sometimes before this, a world of imaginations. In the tale she tells about the Rock-Spring Wonder, the soul of Capesius is carried into a world of pictures that take him far away into cosmic distances and then to a perception of his former life as a Knight Templar.

Scenes Six to Nine depict certain decisive moments of the medieval times, in which the persons of the drama are all brought together. These scenes have a historical background, although here they are compressed into the frame of the particular action of this play. One may well assume that they reveal a reading in the book of cosmic memory, the Akasha Chronicle. The character of such a reading is that it condenses the events to their essentials. Nevertheless, actual history speaks through it. First of all, the place itself: it is the countryside and one of the castles, Burg Lockenhaus, of the Austrian Burgenland. There is to this day a legend about the Knights Templar living in the castle for a time, which is a similar story to the one in the play. The action takes place shortly after the execution in 1314 of Jacques de Molay, the Grand Master of the Templars, of whom the Grand Master in the play speaks.

In Scenes Ten to Thirteen the results of the retrospect for the different individualities are shown. First, Capesius gives a spontaneous but exact description of the way he gained the vision of his former life. This is a unique monologue of a kind which has never before existed in world literature. We witness the reality of spirit experience. Capesius follows the events backwards, from the present awakening leading back in stages to the culminating sight of the actual pictures of his medieval life, and then to the preceding stages of consciousness by which he was gradually carried into this picture world. Finally he ends where he started from, but now the shock of re-embodiment is too great. His longing takes him back into cosmic regions. There he feels at home, estranged from his present life.

In Scene Eleven Maria displays courage, awareness and insight, which enable her to defeat Ahriman. She can prove to him that he lacks the organ of perception for those decisive moments in human evolution when future events have to be prepared: the turning points of time.

In Scene Twelve Lucifer is triumphant over Johannes, who cannot free himself from the impression that Thomas, the miner, made on him. He feels the impact of the conflicts of that earlier time more strongly than the tasks of the present incarnation. This weakness of his gives Lucifer power over him.

In Scene Thirteen, we witness again the Sun Temple, as it was revealed at the end of THE PORTAL OF INITIATION. Benedictus rules in the East, Theodosius in the South and Romanus in the West. This time, Lucifer takes his place at the Northern altar as the result of Johannes' failure. The forces maturing in Strader, even though he has not yet reached full consciousness, cause Ahriman to leave the temple. Strader enters as a sleeping soul, under the guidance of the soul forces. To Maria falls the task of harmonizing the complications brought about by karma, which prevent Capesius and Johannes from being present. In her words about the 'springs of love', she refers to the Christ Being, without mentioning His

9

name, as the Lord of Karma. It is in this spirit that Benedictus sums up the temple's task at the end of the play. The 'three human lives interwoven' (Johannes, Capesius and Strader) will be as a triad from now on under the guidance of the Sun Temple.

# SCENE ONE

*The library and study of Capesius; prevailing color brown. An evening mood. First Capesius; then the spirit figures who are soul forces; later Benedictus. This scene and the following scenes of this play represent events which take place several years after the time of* The Portal of Initiation.

CAPESIUS (*reading from a book*)
    'By looking with the inner eye upon non-being
    and dreaming in thought's shadow-images
    with self-created rules:
    thus erring human nature wants to seek
    the meaning and the goal of life.
    From soul depths he would draw the answers
    to questions of the universe.
    Already-even at the outset—
    such musing brings to life delusions
    and sees at last its view of spirit
    consume itself, deprived of strength.'

    (*he speaks*)

So Benedictus' noble spirit-sight
portrays with serious words
the inner path of many human beings.
To me each word hits heavy as a blow.
With cruel truthfulness they show
the path of my own life.

And if a god in wildly raging storm
should now descend on me in wrath,
his fearful power could not torture me
with more appalling terror
than do these fateful words.
In my long life I have but spun
the images that move like shadow-drawings
within a dream of soul.
And all this merely mirrors, as delusion,
the world of nature and the spirit's action.
Out of this ghostly web of dreaming
I've tried to solve the cosmic riddle.
Down many a path I turned
my restless soul, impatiently.
But now I recognize
that, tricked, deluded, I myself,
*I* did not live within my soul,
when threads of thought
tried to expand themselves far out to cosmic reaches.
_ _ _ _ _ _ _ _ _ _ _ _ _ _ _

Thus what I proudly pictured
remained an empty image.
Then came into my way
Thomasius, the youthful painter.–
With genuine energy of soul,
he was aspiring to the lofty attitude of spirit
that changes human beings
and frees from hidden depths
the forces to create the springs of life.
What rose out of his inmost grounds of soul
reposes within every human being,
and since it was revealed through him,

I've understood: the greatest sin in life
is to ignore the treasures of the spirit.
— — — — — — — — — — — — — — — —

I know now, I must search,
and not continue endlessly to doubt.
In earlier years, my vanity of thought
could have enticed me to the false belief:
that man aspires in vain to knowledge,
and only resignation can be fitting
for him who strives to find the springs of life.
— — — — — — — — — — — — — — — —

If I had had to recognize
as height of wisdom
that powers of human destiny demand
I sink as individual being
into the gulf of nothingness:
I would have dared to do it, unafraid.
Today such thinking would be sacrilege
since I have learned so clearly
that I should never rest
until the spirit treasure in my soul
has found the light of day.
— — — — — — — — — — — — — — — —

The fruits of spirit beings' work
have been implanted in the human soul;
the gods' own work will be destroyed by those
whose heedlessness lets seeds of spirit wither.-
I recognize what is the highest duty of my life.
But if I dare to take one single step
into that realm from which I cannot turn
I feel how just those forces leave me
by which my vanity of thought once tried
to throw some light

on time and space and goals of life.
Once I believed that it was easy
to press the thoughts out of my brain
and they would grasp realities.
But now – in trying to behold
the springs of life illumined by the light of truth,
my thinking's instrument seems dull.
I torture myself fruitlessly
to form clear images of thought
out of the earnest words of Benedictus,
directing me upon the paths of spirit:

*(resumes his reading)*

'Enter calmly into depths of soul
and let strong courage be your guide.
Cast off your former ways of thought
when you descend into yourself
to guide yourself toward selfhood.
As you extinguish self-engendered light,
the spirit's brightness will appear to you.'

*(speaks again)*

It is as if my breath had stopped
when I attempt to grasp the meaning of such words.
Before I sense what I should think,
anxiety and fright take hold of me.
I have the feeling: all the things
which until now had filled my life
were crashing down, and in their ruin
they soon must crush me into nothingness.
Alas! I've read a hundred times
the words which follow now . . .
and every time, the darkness

has broken in upon me
with ever-deepening gloom.

(*reading again*)

'Within your thinking cosmic thoughts hold sway,
Within your feeling cosmic forces weave,
Within your willing cosmic beings work.
Lose yourself in cosmic thoughts.
Experience yourself through cosmic forces.
Create yourself from beings of will.
In worlds' far reaches do not end
through thinking's play of dreams.
Begin within expanded spirit spheres
and end in depths of your own soul:
you'll find the aims of gods
when you can know in you your self.'

(*sinking into his thoughts, he is made faint by a vision;
then comes to himself and speaks*)

What was this?

(*Three figures as soul forces hover around him*)

LUNA      You do not lack the strength
for lofty spirit flight.
It's founded well
upon the human will;
It's hardened well
by certainty of hope.
It is well steeled
by sight into the future.
You only lack the courage
to pour into your willing
new confidence in life . . .

Into the vast unknown
with courage dare to venture forth.

ASTRID        From worlds afar
out of the joyful sunlight, –
from distant stars
out of the magic power of worlds, –
from azure heavenly ether
out of the mighty spirit heights, –
strive for power of soul
and send its radiant beams
deep down into your heart;
then knowledge will with warmth
create itself in you.

THE OTHER PHILIA
They are deceiving you,
the wicked sisters;
they wish to spin a web for you
of fanciful tricks of life.
The vain delusion of their gifts
which they are offering you
will vanish into air
if you attempt to hold it fast
with human force.
They lead you on
to worlds of gods
and will destroy you,
if you make bold within their realm
to hold yourself
as human being.

(*The soul forces disappear.*)

16

CAPESIUS          It was quite clear . . .
                  beings spoke here . . .
                  yet it is certain . . .
                  no one is here beside me
                  in this room . . .
                  _ _ _ _ _ _ _ _ _ _ _ _ _ _ _ _
                  Have I then spoken only to myself? . . .
                  That, too, seems quite impossible;
                  for never could I have imagined
                  what I think I heard . . .
                  _ _ _ _ _ _ _ _ _ _ _ _ _ _ _ _
                  Am I still the one
                  I was before?

                  (*In his gestures, one can notice that
                  he feels unable to answer 'yes'.*)

                  O . . . I am . . . I am not.
                  _ _ _ _ _ _ _ _ _ _ _ _ _ _ _ _

SPIRIT VOICE, *the spiritual conscience*:
                  Your thoughts are now descending
                  To depths of human life.
                  What as soul enfolds you,
                  what as spirit is bound to you
                  soars up to cosmic grounds,
                  out of whose fullness, drinking,
                  men live in thinking;
                  out of whose fullness, living,
                  men weave in seeming.

CAPESIUS          Too much . . . too much . . .
                  Where is Capesius?
                  I implore you,
                  unknown powers,

where is . . . Capesius?
Where am I myself?

(*Once more he is absorbed, brooding in himself.*)

BENEDICTUS (*enters, unnoticed by Capesius. Benedictus touches him on the shoulder.*)

It has come to my attention
that you wish to speak to me,
and so I've sought you out at home.

CAPESIUS    It is most kind of you
to grant my wish,
yet you could hardly find me
in a worse position.
– – – – – – – – – – – – – – – –
That after so much pain
which just has racked me
you do not find me paralyzed
upon the ground before you,
I owe to your kind glance alone
that met my eye when gently
you roused me from the horrors of my
dream.

BENEDICTUS    It is not hidden from me
that I find you in life's battle.
I knew already long ago
that we would meet some day like this.
Prepare to change the sense of many words,
that we can fully understand each other,

18

and do not marvel
if in my way of speaking
your suffering must change its name.

- - - - - - - - - - - - - - - -

I find you in good fortune.


CAPESIUS        Then you increase my pain
which throws me into darknesses.
My very self, it seemed,
had fled to cosmic depths
and through the sheaths, strange beings
had spoken in this room. –
That I saw through such spirit trickery
as mere illusion, and that soul-deception
provided so much pain:
only this could help sustain me.
O do not rob me of such feelings' firm support! . . .
Do not call this good fortune –
it is to me but feverish illusion –
or else I shall be lost indeed.


BENEDICTUS     In truth, a man can only lose
what severs him from cosmic being,
and if it seems to him that he has lost
what in his thinking's dreamlike mood
he has abused in worthless effort,
then let him search for what has gone from him.
If he can rediscover it,
he may at last be able
to dedicate it rightfully to man's endeavors.
To try to comfort you in such an hour
would only be a play on words.

CAPESIUS     No. – Teachings which would satisfy mere reasoning
will never come from you.
I've had to realize this bitterly.
As actions sometimes lead us up to heights
but also hurl us down into abysses,
your words pour streams of fiery life
and also deadly chill
into men's souls, with mighty power.
They have the same effect as blows of destiny
or as the storms of love in life.
Much had I thought and searched
before we met . . .
but I have learned to know
creative forces of the spirit
as well as its destructive power
only since I've followed in your steps.

– – – – – – – – – – – – – – – –

The havoc that your words caused in my soul
you could perceive
on entering my room just now.
I've often been tormented
when meditating on the content of your book.
Today, however, painful sorrow filled my cup
and my distress of soul flowed over
while reading in your book those words of destiny.
To understand their meaning
was not yet granted me,
but they gushed forth into my heart
like springs of life,
arousing world-enchantment –
this robbed me of my clarity of mind.
And ghostlike beings were surrounding me;
significant, dark words I heard,

resounding from erratic sickliness.
I know that you do not confide to writing
all that you must hold safe for souls of men,
and that you only grant a riddle's answer
to each, according to his need.
So grant me what I sorely need;
for I must know
what robbed me of my reason and my senses,
as it surrounded me
with an ephemeral magic spell.

BENEDICTUS    I do not wish my words alone to say
what they convey as covering for concepts.
They turn the natural forces of the soul
to the realities of spirit.
Their meaning is first reached
when they unlock the power of seeing
in souls surrendered to their force.
They do not spring from my research
but are entrusted to me by those spirits
who read the signs
by which world karma manifests itself.
It is the nature of these words
to lead to founts of knowledge;
yet it remains with him
who hears them in their own true sense,
to drink the spirit water at the source.
It is not counter to the purpose of my words
to lift you into worlds
which must to you seem ghostly.
You've entered now a realm
which will remain illusion
as long as you can lose yourself in it.

However, if you here sustain yourself,
this realm will surely open its first portal
of highest wisdom to your soul.

CAPESIUS      And how can I sustain myself?

BENEDICTUS    The answer to this riddle you'll be granted
if you can face with an awakened eye of soul
the many wondrous things
which soon will come your way.
Ordained I see you now to a probation
by spirit forces and powers of destiny.

(*Exit*)

CAPESIUS      Although the meaning of his words I can't explain,
I feel them working actively within me.
He's allotted me a goal: . . .
and I am ready to obey.
He does not ask for striving in mere thoughts;
he wants me to direct my steps
into realities of spirit, searchingly.

— — — — — — — — — — — — — — — —

I do not know the nature of his mission,
and yet his action here compels my trust.
He's brought me to myself again.
So may the magic spell,
which frightened me,
at present still remain unsolved.
And openly and freely I will face
those future happenings which he has promised.

(*Curtain, while Capesius remains standing.*)

22

# SCENE TWO

*A meditation room; prevailing color violet. Serious but not gloomy atmosphere. Benedictus and Maria; later, spirit figures that represent soul forces.*

MARIA

Grave inner battles urge me in this hour
to turn to you for guidance and wise counsel.
Dark premonition rises in my heart,
and I'm unable to oppose the thoughts
that storm upon me constantly.
They strike me in my being's deepest core;
they want to lay upon me a command
which to obey would seem like sacrilege.
Deceptive powers are trying to beguile me; . . .
I beg you . . . help . . .
that I can banish them.

BENEDICTUS

You never need forego
what you must ask of me.

MARIA

I know how closely to my soul
are linked Johannes' paths of life.
A thorny road of destiny united us,
and in high spirit-realms our bond
was consecrated by the will of gods.
All this presents itself to me as clearly
as only images of truth can do.

And I feel horror taking hold of me
when I am forced
to utter such a sacrilegious word,
and yet – deep in my soul I hear a voice
which says distinctly, repeating
despite my will to fight it down:
 'You must give up Johannes, let him go:
 you cannot keep him at your side
 if you would not do harm to him.
 Alone he must pursue the path
 which leads him onward to his goal.'
I know if you but speak one word,
delusion's web will cease to haunt my soul.

BENEDICTUS  Maria, noble grief leads you astray:
you see the truth in image of illusion.

MARIA  It could be . . . truth . . .
It cannot be! between your guiding words,
and my own hearing, delusion also creeps.
O speak to me again.

BENEDICTUS  You've understood me rightly . . .
your love is noble and Johannes
was closely linked to you.
But love should not forget
that she is wisdom's sister.
Johannes was united long indeed
with you, for his own good. And yet
his soul demands that he pursue his aims
upon his further path in freedom.
The will of destiny does not decree

that you should break your outer bond of friendship;
but this it does demand, severely:
Johannes' freedom in the spirit realm.

MARIA  I hear what must be still delusion!
Allow me to speak further
until you understand me.
No spectral shape will dare
so near your ears to twist these words.
All doubts were easily dispersed
if only earth-life's tangled path
had bound Johannes' soul to mine.
But consecration was bestowed upon our bond,
uniting soul with soul eternally;
and spirit powers gave their benediction
by speaking words which banish every doubt:
 'He conquered for himself the truth
 in realms eternal
 because in worlds of sense his inmost self
 had joined itself with you.'
How can I understand this revelation
if now its very opposite is true?

BENEDICTUS You must find out how much indeed
is lacking toward maturity in even those
to whom already much has been revealed.
The paths of higher wisdom are entangled; –
and only those will find their way aright
who walk in patience through the labyrinths.
You could but see one part of full reality
in realms of everlasting light
when to your eyes of soul appeared
an image of the spirit land.

This image is not yet complete reality.
Johannes' soul and yours
have been united by such earthly bonds
as make it possible for each of you
to find the way into the spirit realm
by means of forces that you owe each other.
So far, however, it has not been shown
that you have both fulfilled all the demands.
You were allowed to see a picture
of what the future holds in store for you
if you can stand the full ordeal.
That you've been shown the fruits of striving
does not yet prove that you have reached
the goal of all your efforts.
You have beheld a picture . . .
your power of will alone, however,
is able to transform it to reality.

MARIA Although your words affect me
like bitter grief that follows after joy,
there is at least one lesson I have learned:
to yield myself to wisdom's light
when it becomes alive through inner force.
Already something is becoming clear
that lay in darkness for my heart till now.
Yet when in times of highest bliss
delusion presses in upon the mind
in the deceptive mask of truth,
a darkness of the soul is difficult to ban.
I need still more than you have given,
if I'm to grasp the meaning of your words.
You've led my Self to depths of soul
where light was granted me

to look into those lives on earth
which were allotted me in times long past.
I could experience how Johannes' soul
and mine had found each other.
That I could bring his soul
so long ago to the pure spirit Word –
I could consider this to be the seed
which, growing, could become the fruit of friendship
to be found ripe for all eternity.

BENEDICTUS    You were accounted worthy to retrace
the earthly paths allotted you
in days long past.
But you should not forget to ask yourself
if you are also certain
not any of your paths of life conceals itself from you
when backward you direct your spirit eye.

MARIA (*after a pause which indicates deep self-reflection*)

O how could I have been so blind?
The blissfulness I felt
when I could see a part of bygone times
made me forget then with false vanity
how much is lacking still.
And only now it dawns on me
that I must pierce through darknesses
if I would find the way
from present days to days of old
when my friend's soul
inclined itself toward mine.
To you, my guide, I'll make my vow
to tame my soul's proud arrogance . . .!

Right now I recognize how vanity
of knowing can deceive the soul.
Instead of gaining strength
from freely offered spirit treasures,
it uses them for wanton mirroring of self.
And at this very moment
my heart's forewarning voice,
encouraged by the power of your words,
has told me I must feel how far
I am from reaching still the nearest goals.
No more will I too hastily interpret
the knowledge granted me from spirit lands.
I will esteem it as a force
which helps to shape my soul, –
not as persuasion,
which spares me efforts of my own
to recognize the life-goals of my actions.
If I had only heeded sooner
this word, which asks humility of me,
the truth could not have been obscured:
my friend's so richly gifted soul
can only grow and then unfold in freedom
when he can find such paths
as are not drawn by me beforehand.
And now that this is clear to me
I shall not fail to gain the strength
to do what love and duty ask.
Yet in this hour I feel more deeply
than I have ever felt before,
a hard probation of my soul draws near.
When men must tear out of their hearts
what of the loved one lives in them,
love has been changed into its opposite.

They of themselves change what unites them
because they gather strength from passion's urge.
But now of my free will must I abolish
the influence which my soul life
had on the actions of my friend;
and yet my love must still remain unchanged.

BENEDICTUS  You'll find your way
if you will recognize
what you most valued in this love of yours.
For if you know which force
leads you unconsciously within your soul,
you'll find the power
to do what duty must require of you.

MARIA  In saying this, you've given me the help
of which my soul is in such need.
Within my being's inmost depths
this weighty question I must ask:
what in this love is urging me so strongly?
I see my separate soul life working
within Johannes' being and within his art,
and thus what I am searching for is satisfaction
which I can feel in my own self
and live in the delusion that I'm selfless.
It has remained concealed to me
that in my friend I mirrored but myself.
It was the dragon self-conceit
that veiled deceptively from me
what was in truth impelling me.
For self-conceit transforms itself a hundredfold;
I recognize it now.
And when one thinks it overcome,

it only rises with much greater force
out of the ruins of its former tyranny.
Moreover, it will gain more strength
in showing the illusion
deceptively in mask of truth.

(*Maria sinks into concentrated thought. Exit
Benedictus. The three figures of the soul
forces appear.*)

MARIA
You, my sisters,
I find when in the depths of being
my soul, expanding, guides itself
into the reaches of the universe.
Release for me the powers of seeing
out of etheric heights
and lead them down to earthly paths
so that I may explore and find myself
in course of time
and give direction to myself
to change old ways of life
into new spheres of will.

PHILIA
I will imbue myself
with striving light of soul
out of the heart's own depths;
I will breathe in
enlivening power of will
out of the spirit's urging;
that you, beloved sister,
within old spheres of life
may feel and sense the light.

ASTRID

I will weave into one
a selfhood's feeling of itself
with love's forbearing will;
I will release
the burgeoning powers of will
from fetters of desire,
transform your languid yearning
to certainty of spirit sensing;
that you, beloved sister,
on paths of earth far distant
explore and find your Self.


LUNA

I will call forth renouncing strength of heart
and will confirm enduring soul-repose.
These shall unite and raise
empowering spirit light
out of the depths of soul;
they shall pervade each other
and shall subdue far distances of earth
to the listening spirit ear;
that you, beloved sister,
in time's wide ranges
may find the traces of your life.


MARIA (*following a pause*)

When I can tear myself away
from the bewildering sense of Self
and give myself to you
so that you reflect to me my soul
from world-wide distances:
then I can free myself

out of this sphere of life
and can explore and find myself
in other states of being.

(*A long pause, then the following:*)

In you, my sisters, I see spirit beings
that quicken souls out of the cosmos' life.
You bring to full maturity in man himself
the forces germinating in eternities.
Through portals of my soul I often
could find my way into your realm
and could behold with inner eyes
the archetypes of earth existence.
I now must ask your help:
it has become my duty
to find the way that leads
from present life on earth
to long past ages of mankind.
Release my soul-life from its sense of self
in time-enclosed existence.
Open for me the sphere of duty, brought
from my life journey in ancient days.

— — — — — — — — — — — — — — — —

SPIRIT VOICE, *the spiritual conscience*:

Her thoughts are searching
in traces left by time.
What remains for her as debt,
what is bestowed on her as duty:
arise out of those soul foundations
from whose deeps

men guide their life,
dreaming;
in whose deeps
men lose themselves,
erring.

(*Curtain, while everyone is still on stage.*)

# SCENE THREE

*A room in rose-red; cheerful atmosphere. Johannes at an easel. Maria enters later; then spirit figures as soul forces.*

JOHANNES   Maria remained silent
when last she saw my painting. –
Before, she always gave me
rich treasures of her wisdom
to aid the progress of my work.
As little as I trust myself to judge
whether my art fulfills the inspiration
that flows out of our spirit teaching,
so much I put my trust in her.
And ever and again I hear the words in spirit
which, strength-bestowing, brought me joy
when first I dared to start this picture:
'Begin to paint,' she said, 'in such a way
that you, with courage, venture
to show to earthly senses
what spiritually the soul alone beholds.
You will not fail to see
how forms, resembling thoughts,
can conquer matter,
and how the shades of colour, akin to feelings,
enwarm the force of life.

34

Thus with your skill you also may
portray the higher realms.'
I feel the power of these words
and humbly yield to the belief
that I draw near the goal
that Benedictus has appointed me.
Often I sat discouraged at my painting;
presumptuous it often seemed to me,
at other times almost impossible,
to represent in colour and in form
what I am granted to behold.
How can the weaving life of spirit,
so far removed from earthly sense,
and to the seer's eyes alone unlocked,
reveal itself by means
belonging to the world of sense?
This I have often asked myself.
Yet when I set aside the personal
and, following spirit teaching,
can feel myself removed in blissfulness
to cosmic powers of creation,
the firm belief in such an art awakens
that is as true
as is the science of the spirit.
I learned to live within the light,
to recognize the deeds of light as colour,
just as the student of this science
sees spirit deeds and soul realities
in realms of life devoid of form and colour.
Relying on this spirit light
I gained ability
to feel as one with flowing seas of light,
to live with colours' streaming glow

and to divine the spirit powers holding sway
in weaving light, released from matter,
in living colour, filled with spirit.

(*Maria enters, unobserved by Johannes*)
— — — — — — — — — — — — — —

And when my courage fails me,
I think of you, my generous friend. –
In your soul's fire is warmed
my urge to work creatively;
within your spirit light is wakened
in me the power of faith.

(*He sees Maria*)

O . . . you are here . . .
Impatiently I've waited
and then could miss your coming!

MARIA          I must rejoice
to see you so absorbed in your own work
that you forget your friend.

JOHANNES      O you should not say that! You know
that I myself cannot create one picture
that is not blessed by you.
There is no work of mine
that does not owe its origin to you.
You've purified me in the fire of love
to make me capable of shaping through my art
what shows itself to you in shining glory.
This shining, warming, life-transforming glory
reveals in radiance the spirit world.
And I must sense how my creative flow
streams forth from your soul's fountain into mine.

36

Then I can feel the wings that lift me
to heights of spirit, far from earth.
I love what lives within your soul
and loving, can bestow upon it image form.
This love alone produces forces in the artist
which fruitfully live on in all his work.
If as an artist I should carry pictures
from spirit realms into the world of sense,
the cosmic spirit must appear through me
and my own person only be its instrument.
First I must break the bonds of selfishness
that I do not portray, instead of spirit realms,
my own delusion's fantasies.

MARIA     And if you would receive out of yourself,
and not through me, the primal source of your
creation, the beauty of your paintings would
appear more unified, from regions of *one* soul.

— — — — — — — — — — — — — — —

JOHANNES     I would be spinning webs of idle thought,
were I to speculate on what for me is best:
whether to embody your spirit vision in my art
or whether I should seek
the origin of images within myself.
I know I could not find them in this way.

— — — — — — — — — — — — — —

I can dive down into soul-grounds
and find myself with bliss in spirit worlds;
and I can lose myself in realms of sense,
pursuing with my eyes the miracles of colour
that to my sight reveal creation's deeds.
Yet left alone,

whatever I experience within my soul
must lead a life devoid of all creative urge.
But if I follow you to cosmic heights
and re-experience in blissful warmth
what you have seen already in the spirit,
within that vision I can feel a fire
whose flames burn on within me and, thus flaming,
enkindle powers, forcing me to work creatively.

_ _ _ _ _ _ _ _ _ _ _ _ _ _ _ _ _

If I were to express in words to others
what I can bring to clear cognition
within the higher worlds,
then I could lift myself
to spheres where spirit speaks to spirit.
An artist has to find that fire
which, radiating from his work, burns on in
     human hearts.
And I can only pour into the picture
what streams as magic spirit-fervour into hearts,
if first my soul can drink
from *your* heart's depths the spirit revelation.

_ _ _ _ _ _ _ _ _ _ _ _ _ _ _ _ _

How primal powers condense themselves in longing,
and how creation's forces strike sparks in spirit
     action
and how, divining man, in need of being,
they soon create themselves as gods in time's
     beginning, –
of this my friend so often spoke in lofty words
so that the unseen I might grasp.
Then in the gentle ether-red of spirit worlds
I tried to densify what is invisible,
by sensing how the colours nurse a longing

to see themselves in souls, transfigured into spirit.
So speaks the inmost being of my friend,
as does my own,
to human hearts out of my pictures.

MARIA        Consider well, Johannes, that an entity of soul,
severed from others, has to unfold itself
from world beginning as a single being.
Love that unites the severed beings
will not destroy their selfhood's life.
The moment has arrived for us
when we must test our souls
in how to guide their further steps
on spirit paths for each one's separate good.

(*Exit Maria*)

JOHANNES    What did my friend just say?
I can not understand her words!
Maria . . . let me follow you!

(*The three figures of soul forces appear.*)

LUNA        You cannot find yourself
within the mirror of another soul.
The force of your own being
must root itself in cosmic ground,
if from the heights of spirit
it would implant their beauty
in depths of earth in its true form.
Be bold enough to be yourself,
that you may offer up that self
as valiant shape of soul to cosmic powers.

ASTRID      You must not lose yourself
            upon your cosmic paths;
            men do not reach far-distant suns
            by robbing their own being from themselves.
            Prepare yourself,
            transcending human love, to penetrate
            to inmost depths of heart
            where cosmic love will ripen.

THE OTHER PHILIA
            O do not listen to the sisters.
            They lead you into cosmic reaches
            and rob you of earth nearness. –
            They do not see how earthly love
            bears all the traits of cosmic love.
            Their beings rule in coldness;
            their forces flee from warmth.
            They want to lure each man
            out of his depths of soul
            to freezing worlds on high.

            (*Curtain falls, with Johannes, Luna, Astrid,
            the Other Philia standing quietly.*)

# SCENE FOUR

*The same room as in Scene One, Capesius and Strader.*

CAPESIUS (*to Strader, who has just entered*)

> A hearty welcome, friend, to you
> who used to stand up valiantly
> against me in our heated arguments.
> It's been too long
> since you last visited my house –
> you used to like to come more often.

STRADER

> I've had so little time.
> My life has changed immensely.
> No longer am I torturing my brain
> with spectres of despairing thoughts.
> I dedicate the knowledge I have won
> to honest work,
> that will in some way be of use in life.

CAPESIUS

> Then you have left your line of research?

STRADER

> You could say too that it's left me.

CAPESIUS

> What goals have you now set yourself?

STRADER

> Our life is far from able
> to point out goals

that men can clearly understand.
It is a treadmill, a mere engine,
that pins us by its whirring wheels
and hurls us, wearied, into darkness
when the measure of our strength is spent.

CAPESIUS    I've known you when you dared to grapple
courageously with all the riddles of existence.
I've also seen how you experienced
your hard-won knowledge slipping
away from you into the void
and, deeply shaken, you as searcher had
to drink the bitter cup of disappointed dreams.
Yet I could not conceive you would be able
to tear out of your heart
the urge that filled you so completely.

STRADER    Do you remember still the day
on which a seeress through the truth of what she
      said made clear to me the error of my path?
I had no choice but to acknowledge then
that all our toil of thinking
can never find the fountainhead of life.
For what we think must be indeed mistaken
when to the force of soul
this woman called her own,
the light of highest wisdom is revealed.
I'm certain that stern science
would aim in vain at such a revelation.
If there had been this one defeat
of my conceited searching,
I think I could have made a new beginning
and joined my path to all those other ones.

But seeing how this strange approach to spirit,
which seemed to me at times sheer madness,
could change mere impotence into creative force –
then all my hope was lost.

_____

Do you remember the young painter
we met together
upon those doubtful spirit paths? . . .
After such blows of fate
I lived for many weeks
benumbed and near to madness.
As nature brought me back to sanity,
I formed the firm decision
to stop all further searching.
I needed time to gain once more
my health in mind and body.
I've passed it joylessly.
I made myself proficient in those things
which lead to practical accomplishments.
Today I supervise a shop
which manufactures screws,
and thanks to this activity
I can for many hours forget
how torturing my worthless struggle was.

CAPESIUS     I must confess
that I can hardly recognize
the former friend in him
who stands before me now . . .
Besides those hours of which you spoke
do you not also live through times
in which old tempests are renewed
which force you out of that dull mood?

43

STRADER	The hours are not withheld from me
when weakness fights
with weakness in my soul.
But destiny withholds from me,
in this completely wasted life,
new rays of hope
to penetrate my heart.
Renunciation will I conquer for myself;
the strength which it demands
may give me the ability
to follow in another way the path of research, –
– – – – – – – – – – – – – – – –
if perhaps my life on earth repeats itself.

CAPESIUS	You spoke – O did I hear you rightly? –
of repetition of your life on earth.
So have you then attained
that crucial truth upon those spirit paths
which even now
you still esteem as dubious?

STRADER	So now you've found the third essential cause
that strengthened my resolve
to make a new start in my life.
There on my sick-bed I surveyed once more,
before I turned to other goals,
the sum of knowledge I'd acquired.
A hundred times I asked myself:
what can our natural science teach us
as we can summarize it all today?
– There is no way around it –
the repetition of our life on earth:
our thinking neither can nor dare deny it,

unless we break with everything
that steady research has discovered
throughout the course of time.

CAPESIUS    Could I have had such an experience,
it would have spared me bitter pain,
for many sleepless nights I've passed
and longed that thoughts like these
might bring relief and liberation.

STRADER    And yet this spirit flash has robbed me
of my remaining powers. I always felt it
as strongest urging of my soul
to test through life itself
what thinking gave to me as truth.
It seemed that chance desired to prove
by my own life in all those days of anguish
how cruel and influential is this truth.
It makes life's joys and sorrows seem
to be the consequence of what we really are,
and this indeed is often hard to bear.

CAPESIUS    This seems impossible to me. –
What can transcend a truth
for which we search unceasingly and which
can give us spirit certainty?

STRADER    That may be so for you,
but I feel otherwise.
You know my life's strange course . . .
It seemed but chance that crossed my parents'
        hope for me . . .
They wished me to become a monk.

45

They've often said
that they look on their son's apostasy
as the great sorrow of their life.
I bore all this . . .
much more, indeed, besides,
as one is prone to bear one's life
when birth and death become
the limits of our earthly pilgrimage.
Also my later life with all its crumbled hopes
appeared to me so shaped
that it could only through itself be understood.
O had the moment never come
that brought me to a different opinion.
For you must know, I've not related all
that destiny has put upon me.
I'm not the child of those
who wished me to become a monk;
they had adopted me
when I was but a few days old.
I was a stranger even in my boyhood home.
My actual parents are unknown to me.
Estranged have I remained to all
that has gone on around me in my later life.
My thinking now requires of me
that I look back to former times
when I deprived myself of contact with the world.
Indeed, this thought must follow thought:
whoever has become a stranger in the world
before his consciousness has dawned in him
has truly willed this destiny
before his will was guided by his thought.
Because I have remained just what I was at first,
all doubts in me have vanished:

with apathy I must succumb to powers
that spin my threads of destiny
and will not show themselves to me.
What more of cruel proof is left
to show how dense the veils are that conceal
my inmost being from myself?
Now, judge without false thirst for knowledge:
has this new truth brought any light to me?
It gave me certainty indeed
that in uncertainty I must remain.
It showed to me my destiny;
half filled with sorrow,
and half with irony,
I could repay in the same coin.
It overwhelmed me:
tortured by bitter scorn
I had to face my life,
and scoffing at the magic trickery of fate
I yielded to the darkness.
Yet there remained one single thought:
enmesh me, life, in your machinery;
I am not curious what makes your cogwheels work.

CAPESIUS    The man that I have known in you
could not remain for long
in such a barrenness of thinking,
even if he wished.
Already I can see the days approach
when, changed, we'll find each other once again.

(*Curtain falls while the two are still
facing each other.*)

47

# SCENE FIVE

*A landscape with Balde's lonely cottage; mood of evening. Felicia Balde, Capesius, then Felix Balde; later, Johannes and his Double, then Lucifer and Ahriman.*

CAPESIUS (*enters and comes towards Felicia, who is sitting on a bench in front of her cottage*)

> May your old friend walk up
> and rest a little while with you?
> Now more than ever does he feel in need
> of what he's found so often at your house.

FELICIA

> When I could see you coming in the distance,
> your weary steps foretold –
> and near at hand your eye reveals it, too –
> that sorrow dwells within your soul today.

CAPESIUS (*sitting down*)

> To bring much gaiety into your home
> was never possible for me.
> Today I ask for special patience
> when, with a restless heart,
> I trespass on this peaceful spot.

FELICIA

> You've been so gladly welcomed here
> at times when hardly anyone came near our house,

48

and now despite events that came between us,
you have remained our friend –
though many people now are looking up
this lonely place of ours.

CAPESIUS    Then is it true what I have heard,
that our dear Felix,
so taciturn till now,
has in these days become
a much sought-after man?

FELICIA    Ah, yes. Good Felix used
to shut us off from all the world . . .
Now he is forced to talk to many people:
his duty, this new life appears to be to him.
In former days he wanted to confide
to his own inner self alone
what woods and cliffs revealed to him
of spirit-deeds and nature's power.
Besides, it seemed to no one else worth knowing.
– – – – – – – – – – – – – – – –
How much the times indeed have changed!
Right many people
now listen greedily to what my Felix
reveals·to them about his knowledge,
which in the past they found most foolish.
And when my dearest husband

(*Felix enters from the house*)

for hours on end must talk,
I really long for those old, quiet days;
at that time he had pointed out so earnestly
that only in the silent heart

the soul should bear the spirit gifts
bestowed on it in grace from godly realms.
He called him traitor to the spirit world
whoever would reveal it to a hearing
that opened only to the world of sense.

FELIX BALDE    Felicia finds it hard to reconcile herself
to our completely altered life.
She once complained about our loneliness
and now complains no less
when many a day
we have few hours to ourselves.

CAPESIUS    And what has moved you
to receive and welcome people
in your secluded home?

FELIX    Obediently I followed spirit guidance
that speaks within my heart
when it demanded of me silence.
And just as faithful to its call to speak
I shall now yield myself.
The being of humanity transforms itself,
as earth existence gradually moves on.
We're standing at a turning-point of time.
Some part of spirit knowledge
must be unlocked for every man
who wills to open mind and heart to it . . .
I know, my kind of speech
has little of the form that counts today.
The spirit life, they say, must be expressed
with strictly logical thought-structure,
and this is lacking in my speech.

They claim that genuine science,
which should be based on firm foundations,
cannot regard me otherwise
than as a visionary soul who seeks
a solitary road to wisdom
and knows no more of science than of art.
But others find it well worthwhile
to peer into the tangle of my words
discovering things from time to time
that can be grasped by common sense.
I am a man who artlessly
lets stream into his heart
each revelation that may come to him.
I do not know a knowing without words . . .
When I hold converse in my inmost heart,
when I take heed of nature round about me,
there lives in me a knowledge
that does not search for words . . .
Speech is as closely bound to it
as is his body's form to earthly man . . .
A knowing, which in such a way
reveals itself from spirit worlds,
can be of service also
to men who do not understand it.
So everyone's allowed to come to me
who will attend to what I have to say.
I know full well that curiosity
and other poorer reasons bring some people here.
Yet if in this time now on earth
such people's souls are not yet stirred,
the good has been implanted
and will work on in them.

CAPESIUS     I'd like to say to you quite frankly, –
for many years I have respected you,
yet up to now the sense
of your strange words is closed to me as well.

FELIX     It will unlock itself to you most certainly.
You strive with noble heart and spirit.
The time will come
when you will hear the voice of truth.
Just look what rich endowments
man has, as image of the kingdoms of the worlds.
His head: it is the heaven's mirror-image;
and through his limbs work spirits of the spheres;
within his breast the beings of the earth are moving;
and stemmed against them all, there wrestle mightily
the demons of the province of the moon,
who have to cross the spirit beings' aims.
What as a human being stands before us,
what as a soul we take in livingly,
what as a spirit shines upon us,
has been envisioned by the gods
from all eternity.
Their purpose was to bring together
the forces out of all the worlds
which, thus united, shape the human form.

CAPESIUS     I'm almost frightened by this word,
which boldly would consider
the human being the achievement of the gods.

FELIX     Yes, therefore high humility is needed
by him who would attain to spirit knowledge.
For him who strives to know himself

in arrogance and vanity,
the gates of wisdom do not open.

(*Felix returns to the house.*)

CAPESIUS    Now help me, dear Felicia, as so often
you've done before, so that my soul
may turn itself to pictures and is able,
enwarmed by living images,
to grasp these words as rightly they should be.

FELICIA    My Felix has repeated frequently to me
the words he spoke just now.
And they released out of my heart
a picture, which I've often told myself
I should relate to you.

CAPESIUS    Do so, dear friend!
I long for the refreshment
that flows out of your picture treasury.

FELICIA    So be it! . . .
Once upon a time there was a boy
who lived – the only child of a poor forester –
within a woodland solitude. He knew
besides his parents hardly any other people.
His build was slender,
his skin almost transparent.
One could look long into his eyes:
they treasured deepest spirit wonders.
And though indeed few people entered
the circle of his life,
he never was in need of friends.
When in the nearby mountains

53

the golden sunlight glowed and glimmered,
the boy's rapt, musing eye drew forth
the spirit gold into his soul
until his heart resembled
the morning brightness of the sun. –
But when through darkening clouds
the morning sunrays could not pierce
and dreariness hung over mountain heights,
the boy's eye, too, grew dull;
a mood of sadness filled his heart. –
The spirit weaving of his narrow world
took hold of him so fully
that it was no less strange to him
than were his body and his limbs.
The trees and flowers of the woods
were all his friends:
there spoke to him from crown and calyx
and from the lofty tree-tops spirit beings
and what they whispered, he could understand. –
Such wondrous things of worlds unknown
unlocked themselves before the boy
whenever his soul conversed
with what most people would regard as lifeless.
At evening his anxious parents
from time to time missed their beloved child. –
The boy was at a spot nearby
where from the rocks a spring burst forth,
and waterdrops, dispersing thousandfold,
were scattered over stones.
When moonlight's silver glance,
in sparkling colours' sorcery,
was mirrored in the water's misty spray,

the boy could sit for hours on end
beside the rock-born spring.
And figures, formed by spirit-magic,
arose before his youthful vision
in rushing water and in moonlight's glimmer.
They grew into three women's forms
who told him of those things
toward which his soul's desire was turned. –
And when upon a gentle summer night
the boy was sitting at the spring again,
one woman of the three caught up a myriad of drops
out of the glittering spray
and gave them to the second woman.
She fashioned from the tiny drops
a chalice with a silver gleam
and passed it to the third.
She filled it with the moonlight's silver rays
and gave it to the boy,
who had beheld all this
with youthful inner sight. –
Now in the night
which followed this event,
he dreamed that he was robbed
by a fierce dragon of the chalice.
After this night the boy beheld
just three times more the wonder of the spring.
Henceforth the women came no more
although the boy sat musing
beside the rock-born spring in moonlight's silver
        sheen.
And when three hundred sixty weeks
had run their course three times,
the boy had long become a man

and left his parents' home and forest country
to live in a strange city.
One evening, tired from the day's hard toil,
he pondered on what life had still in store for him,
when suddenly he felt himself a boy,
caught up and carried to his rock-born spring.
Again he could behold the water-women
and this time heard them speak.
The first one said to him:
  Remember me at any time
  you feel alone in life.
  I lure man's eye of soul
  to starry spaces and ethereal realms.
  And whosoever wills to feel me,
  I offer him the draught of hope in life
  out of my wonder goblet. –
And then the second spoke:
  Do not forget me at the times
  when courage in your life is threatened.
  I lead man's yearning heart
  to depths of soul and up to spirit heights.
  And whosoever seeks his strength from me,
  for him I forge the steel of faith in life,
  shaped by my wonder hammer. –
The third one could be heard:
  To me lift up your eye of spirit
  when your life's riddles overwhelm you.
  I spin the threads of thought that lead
  through labyrinths of life and the abyss of soul.
  And whosoever harbours trust in me,
  for him I weave the living rays of love
  upon my wonder loom. –
Thus it befell the man,

and in the night that followed this
he dreamed a dream:
a savage dragon prowled
in circles round about him, –
and yet could not come near him.
He was protected from that dragon by
the beings he had seen beside the rock-born spring
and who with him had left his home
for this far-distant place.

---------------

CAPESIUS   Warm thanks to you, dear friend, –
I leave you with rich blessings.

(*He rises and walks away; Felicia enters the house.*
*Capesius at some distance, alone, speaks as follows.*

I feel how such a picture
works on within my soul, bestowing health;
how to my thinking it is able
to restore the forces I have lost.
The story was so simple that she told.
And yet it stirs in me the powers of thought
that bear me into unknown worlds . . .
In this fair solitude I will indulge
in dreaming.
This has so often
endowed my soul with thoughts
that proved far better
than many fruits of endless brooding.

---------------

(*He goes down a path between the bushes*
*and disappears.*)

JOHANNES (*appears in deep contemplation in the same part of the forest glade*)

Was it a dream? was it reality . . .?
I cannot bear what my friend said
in gentle calmness, yet so firmly,
about our separation.
If I could only think that reasoning,
antagonistic to the spirit,
had set itself between us
as a deceptive image . . .

— — — — — — — — — — — — — — — —

I cannot, will not follow
the counsel that Maria gave
to drown the voice in me
that speaks unceasingly: I love her . . .
This love remains for me the only spring
of action that I wish to know.
What is all the creative urge to me,
what is the outlook toward high spirit goals,
if they can rob me of the light
illuminating my existence? —
Within this light I have to live.
If it were taken from me,
I'd wish for death through all eternity.
I feel my strength is ebbing
when I attempt to think:
I'd have to follow paths
no more illumined by her light.

— — — — — — — — — — — — — — — —

There weaves before my eyes
a mist. It's shrouding in confusion
the marvels which this forest and these rocks

had painted gloriously before my eyes . . .
A wild dream rises out of the abyss . . .
*O terribly it shakes me through and through* . . .
_ _ _ _ _ _ _ _ _ _ _ _ _ _ _

Away from me! . . .
I thirst for solitude,
for it will let me keep the dreams
that are my own.
In them I still may yearn
for what seems lost to me . . .
_ _ _ _ _ _ _ _ _ _ _ _ _ _

. . . It will not leave me! . . .
so I must flee from it –

*(feels himself fastened to the ground)*

What chains are these
that hold me fettered to the ground?

*(The Double of Johannes Thomasius appears.)*

Alas . . .
Whoever you may be,
if human blood is flowing in your veins
or if alone as spirit you exist . . .
leave me alone . . .
_ _ _ _ _ _ _ _ _ _ _ _ _ _

Who are you? . . . has a demon
thrust myself before myself?
He will not go . . .
It is the image of my self . . .
It seems to be still stronger
than is my being in itself . . .

THE DOUBLE    Maria, how I love you . . .
near you

with beating heart,
with feverish blood,
I am consumed . . .
and when your eyes meet mine,
hot waves pulse through me,
and when you put
your loving hand in mine,
blissfulness
pervades my limbs . . .

JOHANNES     You phantom, woven out of vapor mist,
you dare blaspheme
the purest feelings of my heart . . .
What weight of guilt is laid upon me
that I must now perceive
a lewd distortion of the love
I look upon as holy? . . .

THE DOUBLE     I've often listened to your words . . .
I seemed to swallow them into my soul
as message from the land of spirits . . .
But more than by such revelations
I was impelled to love your nearness.
And when you spoke of paths of soul,
there streamed through me a rapture
that surges turbulently in the blood.

THE VOICE OF CONSCIENCE
So speaks revealing
not yet concealing
from shine receding
in blood proceeding

the secret fire
fanning desire.

THE DOUBLE (*with somewhat altered voice*)

I cannot forsake you;
you'll find me often at your side.
I will not leave you
till you have found the strength
to shape me to a likeness of the being
that you will some day be
but are not yet.
In the illusion of your narrow self alone
can you behold that likeness.

_ _ _ _ _ _ _ _ _ _ _ _ _ _ _ _

(*Lucifer and Ahriman appear.*)

LUCIFER

O man, conquer yourself,
O man, redeem me.
You have defeated me
in your soul heights,
but I stay bound to you
in being's depths.
You'll always find me
upon your path of life
when you attempt completely
to shield yourself from me.
O man, conquer yourself,
O man, redeem me.

AHRIMAN

O man, embolden yourself,
O man, experience me.
You've gained for yourself

the seeing of spirit beings.
I had to spoil for you
the quickening of your heart;
often indeed you'll suffer
the hardest agony of soul,
if you'll not bend yourself
to powers of mine.
O man, embolden yourself,
O man, experience me.

(*Lucifer and Ahriman disappear, the Double
also. Johannes goes further into the darkness
of the forest in deep musing. Capesius
reappears. From behind the thicket he has
followed the scene between Johannes and the
Double as in a vision.*)

CAPESIUS    Whatever came upon me? Like a depressing
        nightmare
it weighs on me. Thomasius came this way;
he seemed absorbed in quiet meditation.
Then he stood still as if he spoke to someone,
yet no one else was there.
I felt as if dread fear were weighing down on me.
But then I saw no more of anything around.
As if asleep, unconscious, I seemed
to have been drawn into a world of pictures,
which I can recollect quite well.
It could have only been a short time then
that I sat dreaming, – lost to myself.
How rich, however, was this world of dreams,
and ever stranger does it seem to me.
I could distinctly see the people
of bygone days and hear them speak.

About a spirit – brotherhood I dreamed,
which strove toward mankind's highest goals.
Within their midst I clearly saw myself;
I felt familiar with it all.
A dream? . . . and yet, soul-stirring was the dream.
I know that I could never have experienced
the like of it within this present life.
The after-feeling which remains with me
pervades my soul, as real life would do.
An elemental power draws me to these pictures . . .
O could I but behold that dream again!

(*Curtain falls while Capesius remains standing.*)

# SCENE SIX

*Scenes Six, Seven, Eight and Nine take place during the first third of the fourteenth century.*

> *A forest glade. In the background a high*
> *cliff on which stands a castle. A summer*
> *evening. Peasants pass through the glade and speak*
> *together as they pause along the way.*

FIRST PEASANT See here, the wicked Jew;
he will not dare
to take the same path as we,
for he might hear such things as burn his
ears.

SECOND PEASANT
We should show him for good and all
we shall no longer tolerate his boldness,
sneaking across the border into our quiet
homeland!

FIRST WOMAN He is protected by the lords
who live there in the castle.
Not one of us is given entrance;
the Jew they readily admit. He does
whatever they would have him do.

THIRD PEASANT

> 'Tis hard to know who's serving God,
> who's serving Hell.
> We should be thankful to our knights;
> they give us bread as well as work.
> Where should we be without them?

SECOND WOMAN

> Now I must say a good word for the Jew.
> He freed me of my cruel sickness
> by his own remedies.
> He was so kind and good beside.
> He's done the same for many others, too.

THIRD WOMAN A monk, however, has divulged to me

> that devilish are the means by which he heals.
> Be well on guard against his poison.
> 'Tis said to change within the body,
> and offer entrance to all sins.

FOURTH PEASANT

> The men who serve the knights
> combat our ancient customs.
> They say the Jew knows much
> that good and blessing brings,
> but will be rightly valued
> only in days to come.

FIFTH PEASANT New and better times are soon in store:

> I can foresee them in the spirit
> for pictures from the soul show things
> my body's eyes cannot behold.
> The knights are willing
> to bring all this about for us.

FOURTH WOMAN

        It's to the church we owe our loyalty;
        it saves our souls from devil pictures,
        from death and from the pangs of hell.
        The monks do warn us of the knights
        and of the sorcerer, the Jew.

FIFTH WOMAN  We shall not bear this yoke much longer
        imposed upon our patience by the knights.
        The castle will soon lie in ruins;
        a vision in a dream revealed all this to me.

SIXTH WOMAN  The fear of heavy sin torments me
        when I listen to the people say
        the knights are plotting to destroy us.
        I see but good in all that comes from them.
        I needs must call them Christian too.

SIXTH PEASANT  How men will think in days to come,
        let us leave that to those
        who shall live after us.
        The knights are using us as tools
        to work their devil's arts
        with which they fight
        what's truly Christian.
        When they are driven out,
        we shall be free of their control
        and live our lives as we shall choose,
        here in our native land. –

        Let us now go to vespers;
        we find there what our souls require

and what's in keeping
with the customs of our fathers.
New teachings are not right for us.

(*The Peasants go out*)
(*Simon, the Jew, enters from the wood.*)

SIMON  It always is the same old hate and scorn
which I must hear from every side.
Yet ever and again I'm filled with pain
that I'm unable to defend myself.
There seems to be no reason for the way
I'm persecuted by the people.
And yet one thought pursues me often
that brings this truth before my soul:
that meaning lies in all that we experience.
And therefore, too, there's reason
for what the people of my race must bear.
And looking at the knights there in the castle,
I find their destiny akin to mine.
But purposely they took upon themselves
what powers of Nature have imposed on me.
They set themselves apart from other men
in lonely striving to develop forces
by means of which they win their goals.
I feel how much I owe my destiny
for blessing me also with solitude.
Depending on myself alone,
I could devote myself to science.
Its teachings made me realize,
our time is reaching toward new goals.
There must reveal themselves to man
such laws of Nature as 'til now were strange to him.
He will soon conquer for himself the world of sense

and out of it will liberate the forces
that he will make subservient to himself.
As far as I am able, I have tried
to foster in this way the art of healing.
These efforts have endeared me to the knights.
They have permitted me to study on their land
the forces that reside within the plants
and can be found within the soil,
so that I learn the future ways of healing.
I labour so according to their aims
and may confess that on my path
I've gladly gathered some good fruit.

(*He goes further into the wood.*)
(*Thomas, the master miner, enters from
the wood. The Monk meets him.*)

THOMAS

I'll rest a little here. I need tranquility
so that my soul again recovers from the storms
that have been breaking in upon me.

(*The Monk meets him*)

MONK

I greet you heartily, my son.
You've come here seeking solitude.
After hard work you look for quiet peace
to turn your mind towards spirit worlds.
It pleases me to find my pupil in this mood.
But why does sorrow cloud your eye?
It seems that cares are burdening your
      soul.

THOMAS

Pain is so often close to highest bliss, –
my life has shown me this today.

| | |
|---|---|
| MONK | Have you encountered pain and bliss at once? |
| THOMAS | I have confided in you, reverend father, <br> how much I love the overseer's daughter; <br> she, too, has given me her heart, <br> and as my wife she'll share my life with me. |
| MONK | She'll stand by you in joy and sorrow, <br> a piously devoted daughter of the church. |
| THOMAS | It's only such a wife I want, <br> because from you, beloved teacher, <br> I've learned submission to the will of God. |
| MONK | And are you also sure of your own soul? <br> Will it persist along the path <br> which I could show you as the right one? |
| THOMAS | As truly as this heart beats in my body <br> so faithful shall your son forever be. <br> Submissive will he be to that high teaching <br> which from your lips he has received. |
| MONK | And as you've told me of your bliss, <br> now let me hear about your sorrow too. |
| THOMAS | I've told you often of my life. <br> When I had hardly grown beyond my childhood <br> I started journeying from town to town. <br> I often changed my place of work. <br> There lived within my heart the constant wish <br> to meet again my father whom I loved <br> although I had not had much good from him. |

He had deserted my dear mother
because, unhindered by a wife and children,
he wished to gain a new life for himself.
The craving for adventure lived in him.
I was a child still when he left us;
my sister was just born.
A short time afterward my mother died of grief.
My sister was looked after by good people
who later left my native town.
I have heard nothing further of her life.
Some kinfolk helped me to learn mining,
and I progressed so far in it
wherever I sought work, I always found it.
The hope has never left me
that I would find again my father.
And now, this hope, fulfilled at last,
has gone from me for evermore. –
On an official matter I reported
to my superior yesterday.
You know how I dislike the knight
who is the supervisor of my work
since I discovered you oppose him.
From that time on I've been determined
to serve no longer at the castle.
But in our meeting, for some unknown reason,
the knight could give our conversation
a turn that made it possible for him
to declare himself to be . . . my father . . .
What followed – O I cannot bear to speak of it – . . .
I could have quite forgotten all the sorrow,
which he inflicted on my mother and myself,
when now at last I stood before my father
who, bowed by sorrow, spoke of bygone days.

But in him, *your* opponent stood before me.
One thing alone was clear to me,
the deep cleft that must sever me forever
from him I wished so much to love,
whom ardently so long I sought. –
I've lost him now a second time.
And so I feel the suffering I've had.

MONK        I never would estrange you from the bonds
your blood-ties lay upon you.
And yet, what I can offer to your soul
indeed shall lovingly be given you.

*(Curtain during their exit.)*

# SCENE SEVEN

*A room within the castle which in Scene Six was viewed from outside. It is decorated with symbols of a Mystic Brotherhood. – First, the Knights are shown during a meeting, then the Monk with one of the Knights; later there appear the Spirit of Benedictus, who has died fifty years earlier, Lucifer and Ahriman. The Grand Master with four Knights are gathered about a long table.*

GRAND MASTER

You have become companions to me
in search of mankind's future goals.
We are directed by our Order's precepts
to bring these aims from spirit regions
into the realm of earth activity.
So loyally stand by me now
within this hour of grave concern.
Our venerable leader fell
a victim to those powers of darkness
which draw their strength from evil
and yet promote the plan of wisdom
by opposition's force. This plan
seeks to convert the evil into good.
But since our leader's death,
our earthly strivings are in vain.
Our enemies have overthrown already
many a castle of our brotherhood, – –
and fighting, many of our valiant brothers

have followed the great master
into the bright realms of eternity.
For us, too, the hour is close at hand
when these protecting walls must fall.
Our enemies are spying out the means
by which they can take hold of our possessions.
These we've surely not acquired for profit,
but as a means to gather round us people
into whose souls we can implant
seeds for the future.
These seeds will ripen in their souls
when out of spirit realms they find their way
into a later life on earth.

First Master of Ceremony

Our Order must endure whatever dark design
our destiny has yet in store.
This, one can understand.
But that in perishing, our whole community
must sweep with it
so many brothers' individual lives,
seems an injustice in the light of cosmic laws.
My lips will not complain,
for manfully our brothers died;
but still my soul desires to understand
the sacrifice required of a man
united with a group
when powers of destiny have doomed
that group to its destruction.

Grand Master

The individual's separate life
is linked most wisely with the cosmic plan.

Among our brothers one proves often able
to serve our Order with his spirit forces
although his life is not unblemished.
His erring course of heart and mind will find
atonement through the sufferings
he has to bear in service to the whole.
On him who bears no guilt from his own deeds
yet has to walk the thorny path
marked out by karma for our Order,
pain will bestow new strength
to raise himself to higher life.

FIRST MASTER OF CEREMONY

Then does our Order tolerate within itself
men also, lacking purity of soul,
who consecrate themselves to its high goals?

GRAND MASTER

The one who works devotedly for lofty aims,
he weighs the good alone in souls of men
and he allows the bad to find atonement
within the course of cosmic justice. –
I've summoned you, my brothers,
in these our days of grief
in order to recall to you with earnest words,
that it behooves us joyfully to die –
for goals to which we pledged ourselves
to dedicate our lives.
In the truest sense you are my brothers
when in your souls resound courageously
our Order's words of consecration:
'The separate life and being must be sacrificed
by him who would set eyes on spirit goals

74

through sense-world revelation;
who would, with courage, dare
to pour into his individual will
the spirit's power of will.'

FIRST PRECEPTOR

Most worthy master, if you would test
the hearts of all our brothers,
in clearest echo will resound to you
those words of consecration.
But we would hear from your own lips
how to construe the fact
that with our lands and lives,
the enemy robs us of souls as well
whom with our love we nurtured.
For every day makes it more clear
our people will surrender to the victors
not only through compulsion
but through the hate our foes have taught them
against the spirit path which we have shown.

GRAND MASTER

What we have planted in their souls
indeed may for the present die.
But those who breathed our spirit light
will come again, and then bestow
upon the world what we intended in our work. –
Thus to my spirit from realms of death
our mighty leader often speaks,
when I descend in hours of silence
into my inner depths,
and forces then awaken,
to hold me in the spirit land.

I feel the presence of our leader then
and hear his words
as often I have heard them
in earthly life.
He does not speak of our work's ending,
but of fulfilment of our goals
in later days on earth.

*(The Grand Master and two Knights go out,
while two remain.)*

FIRST PRECEPTOR

He speaks of spirit worlds in just the way
that others speak of villages and towns – – –.
To me this manner is oppressive
in which our consecrated brothers talk
of other regions of existence.
Yet I am sternly bound
to all our earthly aims.

SECOND MASTER OF CEREMONY

I hold fast to our masters' words:
the one who cannot hear with full belief
the truth of spirit and of spirit worlds, –
he does not lack capacity
to grasp such revelation.
The things he lacks are of a different nature.
If he does not feel worthy of
belonging to the higher worlds,
he can well sense it,
but he would like to hide it from himself.
The soul that has some hidden stains
and must deceive itself about them
can never yield itself to spirit knowledge.

*(They go out. The Monk appears in the same hall,*
*and is met by the Second Preceptor.)*

SECOND PRECEPTOR

What brings you here into this house
which you consider enemy domain?

MONK

I must include among my friends all those
who bear the countenance of man.
This is our stringent rule.
Yet hostile may quite well appear to you
what, duty bound, I am obliged to claim.
I'm here at my superiors' behest.
They want by peaceful means
the land restored to them
belonging to the church by reason of old deeds.
The piece of ground you made into a mine
remains in fact our church's legal property.
The way in which you have acquired the land
can never be upheld before the law.

SECOND PRECEPTOR

Whether by law we call it ours or not,
the judges might dispute for a long time.
It nonetheless belongs to us
in light of higher justice.
The piece of ground was undeveloped soil
when it was purchased by our Order.
It was unknown to you
that under it rich treasures lay concealed.
We've won them by and for the work of men.
Today these treasures travel to far-distant places
to further human progress.

77

And many honest people work
within the mine-shafts of that ground
which when you held it was plain wilderness.

MONK    Then you do not consider it your duty
that you prevail upon your Order
to reach a peaceful understanding with us
and satisfy our rights?

SECOND PRECEPTOR
Since we are not aware of any guilt,
nay more, are certain of our rights,
we'll calmly wait
to see if you will feel obliged
to add injustice to your cause.

MONK    You must ascribe it to your stubborn will,
if we are now compelled to other means.

SECOND PRECEPTOR
The honor of our Order
demands that only on the battlefield
can it be robbed of its fair rights.

MONK    So then my mission is fulfilled,
and we can save all further words.
Would it be possible to see
the master who gives orders here?

SECOND PRECEPTOR
He very likely will be at your service.
But I must ask you, wait a little while.
He cannot come at once.

(*He goes out.*)

MONK (*alone*)    O that my office forces me to enter
the hall of this most hateful Order.
On every side my eye encounters
these devilish designs and sinful images.
An agonizing horror grips me . . .
It's crackling – – O it's rumbling through the hall;
I feel how evil powers want to encircle me . . .
– – – – – – – – – – – – – – –
As I am not aware of any sin,
I bid defiance to the adversaries
– – – – – – – – – – – – – –
The horror grows . . . . . . .
O – – – – – – – – – – – – – –

(*The Spirit of Benedictus appears.*)

All good spirits, stand by me now!

BENEDICTUS    Take heed, my son!
I could draw near you frequently
when fervent prayer
transported you to spirit worlds.
So hear with courage also in this hour
what you must bring to clear cognition,
if spirit light in place of darkness
should now hold sway within your soul.

MONK    When I begged earnestly for clarity
in moments of distress
and my devoted prayer
was granted hearing in the spirit land,
then you appeared to me, great master,

79

who was the glory of our Order
in days you lived on earth.
You spoke to me from higher realms,
illumining my sense
and strengthening my power.
My soul's eye could behold you,
my spirit ear could hear you.
And now devoutly in this hour
I'll listen to the revelation
which flows from you into my soul.

BENEDICTUS     You find yourself within that Order's house
which you accuse of evil heresy.
It seems to hate all that we love
and to revere what we deem sin.
Our brothers hold themselves obliged to hasten
the downfall of this sin against the spirit.
In this they are supported
by words which formerly I spoke on earth.
They do not dream
these very words can only be renewed
if they are nurtured for their further growth
by those who are successors in my work.
So let arise within your soul
what I once thought in former days on earth,
but now what it must be
in view of a new age.
The Order here accepts its goals
from occult heights.
Look on it in that light
as I myself would do
if I could walk among you actively
within an earthly body.

This Order strives towards highest goals.
And those who dedicate themselves to it
divine already future times on earth.
Their leaders see with a prophetic eye
the fruits that ripen in a later age.
Both science and men's way of life
will change in form and aim.
This Order, whose persecution you support,
now feels impelled to undertake
the deeds which serve this change.
And only when our brothers' aims
unite for peaceful purposes
with those the heretics pursue,
can good in earthly progress blossom forth.

MONK                The admonition you have found me worthy of,
how can I follow it – – –?
It deviates most forcefully from all
that in the past seemed right to me.

(*Ahriman and Lucifer appear.*)

What other beings now are drawing near!
What wills them here and at your side?

AHRIMAN            More counsel comes from other corners.
You cannot deem it easy to obey
your former master's warning. Just reflect
that he is living in the realm of blessedness.
What works toward law and duty there,
can only cause confusion for
your present situation on the earth.
Lift up your eyes unto his heights
when you seek comfort in the bliss

which will be granted by world spirits
to distant days on earth.
But if at present you would act aright,
be guided then alone
by what your reason and your senses teach.
You have succeeded well
in fathoming these brothers' sins
which they must hide from all the world.
It shows how their ideals
can live quite well in sinful souls.
Faced with the brothers' sly designing,
how can you care to live in peace with them?
For error is a barren soil;
it does not let the good fruit ripen.

LUCIFER      Your pious mind and heart
have shown to you the right direction.
The aims of every age transform themselves;
but heretics should not lay out
the future paths of men.
The danger of this Spirit Order
lies in its words that speak the truth,
yet may be given such a turn
that makes the truth more dangerous than error.
How foolish is the man who lives in the belief
that when he shows his falsehood openly
all men will follow him as leader.
The Spirit-Knights are not so ill-advised. –
Indeed, they speak about the immanence of Christ
because they know this name will open
the portals leading to the souls of men.
To capture for Christ's counter-image

the hearts of men, you best must give
this image the very name of Christ.

MONK

There sound confusingly from worlds of soul
those voices often heard,
that always wished to fight
what pious thought demands.
How shall I find paths leading to the good
if they are praised by powers of evil?
It almost seems to me as if – – –;
no, may this word remain unthought –.
My leader, in his wisdom will still guide me
so that the meaning of his words,
now so obscure,
will be disclosed to me.

BENEDICTUS

I can direct you to the rightful path
if you will permeate yourself in deepest soul
with words which formerly I spoke on earth.
And if you then will search
for those words' power of life
within the worlds
in which you can behold me now,
the rightful path will be revealed to you.

(*The curtain falls while the Monk, the Spirit of
Benedictus, Lucifer and Ahriman are still
present in the hall.*)

# SCENE EIGHT

(*The same room as the previous one. The First Preceptor, Joseph Kean, then the Grand Master with Simon; later, the First and Second Masters of Ceremony. – Joseph Kean is the first to enter; the Preceptor comes to meet him.*)

FIRST PRECEPTOR

> You wished to speak with me.
> What is it that you have to say?

JOSEPH KEAN  Of import for yourself and me
> is what has caused my coming here.
> Thomas you know, the master workman at the mines?
> He is in your employ.

FIRST PRECEPTOR

> Well I know the stalwart man,
> whose ingenuity we greatly value.
> He has endeared himself as well
> to all the workers under him.

JOSEPH KEAN  And Celia, my daughter, is also known to you?

FIRST PRECEPTOR (*moved*)

> I've sometimes seen her
> when I met you and any of your people.

JOSEPH KEAN  It's so that we saw Thomas often in our home
> soon after he arrived.

His visits then became more frequent.
We saw that for our Celia
there grew in him a deep affection.
This certainly was not too strange to us.
But all along we could not think
that Celia would return his love.
Her life was only spent in prayer;
she ran away from people's company.
But now it's more and more apparent
that she's devoted to the stranger
with all her heart.
And as things stand,
we find we're forced not to oppose
our child's desire to give herself
to Thomas as his wife.

FIRST PRECEPTOR (*with uncertain gesture*)
    Why is this marriage then against your will?

JOSEPH KEAN    My lord, you know I'm faithfully devoted
to what this Order stands for.
With heavy heart I know
my daughter turns her love
to those who charge
both you and me with heresy. The monk,
who is the head now of our neighboring cloister
and constantly combats this Order's aims,
has won outright our daughter's soul.
As long as she remains within my house
I'd never give up hope
that she might find the pathway back
from spirit darkness into light.
Yet I must give her up for lost

if she becomes the wife of him
who seeks salvation like herself
according to the teachings of the monk.
And that one has succeeded
in foisting upon Thomas his opinions
as dogma that requires firm belief.
With horror I have heard the curses
which burst from Thomas' lips
whenever there was talk about this Order.

FIRST PRECEPTOR

We've many enemies.
It means but little if one more
is added to their number.
Your words do not make clear
what I can have to do with this.

JOSEPH KEAN  My lord, you see this packet –
these papers are reliable.
My wife and I alone have read them up to now.
Beside us, no one knows their content.
But now it has to be entrusted
to you as well.
The girl who passes for our daughter
is not our child.
We took her in our care
when her own mother died.
I think there is no need to tell you
how all this came about.
For long we did not know our foster-daughter's
         father,
and Celia still today knows nothing of her origin.
She sees in us her own true parents.

It could have always stayed the same,
because the child is dear to us and like our own.
But long years after Celia's mother died,
these papers came to us.
They make it clear who is our foster-daughter's
    father.

(*The Preceptor shows his disquiet.*)

I do not know if he is known to you.
But I am now quite certain
that he is . . . you yourself. –
I think there's not much more to say.
But since this is your flesh and blood,
I beg you for your help.
Perhaps together we can try
to save the girl from future darkness.

FIRST PRECEPTOR

My worthy Kean, – faithful you have always proved.
I hope that I may count on you still further.
There is no chance that anyone
within these walls or on the outside
might hear that I'm related to this girl?

JOSEPH KEAN    On this I pledge my word.
I mean no harm.
I only ask you for your help.

FIRST PRECEPTOR

You'll understand, at present
I cannot answer you at once.
I beg you, come to hear me out tomorrow.

JOSEPH KEAN    I will come. (*He goes out.*)

FIRST PRECEPTOR (*alone*)

How grimly is my destiny fulfilled!
I left my wife and children wretched,
because I felt them to be fetters.
My vanity marked out for me the path
which led into this Spirit Order.
I pledged myself to deeds of human love
with words which sound sublime.
I've done this, burdened with a guilt
that's rooted in the opposite of love.
The wisdom of this Order's guidance
was present clearly in my case.
The Order placed me in its ranks
and gave me its strict rules.
I was compelled to gain insight into myself.
On any other path in life
this knowledge might have been concealed from
    me.
When by a stroke of fate
my son came to this place
I thought that higher powers in mercy
were showing me the way to expiate my sin.
I have long known, the foster child of Kean
is my own daughter whom I once forsook.

– – – – – – – – – – – – – – – – –

The Order faces its destruction,
each brother resolute to meet his death
in full awareness that our goals will further live
for which he gives his life.
For long now I have felt
that I'm unworthy of this selfless death.
And so the resolution grew in me

88

to let the master know my situation
and ask him to release me from the Order.
I wished to dedicate myself then to my children
and bring about whatever of atonement
is possible to me in this earth life.
I see now clearly, it was not
the longing for his father led my son to me
though his good heart made him believe it.
What guided him were forces of his blood
which bind him to his sister.
The other bonds of blood
were loosened through his father's guilt.
The monk would otherwise not have succeeded
in robbing me completely of my son.
He has succeeded well in this attempt,
so that the sister too
will be estranged from her own father.
So nothing else remains for me to do
but to ensure
that they shall hear the truth about themselves,
and then with resignation to await
the penance laid upon me by those powers
which keep account of our life's right and
     wrong.
(*He goes out.*)

(*After a pause the Grand Master and Simon enter
the room.*)

GRAND MASTER

You must now stay within the castle, Simon.
Since they have spread the lying tale
about the sorcery, each step you take outside
would be most dangerous.

SIMON          In truth, it pains me bitterly to know
               that people through their ignorance
               can be so hostile to the help
               which only wants to serve their good.

GRAND MASTER
               Whoever through the grace of lofty spirit powers
               can turn his gaze upon the souls of men
               will see that there the adversaries
               oppose the souls' true being.
               The war our enemies prepare for us
               is but a picture of that mighty battle
               which ceaselessly one power in the heart
               must wage in enmity against the other.

SIMON          My noble Lord, just now you spoke a word
               which strikes me in my deepest soul.
               Though I'm not born to be a dreamer,
               yet when I walk alone through wood and field,
               often before my soul appears an image
               which I can no more master with my will
               than any object which my eye beholds.
               There stands before me then a human being
               who lovingly extends his hand to me.
               And in his features is revealed a pain
               which I have never seen on any face.
               The greatness and the beauty of this man
               take hold of all the forces of my soul;
               I want to sink upon my knees, and humbly
               submit myself to him, a herald out of other
                  worlds. –
               But all at once a violent rage
               flames up within my heart.

And then I cannot check the urge in me
which kindles opposition in my soul. –
And I must thrust away the hand
so lovingly held out to me.
As soon as I've regained once more my senses
the radiant figure has withdrawn itself.
When then in contemplation I recall
what came before me often in the spirit,
a thought stands forth before my soul
which shakes me to the bottom of my heart.
I feel persuaded by your teaching
that speaks about a Spirit Being
descended from the kingdom of the sun
and in a human form appearing to the senses
in order to be understood by human hearts.
I cannot close myself to all the beauty
which is inherent in your noble teaching.
And yet I cannot yield my soul to it.
I've had to recognize within this Spirit Being
the primal form of man.
Yet my own nature holds me back defiantly
when I would turn to Him in faith.
And so I must experience within myself
a war that is the prototype of outer strife.
The riddle that torments and frightens me
concerns my whole life's destiny.
How shall I fathom that I understand you well,
yet never can devote myself in faith
to things your lofty revelation teaches?
In loyalty I follow your example,
and yet I feel my opposition
to that example's origins and goals.
When I thus come to know myself,

all faith is drowned in doubt
that I will ever find myself in this earth life. –
And often I am filled with fear and dread
that these bewildering doubts may still persist
through all my future earthly lives.

GRAND MASTER

The image you have seen, dear Simon, stood out
before my spirit in full light,
just as you painted it in vivid words.
And while you spoke still further,
the image changed and grew before my gaze,
until I was allowed to see those things
which link world goals with human destiny.

*(The Grand Master* and *Simon exit; after a pause
the two Masters of Ceremony enter the hall.)*

FIRST MASTER OF CEREMONY

I must confess quite frankly, my dear brother,
that the forbearance of our master seems to me
incomprehensible when I must see
the great injustice of our enemies.
They do not want to know about our teachings
but paint them frighteningly to people
as heresy and as the devil's work.

– – – – – – – – – – – – – – –

SECOND MASTER OF CEREMONY

The master's mild forbearance flows
out of our teaching.
Can we proclaim as highest goal in life
the understanding of all human souls
and yet misunderstand our foes?

Among them many follow
Christ's example honestly.
The deepest meaning of our teachings
remains, however, sealed for those
who hear them only with an outer ear.
My brother, remember how reluctantly,
with inner opposition, you grew willing
to listen to the Spirit Word.
From what our masters have revealed we know
how, through the light of spirit, future men
will see the lofty Being of the Sun
Who lived but once within an earthly body.
With joy we can believe the revelation
because we follow trustfully our leaders.
But recently the man that we acknowledge
our Order's head, spoke these important
          words:
'Your souls must gradually mature
if you'd behold prophetically
what will reveal itself to men in future. –
But do not think', he also said,
'that after your first soul probation
this premonition will appear to you.
For even when you have the certainty
of men's return to life on earth,
you'll have to face the second test
which will unloose your vanity of Self
so that it spoils for you the spirit light.'
He also gave this solemn warning:
'In silent hours of your devotion search
how this delusion as soul fiend
imperils the spirit seeker's path.
He who falls prey to it may see

our human nature in those spheres where only spirit
reveals itself to spirit light. –
If you would worthily prepare yourselves
to take in with your eye of soul
the light of wisdom streaming from the Christ,
you must keep careful watch upon yourselves
that self-delusion may not blind you
in moments when you think it far removed.'
By keeping these words well in mind
we'll soon give up the false idea
that we can easily today hand over
the teachings that our souls profess.
We must take comfort from the fact
that we encounter many a soul
who in our day unconsciously receives
the seed for future lives on earth.
This seed may seem at first
in conflict with those powers
to which in later times it will submit itself.
Within that hatred which pursues us now
I can find only seeds of future love.

FIRST MASTER OF CEREMONY

It's certain that the goal of highest truth
can be revealed in words like these.
Yet it seems hard already in these times
to guide our lives according to their wisdom.

SECOND MASTER OF CEREMONY

Here, too, I can accept our masters' words:
'It is not granted to all men
to live earth's future in advance.
But such men always must be found
who can foresee the shape of later days.

They'll dedicate their heart to forces
that can release existence from the present
and guard it safely for eternity.'

(*The curtain falls while the two Masters of Ceremony
are still in the hall.*)

# SCENE NINE

*A forest glade, as in Scene Six. Joseph Kean, Dame Kean, their daughter Bertha; afterwards, Peasants; later, the Monk; finally, Kean's foster daughter Celia and Thomas.*

BERTHA

I'd like so much, dear mother,
to hear from you that story,
the one that Celia used to tell about.
No one can tell as you the tales
which our dear father brings us from the knights.
Indeed, there's surely no one
who does not love to hear them.

JOSEPH KEAN

These stories are true treasures for the soul.
What they can give the spirit stays unchanged
even beyond our death, and will bear fruit
in later lives on earth.
We marvel at their hidden truth
and out of marvelling, our souls
form knowledge, which we need in life.
Yes, if only all the people understood
what gifts the knights bestow on them.
It is a pity, Celia and Thomas,
at present, have deaf ears for them –
for they receive their wisdom somewhere
else.

| | |
|---|---|
| BERTHA | Today I'd like so much to hear the tale<br>which speaks of Good and Evil. |
| | |
| DAME KEAN | Right gladly I will tell it you. Now, listen:<br>Once upon a time there lived a man<br>who pondered much about the world.<br>His brain was tortured most of all<br>by his desire to know the origin of evil;<br>but he could give himself on this no answer.<br>'The whole world comes from God', so argued he,<br>'and God can only have the good within Himself.<br>Then how do evil men come from the good?'<br>Time and again he pondered, all in vain.<br>The answer could not be discovered.<br>One day it came to pass, this gloomy thinker<br>upon his way beheld a tree,<br>which was in conversation with an axe.<br>And mark! the axe was saying to the tree:<br>'What is impossible for you to do, that I can do.<br>I can fell you; but not you me.'<br>The tree then gave this answer to the haughty axe:<br>'A year ago a man cut out the wood<br>from which he made your handle<br>out of my body, with another axe.'<br>And when the man had heard this speech<br>a thought arose within his soul<br>he could not clearly put in words.<br>It gave, however, answer to his question<br>how evil can derive from good. |
| | |
| JOSEPH KEAN | Bear in mind this tale, my child,<br>and you will see how we, in contemplating Nature,<br>arrive at knowledge in the human head. |

I know how much I can explain
by pondering upon the tales
by which our knights instruct us.

BERTHA    Truly I am a simple little thing
and never surely could I understand
what clever people would relate
with learned words about their science.
I have no sense at all for things like that.
I get quite sleepy when our Thomas
begins to tell us of his work.
But when my father, coming from the castle,
brings home the tales, and hour after hour,
puts his own thoughts to them,
right gladly could I listen without end.
Quite often Celia speaks about a pious heart
which to her mind is something that I lack.
But it is truly piety I feel
when I call up these tales before my eyes
and can with all my heart rejoice in them.

*(Joseph Kean, Dame Kean and Bertha go out.*
*After a pause, Peasants enter the glade.)*

FIRST PEASANT    My uncle came home yesterday.
For long he's made an honest living
as miner in Bohemia. Much news he has to tell
of what he heard upon his journey.
Great agitation's everywhere.
They're closing in upon the knights
and everything is well prepared
against the Brothers of the Order here.
The castle will soon be besieged.

SECOND PEASANT

>They should not hesitate too long.
>Full many of us will rush
>to join them in the fight, and you can count
>on me for sure among the first.

FIRST WOMAN  It's headlong into ruin you'll be running.
>Who'd be a fool and not consider
>how well the castle has been fortified.
>In truth there'll be a frightful war.

SECOND WOMAN

>The peasants should not mix themselves
>in things they do not understand.
>But there are many busy ones
>going from place to place
>and stirring up revolt.
>Now it has come so far that helplessly
>the sick must lie untended in distress.
>The kindly man who formerly
>gave help to many a one
>no longer dares to leave the castle.
>They've harmed him dreadfully.

THIRD WOMAN  And that's because so many were embittered
>when they discovered whence the sickness came
>that's broken out among our cows.
>The Jew bedevilled them!
>He cures the people only as a sham
>to serve with hellish arts the evil powers.

THIRD PEASANT

>There was much gossip about heresy
>which came to nothing.

The people prospered
and no better could they do
than pass their leisure time with evil talk.
Then someone, shrewdly working on the people,
made up the nonsense that the Jew
bewitched our cattle – and then, of course,
a storm broke loose.

FOURTH PEASANT
I think you should consider
what war and all its horrors mean.
Our fathers often told us what they endured
in times when everywhere the land
was occupied by troops.

FIFTH WOMAN  I've said it time and time again:
their lordship's rule must vanish.
Indeed a dream has shown to me
how we can serve the troops
and care for them right well
when they arrive to carry out the siege.

SIXTH PEASANT
If dreams are still to be believed,
we do not need to question.
The knights have tried to
make us more intelligent
than were our fathers,
and now they shall find out
just how much cleverer we have become.
Our fathers gave them welcome here,
but we will chase them out.
I know the secret passageways
which lead into the castle.

I used to work up there
until my anger drove me out.
I'll show the noble knights
how science can be useful.


FOURTH WOMAN

He's surely planning nothing good,
I feel quite frightened at his words.


FIFTH PEASANT I have been shown already in a vision
how soon by secret ways a traitor
will lead the enemy into the castle.


SIXTH WOMAN I find such visions most pernicious.
If we can think as Christians still,
then we should know that honesty, not treachery,
will rescue us from evil.


SIXTH PEASANT I let these people talk
and do what brings results.
This one or that calls something wrong
that he's not able to achieve himself,
because he lacks the courage.
But let's go on our way;
There comes the holy father on this path.
He should not be disturbed. –
I always have been able
to follow him so easily;
but what he preached today
had much I could not understand.

*(The Peasants go out in the direction of the forest.
After a pause the Monk enters along the path.)*

MONK       The paths of soul must lead into confusion
when man desires to follow his own being.
It could be only weakness of my heart
which brought before my eyes those phantoms
I saw within the castle.
They showed themselves in conflict; –
this proves to me how little yet in me
the forces of my soul unite themselves.
I will therefore bestir myself anew
to kindle in myself those words
which bring me light from spirit heights.
Another path can lure the man
whose mind stays blinded by his vanity.
The soul can only triumph over falsehood
by showing itself worthy of the grace
that can reveal from fonts of love
the spirit light in wisdom's word.
I know that I will find you, noble power;
you will throw light on what the Fathers taught,
if from the darkness of my self-conceit
with piously devoted heart, I can escape.

*(The Monk goes out. After a pause Celia and Thomas
come into the glade.)*

CELIA       Dear brother, often ardently
I bowed in silent prayer
before the godly fountainhead
and longed whole-heartedly
to be united with it, –
a sheen of light appeared then to my spirit
which radiated gentle warmth.
It shaped itself into a human image

102

and looked at me with tender eyes,
pronouncing words
that sounded thus to me:
'You were forsaken once through man's delusion;
you are supported now by human love.
So wait till longing finds the path
on which that love can guide itself to you.'
So spoke the human image to me often.
I could not solve the riddle of these words;
yet dimly I divined with quickened feeling
that one day they would be fulfilled.
And then when you, beloved brother, came
and when I first set eyes on you,
I felt my senses leaving me:
you bore full likeness to that human face.

THOMAS       Dream and prophetic feeling did not lie;
it was my longing leading me to you.

CELIA       And when you wanted me in marriage,
I thought you destined for me by the spirit.

THOMAS       The spirit wished to reunite us.
Indeed, it's shown us this in perfect clarity,
although at first we did not understand it.
When we first met, it seemed to me as if
the spirit wished to give to me a wife.
But I had found again the long-lost sister.

CELIA       And now there's nothing will divide us.

THOMAS       And yet, there's much that stands between us.
I must reject the Brotherhood
to which your parents link themselves.

| | |
|---|---|
| CELIA | But they are filled with love and goodness. |
| | You'll find in them the best of friends. |
| | |
| THOMAS | My faith will separate me from them. |
| | |
| CELIA | You'll find the way to them through me. |
| | |
| THOMAS | Good Kean is of a stubborn mind. |
| | He will see naught but darkness there |
| | where I perceive the very font of light. |
| | This light of truth did not become |
| | accessible to me until maturer years. |
| | What I had learned of it in childhood |
| | was hardly conscious to my spirit. |
| | And later on it was my sole intent |
| | to work and get the scientific skill |
| | as means to earn a livelihood. – |
| | Then finally I found the teacher and the guide |
| | who had the power to liberate my soul. |
| | The words he lets me listen to |
| | bear certainly the signs of truth. |
| | He speaks in such a way that heart and head |
| | alike can yield themselves to teachings |
| | he gives with gentle kindness. |
| | Till then I had to make the greatest effort |
| | to understand the other spirit path. |
| | I found this path must lead to error, |
| | relying only on those spirit forces |
| | which well may guide aright in earthly matters, |
| | but cannot lead to higher worlds. |
| | And how am I to find the way |
| | into the hearts of men who only |
| | expect salvation from this error. |

CELIA        I hear your words, dear brother;
they do not seem inspired by peace.
Yet they recall before my soul,
from former days, a peaceful image.
It was on a Good Friday, many years ago,
I saw the image I described before.
The man who bore your countenance
at that time spoke these words:
'Out of the Godhead rose the human soul;
dying, it can descend to depths of being;
it will, in time, release from death the spirit.'
Not until afterwards was I aware
that these words are the motto of our knights.

THOMAS     O sister, must I hear from your own lips
the evil words our foes are treasuring
as revelation of the highest spirit truth?

CELIA        In my own heart I am indeed averse
to all the outer doings of the knights.
I'm faithful to the creed that comforts you.
But I will always be convinced that those,
who as the purpose of their teachings
avow such paths of soul,
do follow in the steps of Christ.
In my devotion to the spirit
I must confess that I believe
my brother's spirit wished to speak that day
of inner goals for peace.

THOMAS     Through powers of fate these inner goals for peace
do not seem destined for our life.

Our father they have taken from us
within the very hour that gave him back.

CELIA        Pain robs me of all clarity of sense
when hearing how you speak about our father.
Your heart inclines you lovingly to him
and yet you tremble when you try to think
yourself united with him once again in life.
In loyalty you follow our wise teacher
and cannot hear the message of true love
that streams abundantly through all his words.
I feel a dark enigma looms before me:
I see your honest heart and your firm faith
and can but shuddering stand at the abyss
which deepens dreadfully between them both.
And if as comforter there did not live in me
the hope that love will always overcome,
I'd lack the courage to endure this grief.

THOMAS     It is concealed from you, dear sister,
how power of thought can prove compelling
once it has gripped the human soul.
The son does not oppose the father here;
thought turns away from thought. – –
I feel its force within my soul.
To strive against it means in truth
my own self's spirit death.

(*The curtain falls while Thomas and Celia are still in
the glade.*)

# SCENE TEN

*The following is the continuation of the events which took place in the first five scenes. The same landscape as in Scene Five. Capesius awakens from a vision which brought before his soul the pictures of his previous incarnation.*

CAPESIUS  O this strange countryside! A bench,
a cottage and a glade before me.
Do I know them? They ask insistently
for me to recognize them. Yet they oppress me.
They bear down as a heavy load upon me,
though they seem real. No, all this
is but an image woven of soul fabric.
I know these images were formed
out of the thirst and yearning of the soul.
I have emerged as if awaking from this yearning
out of the wide-spread ocean of the spirit.
Haunting and frightful rises from my soul depths
the memory of all this longing.
How searing was my thirst for worlds imbued with
life.
Delusion's craving grew from want
and burned, consuming my whole being.
I wished tempestuously to be and live,
and all existence wanted to escape me.
A moment that now seems eternity,

poured storms of agony into my soul
as only a full life can bring with it.
Before this yearning's terror seized me,
there rose what had created it for me.
I felt myself expanded to the universe,
bereft of my own being . . .
But no, it was not I who felt this way,
it was another being, sprung from me.
I could see men and deeds of men develop
from cosmic thoughts advancing throughout space,
and pressing to reveal themselves as beings.
Then they unfolded one whole world of life
before my eyes, in pictures, tangible.
They took from my soul-fabric
the power to create existence out of thought.
The more this world condensed itself before me,
the less I could sustain the feeling of myself.
And from the world of pictures words resounded
that thought themselves, and stormed upon me;
from life's deficiencies they fashioned beings
and gave them strength from deeds of goodness.
Out of the wide-flung space they sounded warningly:
'O man, know thou thyself within thy world.'
A being whom I saw confronting me
showed me my soul to be his own.
And then these cosmic words continued:
'As long as in the circle of your life
you cannot feel this being closely interwoven,
you are a dream that only dreams itself.'
I could not form clear thoughts, but I could see
chaotic forces working and upsurging
from nothingness to being, from being into
      nothingness.

But when in spirit I strive further back,
remembering what I could see before this chaos,
there stands before my soul a picture of a life
which is not so confused as all those things
that I perceived in later moments,
but which in all its detail showed me clearly
men's lives and actions.
Within this picture I would seem
familiar with the people and with what they do,
I recognize each soul I see;
their bodies' shapes, however, are transformed.
I look upon all this while feeling: I could be
myself a being of this world.
It shows itself to me as real life
but leaves me cold, without emotion.
It seems as if its working on my soul
restrained itself until the later moment
which earlier stood before my spirit.
Amidst a Spirit Brotherhood
I could perceive myself and others, too,
but as a picture of those times long past
that wrests itself from memory's deep wells.
I can see the miner, Thomas, as my son,
and then my thought must link him to the soul
shown otherwise to me within Thomasius.
The woman whom I know as seeress now
appears as my own child before my eyes.
Maria who befriends Thomasius
reveals herself clothed as a monk
who fights our Spirit Brotherhood.
And Strader bears the mien of Simon the Jew.
In Joseph Kean and in his wife
I see the souls of Felix and Felicia.

I can survey quite clearly
the lives of other people and my own.
But while I am absorbed in them,
they disappear out of my spirit view.
I can perceive how the soul-fabric
that wove these pictures
now pours itself into my soul.
And I feel blissfulness
is permeating my whole being.
Freed I seem from senses' limitations.
My being is expanded
to the far reaches of the universe. –
Again I feel that long extended moment
which I lived through before
I was confronted with that picture of a life.
Now I can look still further back.
Condensing out of cosmic power of thought
there comes before my eyes the glade,
the cottage where Felicia and Felix
so often comforted my sorrow.
I find myself back on this earth
from which I was so far removed
by earthly times and world's far reaches.
But what unfeelingly I could behold before:
the picture that revealed myself to me
is settling like a heavy mist of soul
in front of everything my senses now perceive.
It's changing to a nightmare,
the picture that so weighs on me.
It's writhing in my soul's depths.

– – – – – – – – – – – – – – –

It opens cosmic portals, distances of space.

– – – – – – – – – – – – – – –

What storms into my being's depths?
What surges towards me from far reaches of the
worlds?

_ _ _ _ _ _ _ _ _ _ _ _ _ _ _ _

A VOICE AS SPIRIT CONSCIENCE

Be aware of what you've seen,
be alive to what you've done.
Renewed, you are reborn to being.
Your life you have been dreaming.
Rework it
out of noble spirit light;
perceive the tasks of life
with sight-empowered soul.
But if you fail in this, –
to empty nothingness
forever are you bound.

(*The curtain falls while Capesius is still present.*)

III

# SCENE ELEVEN

*A Room for Meditation as in Scene Two.* (*Maria, Ahriman*)

AHRIMAN      The web of thought you've been pursuing
was spun with crafty care by Benedictus.
It has indeed ensnared you in untruth.
Thomasius and Capesius too
are victims of the same deceptive vision.
Their gaze as well as yours
beheld that earthly life in days long past.
And thereupon you wish to find in just that time
the lives you lived before this present one.
You will breed error out of error only
if you can let yourself determine
as consequence of such imaginings
the duties you aspire to on your earthly path.
That Benedictus merely took the pictures
out of your brain and set them in the past
you can discover clearly with what you know
        yourself.
You saw the people of today
with scarcely any change from those much earlier
        days.
The women you beheld as women, men as men;
their traits of character were similar, as well.
You cannot therefore any longer doubt

that in your spirit vision you transformed
your soul's delusion, not the truth,
into those days of long ago.

MARIA   I see in you the father of deceit.
But yet I know, you often speak the truth.
Whoever would reject each word of counsel
he can receive through what you have to say
would fall a victim to severest error.
Just as illusion wears the mask of truth
in order to ensnare men's souls with certainty,
so can one also yield to such illusion
by always trying like a coward to sneak past
each place where error has its source.
Man does not owe to you delusion only:
from out the Spirit of Deceit
there springs a power as well
which gives men judgment, clear and vigorous.
Therefore in freedom I oppose you face to face.
You have attacked that portion of my soul
that must sustain itself in wakeful vigilance.
In weighing all the evidence which you
present to me in clever calculation
it might well seem that only pictures from my brain
have been transferred to former days on earth.
But now I ask you whether your own wisdom
is able to unlock the portal
to *every* epoch of the earth?

AHRIMAN   No beings live in any spirit realm
who would be hostile to my need
for entrance into any epoch of the earth.

MARIA   The lofty powers of destiny have wisely
        appointed you to be their adversary.
        You further everything you wish to hinder.
        You bring the power of freedom to men's souls
        when you can penetrate their very depths.
        From you springs forth the power of thought,
        the origin indeed of phantoms in men's knowing, –
        but it is guide as well to all men's sense of truth.
        There is one region only in the spirit realm
        in which there can be forged the sword
        before whose sight you have to disappear.
        It is the realm in which the souls of men
        form knowledge out of powers of reasoning
        and then transform it into spirit wisdom.
        If at this moment I forge rightly
        the word of truth into that sword,
        you will be forced to leave this place.
        So hearken – you, who are the father of deceit –
        if what I speak before you is triumphant truth.
        There are such times in earthly evolution
        when gradually old forces pass away
        and, dying, see the growth of newer ones.
        At such a turning point of time my friends
        and I could find ourselves together in the spirit
        while they were seeking out their life on earth.
        True spirit men were active at that time
        united in a brotherhood of souls
        which took its aims from occult heights.
        At such a turning point of time must seeds,
        that need much time for full maturing,
        be planted carefully in human souls.
        Such men will show in their next life on earth
        still traits of character out of an earlier one.

There will be many men at such a time
reborn as men in their succeeding life
and many women reappear as women.
The interval is also shorter then
than usually between two earthly lives.
To understand such turning points of time,
you lack sound insight.
Therefore their coming into being
you cannot unmistakably survey.
Recall when last we met
within the castle of that Spirit Order:
you spoke to me with words of flattery
intending to unloose my deepest self-conceit.
Remembrance of this time bestows on me
the strength to make a stand against you.

(*Ahriman withdraws with a reluctant gesture. Thunder.*)


Defeated he has had to leave this place
which Benedictus has so often blessed.
But gloriously he has revealed to me
how quickly error can take hold of souls
when they incautiously expose themselves
to spirit hearing, and avoid the safer paths.
The adversary has indeed the power
to play upon life's contradictions
and thus to rob men's souls of certainty.
He must fall silent when the light appears
which radiates from wisdom's innate sources
and grants full clarity to spirit sight.

(*The curtain falls with Maria remaining in the room.*)

## SCENE TWELVE

*The same room as in Scene Eleven. Johannes and Lucifer.*

LUCIFER       Perceive within Capesius those fruits
which ripen when a soul attempts too early
to penetrate the spirit world.
He now can read his book of life
and knows his obligations for all coming lives.
But suffering which does not lie
within the plan of destiny
arises out of knowledge that lacks power
to shape itself to deeds in life.
Whatever in a man leads to success
depends upon the ripeness of his will.
At every step that now he takes in life
Capesius must ask himself:
do I fulfil with this an obligation
which is the outgrowth of my former life?
Thus falls on everything a light
that dazzles painfully his eyes,
but can in no way be of help to him.
It deadens forces which, unconscious still,
are trusty guides for every human soul,
and yet this light cannot enhance
clear-minded thoughtfulness.

Through it, the body's mighty strength is lamed,
before the soul becomes the body's master.

JOHANNES   I can perceive the error of my life,
for I deprived my body of soul forces
by carrying them proudly into spirit realms.
A human being, incomplete,
was thus led upward toward the light.
It was a thin soul-shadow only
that was enraptured by the spirit worlds
and felt as one with the creative powers.
He wished to live in bliss within the light
and to behold the deeds of light in colours.
As artist, this soul-shadow fancied
he recreated spirit life in worlds of sense.
This being who had borrowed all my features
has shown me to myself in dreadful truth.
I dreamed about the purest love of soul,
but passion raged through all my veins.
And now I could behold that earthly path
which truly has created all my life today.
It shows me how to strive in honest truth.
How can the ways of spirit I pursued
be still continued by the soul
that found itself before this earthly path
within the body of the miner Thomas?
The way in which he shaped his life
makes me aware of all my present tasks.
In this life I have striven to attain
what only later can bear fruit for me.

LUCIFER   My light must firmly lead you on
as until now you let yourself be led.

The spirit path you have set foot upon
unites the spirit with the higher world,
but shrouds the soul in darkness.

JOHANNES    What has a man achieved if he surrenders
his soulless self unto the spirit world!
The end of all his days on earth will find him
the very being that he was
when in primeval times his human form
was born out of the cosmic womb.
If I surrender to those urges
which force their way with strength toward life's
        reality
out of unconscious depths of soul,
then the whole cosmos will be working in me.
I do not know what drives me on to act,
yet certainly the cosmic will itself
will lead me on, according to its plan.
This cosmic will must know the goal of life
though human knowledge cannot grasp it.
What it creates in man's totality
is wealth of life through which the soul takes
        shape.
I will surrender to it and no longer
suppress it by my worthless spirit striving.

LUCIFER    Within this cosmic will I am at work
when it streams mightily through souls of
        men.
They are but parts of higher entities
until they can experience my power.
I am the first to make them truly men
whose inmost self they bring
into accord with the whole universe.

JOHANNES    For some time have I thought I know you well,
            and yet there only lived in me your shadow
            projected into me by spirit vision.
            Now must I feel you, through my will –
            then I can overcome you later on
            if so the planning of my destiny ordains it.
            Let spirit knowledge that I gained too soon
            repose henceforth within my inmost soul
            till my own impulses of life awaken it.
            With confidence I now surrender to that will
            that is much wiser than the human soul.

            (*Exit Johannes with Lucifer. Curtain.*)

# SCENE THIRTEEN

*The Sun Temple; the hidden mystery place of the Hierophants. Lucifer; Ahriman; the Three Soul Figures; Strader; Benedictus; Theodosius; Romanus; Maria.*

(*Enter at first Lucifer and Ahriman.*)

LUCIFER
Victorious, the Lord of all Desire
stands here before you.
I have succeeded in the conquest of that soul
who, even in the brightness of the Spirit Sun,
feels still related to our realm.
At the right moment I could blind
him to the vision of the shine of light,
to which he only dreamingly had yielded.
But all my hopes that we shall be
victorious in the spirit realm must vanish,
when now I turn to you,
my comrade in the battle.
You could not conquer for yourself the one
who would have brought our labor to its goal.
I can maintain the human soul,
surrendered now to me, within our realms
for but brief spans of earthly time;
yet all in vain,
for soon I must return him to our foes.
To win full victory we'll need the second one
who has withdrawn from your control.

AHRIMAN        The time is not propitious for my action.
I find no means of access to men's souls.
One is approaching
whom I've stirred up tenaciously.
Though he is coming ignorant in spirit,
the drive for reasoning compels him on.
I must give way to him and to this place,
where he can only come unconsciously.

(*exit Ahriman. The Three Soul Figures enter
with Strader.*)

PHILIA        I will imbue myself
with illumining power of faith;
I will inspire myself
with living force of trust
from inner joy of striving,
that thus the spirit sleeper
may be awakened by the light.

ASTRID        I will weave into one
the treasured word of revelation
and humble joy of soul;
I will condense
the shining rays of hope.
They shall ray forth in darkness,
and they shall dimly gleam in light,
that thus the spirit sleeper
may be upheld by powers of hope and joy.

LUNA        I will bring warmth to light of soul;
I will make firm the force of love,
that they take courage for themselves;
that they redeem themselves
and, rising high,
endow themselves with weight;

that thus the spirit sleeper
may be released from cosmic burdens,
and liberated
by inner joy of light.

(*There appear Benedictus, Theodosius and
Romanus.*)

BENEDICTUS    My brothers, I have summoned you,
who are to me companions
in search of spirit light
which shall stream forth to souls of men.
You know the nature of the Sun of Soul;
it radiates at times in midday's perfect brightness;
at other times it weakly penetrates
the mist of dreams in twilight's glimmer,
and often it must yield to darknesses.
The temple-servant's spirit-sight must penetrate
those depths of soul where spirit light
shines mightily from cosmic heights.
However, it must also find those sombre goals
that wish to guide man's growing forces
unconsciously in darknesses of soul.
The spirit beings who bestow on human souls
the spirit nourishment from cosmic powers
are present now within our hallowed temple.
They wish to guide the aims of one man's soul
from spirit night to lofty regions of the light.
The sleep of knowledge still envelops him,
but a summons of the spirit has already sounded
in his unconscious depths of being.
What they have spoken to his inmost soul
will soon pierce through into his spirit hearing.

THEODOSIUS    His soul was not yet able to discover
itself again within the light of spirit

which radiates through senses' revelation
and shows the meaning of all earthly progress.
He saw God's spirit unadorned by Nature
and saw all that belongs to Nature god-estranged.
Through many earthly lives he felt a stranger
confronting the true meaning of existence
and only found as tools of his own being
those sheaths of body
which severed him from world and from mankind.
He will acquire forces in the temple
to feel the alien life outside him as his own
and so be able to attain the power
which frees the soul from labyrinths of thought
and shows the pathway to the springs of life.

BENEDICTUS     Another man is striving for the temple's light.
In future only will he near its portals
and ask for entrance to this hallowed place.
Throughout a life of serious search for knowledge
he has implanted seeds of thinking in his soul.
The spirit light shone on these seeds
and ripened them outside the temple.
He could perceive his present life on earth
as sequence of another life
he had experienced in times long past.
He has become aware of errors in that life
and realizes all their consequences.
He lacks the power to fulfil the duties
which he can sense through knowledge of his
       Self.

ROMANUS     Capesius shall through powers of this temple
learn how a man must, in a single life,
be burdened with the duties which demand
to be absolved in their full measure only
by many of his lives of earthly pilgrimage.

And so he will acknowledge without fear
that he must carry consequences
of former errors still beyond the gate of death.
He certainly will prove victorious
in battles that lay open spirit portals
when boldly he confronts the Guardian
who stands there at the threshold of the spirit land.
This Guardian will make manifest to him
that no one reaches into heights of life
who fears his book of destiny.
With courage he will come to the conviction
that self-enlightenment must come through pain. –
The Will becomes companion to the one
who bravely goes to meet what is to come
and, fortified by Hope's strength-giving stream,
will boldly face the pain which knowledge brings.

BENEDICTUS    You have, my brothers, at this present hour
as faithful servants of our temple
marked out the paths in wisdom
on which you'll lead both seekers for the spirit
to goals that are essential to their souls.
The service of this temple asks for further work.
You see the Lord of all Desire here at our side.
This sacred place he was allowed to enter
because Johannes' soul could open portals
which otherwise are barred to him.
Our brother, whom we've given consecration,
lacks still the power
to resist courageously the words
arising out of darknesses.
Good forces will grow strong in him
when on their opposite they test themselves.
Soon will he be received within our temple
encompassed by our warm fraternal love.

And yet the treasure of his spirit must be guarded
now that his will is to descend into dark realms.

(*turning to Lucifer*)

I must address myself to you who not
for long must rule the place where you are standing.
The temple's power at present cannot wrest
Johannes' soul from your domain.
But in the future he'll be ours again
when those fruits of our sister's deeds,
that now as blossoms we can see, will ripen.

(*Maria appears*)

She was allowed to see in her past life on earth
how closely linked Johannes was to her.
He followed after her in those days even
when she herself tried to resist the light
to which she now devotes herself.
When bonds of love prove strong enough,
they may outlast the spirit's transformations.
Then will the power of the Lord of all Desire
most certainly be shattered by their firmness.

LUCIFER      But it was Benedictus' will itself
to separate Johannes from Maria.
And where men separate from one another,
the field is well prepared for my dominion.
I'm ever searching for those souls
who live completely for themselves,
that I may liberate from cosmic servitude
the life on earth for all eternity.
Maria, in the clothing of a monk,
could turn the soul away from his own father,
the soul indwelling now Johannes' form.
For me this, too, prepared the seeds
which I can surely bring to ripening.

MARIA (*turning to Lucifer*)

In human beings there are springs of love
to which your power cannot penetrate.
They are unsealed when faults of former lives,
which man has brought upon himself unconsciously,
are seen with spirit eyes in later lives on earth,
and by free will of sacrifice
are then transformed to deeds
which fructify true human progress.
The powers of destiny have granted me
the retrospect of former days on earth;
the signs are also now revealed to me
by which I learn to guide my will to sacrifice,
that good may come to those whose threads of life
are interwoven with my own
throughout the evolution of the earth.
I saw Johannes' soul within its former body
withdrawing from his father
and saw the powers which compelled me
to estrange the son from his own father's heart.
Thus does the father now confront me,
reminding of my ancient debt to him.
He speaks distinctly in a cosmic language
whose symbols are the actions of man's life.
What I have set between the son and father
now reappears, though in another form,
within *this* life, which bound again
Johannes' soul so closely to my own.
And in the pain I had to undergo
in severing Johannes from myself
I can see destiny at work in my own deeds. -
If now my soul is loyal to the light
which spirit powers bestow on it,
it will be strengthened by the services
which I may render to Capesius
upon his arduous life-pilgrimage.

With forces won like this, my soul
beholds Johannes' star with certainty,
although at times, misled by fetters of desire,
he does not walk the path illumined by the light.
The spirit vision, which has led me back
to distant days on earth, will teach me now
how *in the present* I must shape those bonds of soul,
so that life forces, once prepared unconsciously,
may work in clarity for man's welfare.

BENEDICTUS   There formed itself in earlier days on earth
a knot from threads
that karma spun in world becoming.
In it three human lives are interwoven.
There shines forth on this knot of destiny
the lofty spirit light within the temple.
To you, Maria, I must address myself,
for you alone of these three souls are present
in this hour and at this holy place.
May in your Self this light now heal
and turn into the good
those forces which once firmly bound
your threads of life with all the others
in a knot of destiny.
In former days the father could not find
the heart of his own son; but now
the spirit seeker will accompany
your friend upon his path into the spirit land.
Yours is the duty to maintain
Johannes' soul within the light.
When once you held him fast in bondage
he could but blindly follow you.
You gave him back his liberty
when he still clung to you, infatuated.
You'll find him once again when he succeeds
in conquering his selfhood for himself.

If your soul can be loyal to the light
which spirit powers bestow on you,
Johannes' soul will thirst for you in realms
where still the Lord of all Desire holds sway.
And through the love which keeps it bound to you,
his soul will find the path into the light.
For he who knowingly beheld
the heights of spirit from his depths of soul
can pass through light and darkness livingly.
From cosmic reaches he has breathed
the air which quickens life to all eternity, –
and living raises every human life
from depths of soul to lofty regions of the Sun.

(*Curtain*)

# THE GUARDIAN OF THE THRESHOLD

SOUL EVENTS IN
DRAMATIC SCENES
*by*
RUDOLF STEINER
*translated by*
Ruth and Hans Pusch

## THE GUARDIAN OF THE THRESHOLD
## THOUGHTS ON THE SEAL

The first impression is that of continuous motion. It is as if a whirlwind is bending, curving and sweeping everything along with it so that no straight line remains. It characterizes the atmosphere surrounding the Guardian, created by the earthly desires souls bring with them. But the seal reveals within this turbulence also a process which develops stage by stage: the building and shaping of a community of free individuals.

This process starts in the centre where two curved lines cross each other. Wherever man experiences such a crossing, whether physiologically in the crossing of the nerves that lead from the eyes to the brain, for instance, or by an outward gesture, crossing his legs or folding his hands, he creates awareness or sustains consciousness. In the central crossing of the seal we become conscious of the four directions aiming out towards the circumference.

But the aim itself seems to be interrupted by the four separate, isolated curves. It is a phase in the attempt towards a community, familiar to those seeking a balance between the individual and the whole. These four forms remain each for itself, and yet they follow nevertheless the radii of the circle.

The periphery is set in motion by a fourfold wave-like thrust. One can feel a pull from the centre which bends the regular circular swing downward. But the dynamics of this form overcomes the pull and it swings energetically back into the circle. Here the individual motion through its own energy and activity joins the all-embracing circle. But out of it something new is created: the small figures above each downward-upward curve are a replica of this happening in the circle. They stand out as individual outposts, breathing the air of the circumference.

What is developed in these several phases of the seal depicts the action in the play leading to the climactic movement at the end: when individuals take over the duties of the Brotherhood. The altars in their sanctuary are still symbols of the overcoming of the downward trend of an earth-bound existence, and the cultivation of a spirit life which follows the guidance of higher beings. Now free individuals take on themselves this spirit-inspired guidance.

Hans Pusch

# THE GUARDIAN OF THE THRESHOLD
by Rudolf Steiner

## THE PERSONS, SPIRITUAL FIGURES
## AND HAPPENINGS.

The occurrences of a spiritual and soul character, which are sketched in the successive scenes of 'The Guardian of the Threshold', represent a continuation of those shown in my previously published 'Portal of Initiation' and 'Soul's Probation'. Together, they form a whole.

In 'The Guardian of the Threshold' the following characters and entities appear.

I. THE BEARERS OF THE SPIRITUAL ELEMENT:

    1. Benedictus, leader of the Sun Temple and teacher of a number of people who appear in 'The Guardian of the Threshold'. (The Temple of the Sun is named only in 'The Portal of Initiation' and 'The Soul's Probation').

    2. Hilary Gottgetroy, The Grand Master of a mystic brotherhood. (He was shown in an earlier incarnation, in 'The Soul's Probation', as the Grand Master of a spirit brotherhood).

    3. Johannes Thomasius – pupil of Benedictus.

II. THE BEARERS OF THE ELEMENT OF CONSECRATION:
(DEVOTION, SACRIFICE)

    4. Magnus Bellicosus, (called Gairman in 'The Portal of Initiation'), the Preceptor of the mystic brotherhood.

    5. Albert Torquatus, (called Theodosius in 'The

Portal of Initiation'), Master of Ceremonies of the mystic brotherhood.
6. Professor Capesius.

III. The Bearers of the Element of Will:

7. Frederick Trautman, (called Romanus in 'The Portal of Initiation'), Master of Ceremonies of the mystic brotherhood (reincarnation of the Second Master of Ceremonies of the Spirit Brotherhood in 'The Soul's Probation').
8. Theodora, a seeress (in her, the will element is metamorphosed into naïve seership).
9. Doctor Strader.

IV. The Bearers of the Element of Soul:

10. Maria, pupil of Benedictus.
11. Felix Balde.
12. Felicia Balde.

Entities from the Spiritual World:

Lucifer                    Ahriman

Entities of the Human Spiritual Element:

The Double of Thomasius
The Soul of Theodora
The Guardian of the Threshold
Philia ⎫  The spiritual entities who further the
Astrid ⎬  uniting of the human soul with the
Luna  ⎭  cosmos.
The Other Philia, the spiritual entity who hinders the uniting of the soul powers with the cosmos.
The Voice of Conscience.

6

These spiritual entities are not meant allegorically or symbolically, but as realities which, for spiritual perception, are the equivalent of physical persons.

1. Ferdinand Reinecke (fox)
2. Michael Edelmann (nobleman)
3. Bernard Redlich (upright)
4. Francesca Demut (humble)
5. Maria Treufels (loyal)
6. Louise Fuerchtegott (God-fearing)
7. Frederick Geist (enspirited)
8. Caspar Stuermer (firebrand)
9. George Wahrmund (truthful)
10. Marie Kuehne (bold)
11. Hermine Hauser (provincial)
12. Katharina Ratsam (prudent)

(These are reincarnations of the twelve peasant men and women of 'The Soul's Probation').

Editor's note:
    The names of the twelve, although they are not used on stage, give a hint as to their character. Therefore an English translation has been added.

The events of 'The Guardian of the Threshold' take place about thirteen years after those of 'The Portal of Initiation'. The manner of repeating earth lives as encountered in 'The Guardian of the Threshold' must not be taken as a universally valid law, but rather as something that can happen at a special turning-point of time. What happens, for example, in the Eighth Scene between Strader and the twelve people is only possible at such a point of time. The Spiritual Entities that appear in 'The Guardian of the Threshold' are never thought of allegorically or symbolically; he who knows a spiritual world as something real may well represent the Beings, who are as valid for him there as are physical human beings in the sense world, in the same way as he shows the latter. Whoever holds these Beings to be allegories or symbols misunderstands the whole way of presenting the happenings in 'The Guardian of the Threshold'.

7

That Spiritual Entities do not have human countenances, as they must have in the stage presentation, is of course obvious. If the author of these 'Scenes Depicting Soul Happenings' held these Entities to be allegories, he would not represent them in the way he does. The arranging of the characters in groups ($3 \times 4$) was not striven for, nor does it underlie the presentation; it arises – subsequently, for one's thinking – out of the events which were conceived quite for themselves, and which of their own accord shape such a grouping. To have had them as a basis is something that would never have occurred to the author. To present them here as a result is permissible.

# SYNOPSIS

SCENE ONE. A group of twelve persons, representing the 'general public' has been invited by a Mystic or Occult Brotherhood. What up to now has been cultivated behind closed doors, traditional mystery wisdom, seeks a contact for the first time with the outside world. The Brotherhood is motivated to this step by the publication of certain books on spiritual science, which reveal basic truths in modern thought-form. The author is Thomasius, whom the Brotherhood wants to honour because of his clearly demonstrated attachment to a spirituality which has its roots in the Rosicrucianism of the Brotherhood itself. They offer to sponsor his work.

SCENE TWO. Thomasius refuses this offer. In reality, what he has written will be utilized by Ahriman, because Thomasius himself is not able to exert full control over his lower self. His own unbalanced nature will influence the destiny of his writings. He describes an actual encounter with Ahriman on his way to this meeting. There is a sketch by Rudolf Steiner* among the preparatory notes to 'The Guardian of the Threshold', which contains a speech by Ahriman directed to Thomasius at their encounter. Although discarded in the final script, it throws light on the words of Thomasius in Scene Two:

AHRIMAN     These wheels of fire I roll and roll
            endlessly up the precipice

*Entwürfe, Fragmente und Paralipomena zu den vier Mysteriendramen. Bibliographie 44.

9

in the everlasting course of human life.
I feel within me
how human souls exult in joy
when I lift mountainward the fiery element.
In me re-echoes the triumphant, loud rejoicing
of human spirits who, advancing,
feel themselves led from step to step.
And yet, however often I've believed
the start and finish of the work complete,
it always came to nothing more
than the beginning of new toil.
Uncertainty thus tortures me
whether the goal will ever be in reach.
And only one thing do I know for sure:
my aim will be achieved
when this titanic work, my undertaking,
ignites within one single human soul
a little spark
which can flare up to steady flame.
Although gigantic is my work,
it needs this one small spark
to reach its final goal.
Till now there have been several souls resolved,
but fear soon quenched their spark of fire,
fear of those worlds
which hold me fettered fast.

SCENE THREE. Maria unexpectedly meets Capesius in Lucifer's realm. Both are outside their physical bodies, surrounded by the alluring picture-world of luciferic astrality. Capesius' soul is a captive of this world, revelling in it to such a degree that he does not welcome Maria's attempt to arouse in him an awareness of his ego's duties within the physical body. But her words will have their effect when Capesius comes to a new awakening in the etheric world, in Scene Six.

Maria's soul had entered Lucifer's realm for the sake of Thomasius. She witnesses the initiative which Lucifer has taken in order to bind Thomasius to himself. He uses Thomasius' Double to inflame a passion for Theodora; it is an illusionary, but magical effort of intervention. To this Maria, with the encouragement of Benedictus, reacts with words that carry in themselves through their selfless energy the final defeat of Lucifer.

SCENE FOUR. A quiet, harmonious conversation takes place between Strader and Theodora on the occasion of their seventh wedding anniversary. The scene ends, however, on a note of doubt and shock. Lucifer's machinations have begun their work.

SCENE FIVE. After Theodora's unexpected death, Strader seeks comfort at the home of Felicia and Felix Balde. Capesius is also a visitor, but in a disturbed state of mind. After the retrospect into his former life, in medieval times, he has lost interest in the present time and place. His mind is absent, dwelling in realms removed from his normal consciousness. From time to time, it breaks through and brings messages from these other worlds to his friends. In this scene, it is Theodora's soul – actually appearing for a moment – with which he is in direct communication, to the bewilderment but also for the benefit of Strader.

*The following three scenes take place in the supersensible worlds.*

SCENE SIX. Capesius' soul finds itself carried into the etheric world by mantric words received in earlier times from Benedictus, and now sounding to him. Benedictus himself intones them, leading Capesius to a situation where his own soul forces reveal these mantric words as thought-beings outside himself. In a dramatic confrontation, Lucifer and Ahriman re-echo the mantric words in

11

sound and movement. Finally, the fairy tale of the child of light ('Imagination') gives Capesius the inner strength and courage to bring back his ego-consciousness into his earthly body.

SCENE SEVEN. Thomasius, accompanied by Maria, appears before the Guardian of the Threshold. He has the vision of a life in pre-Christian times and, still under the spell of Lucifer, interprets it as relating to Theodora. Because Maria vouches for him, the Guardian lets them both pass through into the spiritual world, which reveals itself at first as the icy fields under Ahriman's rule, the realm of death, as shown in the next scene.

SCENE EIGHT. Ahriman in his own domain is not recognized by Hilary, although his companion, Trautman-Romanus, has a frightening reaction to the cold darkness surrounding them. – Strader enters fully aware of Ahriman and is a witness to his power over the twelve souls who in their sleep come under his spell. He recognizes in Ahriman the ruler over those forces which on earth are at work in the laws of measure and number. – The scene ends with Thomasius' initial experience beyond the actual threshold, a renewed encounter with his Double, and his release from Lucifer's magic spell.

SCENE NINE. After the highly dramatic events of the preceding scenes, the conversations that follow, in a pleasant landscape, breathe harmonious tranquillity. At an early morning hour Benedictus meets his friends, Capesius and Strader, who have become his pupils. Thomasius recalls to Maria his shattering experience in Ahriman's realm. She confirms the vital step he has made by crossing the threshold. What is so striking in this scene is the fact that these conversations take place while the various groups are walking in the country, not far from a large city whose outlines are visible on the horizon. Rudolf Steiner has described a similar scene at the time when the mystery centre of Ephesus was flourishing. Priests and neophytes conversed while walking along paths branching out from the temple.

SCENE TEN. The sanctuary of the Rosicrucian Brotherhood is a symbolic temple with three altars. Only Benedictus' presence establishes the link to the supersensible Sun Temple which concluded the First and Second Plays. The duties at the altars in East, South and West are now taken over by free individuals who, under the guidance of Benedictus, have achieved direct insight into the world beyond the threshold. Felix and Felicia Balde join them, although their paths were somewhat different, leading from mysticism in one and imaginative knowledge in the other to the same recognition of the demands of this modern age.

In this scene Maria and Benedictus speak out the name of Christ three times: first in the Paulinian sense of 'Not I, but Christ in me'; secondly as 'With Us Now', and thirdly as the dissolver of karmic blood-ties.

The Soul Forces close the play with words of grace, in which the audience, as well, can feel included:

LUNA       I will implore from primal powers
            courage and strength
            and let them help
            self-sacrifice to grow,
            so that what is perceived
            as temporal
            can be transformed
            to seeds of spirit
            for all eternity.

# SCENE ONE

*A hall in the prevailing tone of indigo blue; the antechamber to the rooms in which a Mystic Brotherhood carries on its work. Twelve Persons are present, conversing, each of whom in one way or another takes an interest in the endeavours of the Brotherhood. Besides these twelve: Felix Balde and Doctor Strader. The events of this scene and those following it take place about thirteen years after the time of* THE PORTAL OF INITIATION.

FERDINAND REINECKE

        It is a most extraordinary summons
        that brings us all together here and now.
        It comes from people who have always thought
        that they were given special spirit-tasks,
        and kept themselves aloof from other mortals.
        But now it must be that the cosmic plan
        has clearly shown their spiritual eyes
        that they must link themselves with other men
        who fight their way through life by their own efforts,
        without all blessing from the spirit-temple.
        I never was attracted by their style;
        they always have recourse to secrecy,
        whereas I want to stay with healthy thinking
        and lay great weight on simple common sense.
        The mystic brotherhood that summons us
        surely does not intend to raise us now
        to knowledge of its highest aims and plans.

15

It will address us in mysterious words,
but keep us in the temple's outer court,
saying that we express the people's will,
but using us to further its own plans.
Thus we are made into the tools and servants
of all those people who look down on us
and think they're born to rule us from on high.
They would not think us yet mature enough
to take a single step that would entail
our getting near their spiritual light
or glimpsing any of the temple's treasures.
When I reflect on their true attitude
I find it naught but pride and trickery
fairspoken though it is and humbly dressed.
It would be best that we avoid, I think,
the so-called wisdom offered to us here.
But still we must not let it seem as though
we blindly set ourselves against the work
that now is praised so much by everyone.
Therefore I say, let us politely listen
to what these lords of wisdom have to say,
and then be guided by our common sense.
One who thus lets discretion be his tutor
will never fall a prey to the temptations
that come upon us from the mystics' temple.

MICHAEL EDELMANN

I cannot tell, I cannot even guess,
what treasures of the spirit have been given
to those who now would find a bridge to us.
But I know many really noble men
belonging to this spiritual league.
Though strictly silent touching all the lore

16

that must have been imparted to their souls,
they clearly show, through deeds and way of life,
the source that feeds them can be only good.
For everything proceeding from their ranks
displays the earmarks of the purest love.
Therefore I think whatever moves them now
is also good, as in the present project
they seek to join themselves with men like us,
who know the striving of the soul for truth
but have no knowledge of the mystic ways.

BERNARD REDLICH

The thing for us to follow here is caution.
The mystics seem to think a time is near
that spells the end of their old sovereignty.
No reasonable person nowadays
asks what the temples say about the truth.
If any propositions made to us
seem sensible to ordinary thinking,
it may behoove us to collaborate.
But they must lay aside the mystic robes
if they would like to step across the bounds
which long have kept them closed off from the world
as if they lived within the realms of light.
Their high opinion of their merits
will carry little weight among us here.
They must not be awarded higher status
than they deserve by normal human rules.

FRANCESCA DEMUT

A large amount of what you're saying here
makes me suspect that you are like those men
who are completely blind to all the light

that long has flowed from out the sanctuaries
in streams of noble wisdom through the world,
to heal and comfort all the souls of men.
Only a man who lets his heart be brightened
and lets his soul be filled with warmth and zeal,
can recognize the meaning of this hour.
The mystic realm is now to be revealed
to those who always felt themselves too weak
to stand the sanctuaries' ancient tests
of fitness to receive the spirit's light.

MARIA TREUFELS

Many sure signs there are that clearly show
how many changes must take place in souls
accepting leadership in their life's course;
but far less certain that the mystic path
can lead us surely to those blessed goals
that stimulate the forces of men's souls.
I sadly fear that leaders now are lacking
who, in their harnessing of nature's forces,
combine both genius and agility,
and thus while working at their earthly tasks
show practical ability in action.
If such men plant the roots of spirit-work
in the good soil of plain reality,
they will be able, soberly,
to work in this world for the good of all.
Being convinced entirely of this view,
I see in Strader, rather than the mystics,
the forces needed for the leadership of men.
How long we have experienced with pain
that all our technical accomplishments
have only added to the heavy fetters

that hindered our free striving toward the spirit.
But now we can begin to have a hope,
a hope of which, till lately, none could dream.
In Strader's workshop one can find already
amazing things still in the model stage,
which, if they work, may change technology
in such a way that it will nevermore
oppress our souls with dreary hopeless weight.

STRADER  Your words are optimistic, but my work
seems headed in the right direction.
It still must cross the gap that separates
experiment from application,
but up to now the expert eye inclines
to find it technically feasible.
I hope that the inventor of the thing
may be allowed to give his own opinion
of what he has accomplished at this stage.
And since my words to some may seem immodest,
I ask indulgence for them in advance.
My aim is only to describe the feelings
from which the forces for my work have sprung.
It happens often in the course of life
that all our labour soon becomes detached
from feeling and from soul, becoming soulless
the more our spirit learns to dominate
the forces found here in the realm of sense.
Our labour in producing needed goods
grows more mechanical from day to day,
and with the labour also life itself.
For years much careful thought has been devoted
to finding measures, finding ways and means,
to rescue labour from technology,

so that the soul would not be lamed by work
but workers feel connected with the spirit.
Yet little was achieved by all these efforts
because one question only was considered –
the right relationship of man to man.
I too devoted many weary hours
to groping for the answer to this riddle.
I always found that my deep cogitations
produced in actual life no real value.
I very nearly reached the harsh conclusion
that in this world our destiny ordains
that our great triumphs in material realms
can only prejudice the spirit's growth.
Then there occurred a seeming accident,
producing a solution from the muddle.
I had to institute experiments
which seemed at first remote from all these problems,
but suddenly the thoughts sprang forth
that showed me the right way.
Through one experiment upon another
I finally discovered at my desk
a way by which to harmonize the forces
so that, when all the details are worked out,
through pure technique there will result that freedom
in which the soul can properly unfold.
No longer must our labourers be forced
to spend their days in soul-degrading sweatshops,
dreaming their lives away like vegetables.
The products of technology will now
be so distributed that every man
will have what he may need for his own work
within a house arranged to suit himself.
I've had to speak first of this hope to you

so as to furnish some foundation
for what I have to say about the summons
the Rosicrucian Brotherhood has sent
to persons standing outside their own ranks.
If in the future we can find ourselves
and let our souls develop properly,
then only health will follow from those instincts
by which one spirit seeks another one.
So now it's fair to say that honest thinking
is bound to recognize the correspondence
between that summons and the signs we see.
The Spirit Brothers want henceforth to offer
their lofty treasures freely to all men
because all men should now demand them.

FELIX BALDE   The words that we have just heard spoken here
have fought their painful way out of a soul
that's able to bestow upon our times
true values in the realm of sense-perception.
In this particular field today, I think,
no one can be compared with Dr. Strader.
I have myself by wholly different ways
discovered what is needed by the soul,
and hence may be permitted a few words.
I was by destiny assigned to the task
of seeking out the treasures that a man
can find within the precincts of his soul.
And there I seemed to find the kind of wisdom
that can illuminate all values here.
I was allowed to study mysticism
in contemplation and in solitude.
And on this path it was not hard to learn
how all that leads us men to mastery

of forces working in the realm of sense
imposes on us too a sort of blindfold,
so that we grope to find our way in darkness.
And all the treasures gained on earth by science
through application of the mind and senses
are still a fumbling in obscurity.
I am convinced that only mystic paths
can lead us to the genuine light of life.
I stood myself upon these paths of truth
as one who worked with no help from outside,
but this is not within the power of all.
Sense knowledge, intellectual thought,
to me seem like a body without soul,
as long as they so stubbornly resist
the light that since the first days of the world
has flowed out from the mystic sanctuaries.
Hence we should grasp in love and eagerness
the overtures made to us by the temple,
upon whose threshold roses bright and red
bedeck the sombre symbol of man's death.

LOUISE FUERCHTEGOTT

A man aware of his own soul's true worth
is able to rely on his own judgment
when he begins to seek out for himself
the spirit and the spiritual worlds.
But one is lost who only in blind faith
surrenders to the leadership of others.
Even the light that one would like to find
within himself as force of higher wisdom
deserves no serious acknowledgment
unless its truth is clearly proved.
The light can be a danger to a man

if he inclines to it without such proof.
For all too often on this path the soul
accepts as valid knowledge of the world
what only springs from its unconscious wish.


FREDERICK GEIST

Every modern man should feel impelled
to understand the workings of the mystics.
It seems to me that if one thinks he knows
just what the goal is like before he starts,
illusion will result instead of truth.
But of the mystic it is said that he
relates himself to his high goal of truth
as men do who desire to see the beauty
of distant views from a high mountain peak.
They do not paint the picture in advance:
they wait until they've climbed up to the top
and actually see what they have sought.


FERDINAND REINECKE

At this time let us not concern ourselves
about the proper attitude toward truth.
The brothers of the league will surely not
be eager for opinions from us.
But recently reports have reached my ears
that an event of very special import
has forced the brothers to consider us.
Thomasius, who for many years already
is active in a spiritual stream
that is devoted to occult pursuits,
has learned to use the thoughts and words of science
(in which our times have perfect confidence)

to clothe a presentation of the wisdom
that was till now initiation-lore.
He has succeeded, through this brilliant work,
in bringing many circles to applaud
writings that have a logical appearance
but actually contain rank mysticism.
Scholars who must be taken seriously
have said enthusiastic things about him
and thus have added to his growing fame,
which now seems dangerous in certain eyes.
The initiates now fear that one effect
will be to undermine the old belief
that they have sole possession of this lore.
Therefore they want to take into their fold
all that Thomasius has brought to light.
Their aim is to make everyone believe
that they have been aware for many years
that this material would be revealed
and this was merely part of their great plan.
If they should now succeed in craftily
enlisting us as members of their circle,
then they will spread the word throughout the world
that both Thomasius and his message were
sent out by mighty lords of destiny,
so that the common race of men might come
to believe in their importance to the world.

CASPAR STUERMER

The mystic school continues as before
to claim the privilege of guiding man.
This shows how little real respect it feels
for all that healthy people have achieved
in the long struggle to uplift mankind

that started with the proof that soul and nature
could be explained by mechanistic laws.
It's painful to a liberated mind
that such a clever man as Doctor Strader
should show himself inclined to mysticism.
One with his understanding of the forces
should certainly be able to see how
modern psychology itself requires
that mysticism be eliminated.
The spurious science that Thomasius
now boldly promulgates to all the world
should show him how the best intelligence
degenerates into mere fantasy
when it succumbs to this delusion.
For had Thomasius only trained himself
to think in strict accordance with Dame Nature,
instead of playing with this mystic trash,
his talents certainly would have allowed
him to produce fine scientific work.
But on the other path that he has chosen
he could not possibly escape great errors.
The spirit-league, however, may believe
that errors can be very useful to it.
It profits from the general impression
that science now has clearly documented
what really is such stuff as dreams are made of.

GEORGE WAHRMUND

The fact that anyone can speak such words
as those that we have just been made to hear
shows us how pitifully undeveloped
in our dark days the understanding is
that stems from cultivation of the spirit.

25

We only need to think of early times
and recollect what lived within men's souls
when science, which is now so dominant,
was not yet present even in the bud.
When we do this, we see the mystic league
is executing at this time a deed
that long was written in the cosmic plan.
The great work had to be anticipated
that's now succeeding for Thomasius.
The way is new by which he's trying now
to bring the spirit's light to human souls.
But this same light, you may be sure, was working
in all that's been achieved by men on earth.
And if you ask where this light had its source,
the signs all clearly point to mysticism
as it was nurtured in the sanctuaries
in times when man could not be led by reason.
The brotherhood that now has summoned us
wants to allow the mystic light to stream
upon the work that boldly tries to wring
real spirit-knowledge out of human thinking.
And we, who stand upon this hallowed ground,
in this brief moment fraught with destiny,
we are the first who, uninitiated,
shall be allowed to see the godly spark
leap from the spirit's heights to human souls.

Marie Kuehne

Thomasius needs not the sponsorship
the Rosicrucians contemplate for him,
since in a serious scientific way
he shows the soul's path through repeated lives
and how it lives in spirit realms between.

His deed has made available to all,
even to those who shun the sanctuaries,
the light to which the mystics used to lead.
Thomasius deserves the recognition
that's been so richly granted him of late,
because he gives our thinking just that freedom
that was denied it by the mystic schools.


HERMINE HAUSER

I think the Rosicrucians have no future,
though they will surely be remembered long.
What they call forth at just this point in time
will undermine the temple's whole foundation
when it becomes aware of its own power.
They have courageously resolved to bind
reason and science to the sanctuaries.
Therefore Thomasius, whom they receive
so willingly into the temple now,
will look to aftertimes like its destroyer.


STRADER

I have been blamed for saying candidly
that we should now express our readiness
to work together with the mystic league
in furthering Thomasius's work.
One speaker said my views were painful to him,
because I ought to know how dangerous
the mystics are to real psychology.
But mysticism often seemed to me
most understandable just at the time
when I was most absorbed with all my heart
in mechanisms I myself had made.
The way I was related to my works

showed me the nature of the sanctuaries.
And while I was at work I often thought:
What can I be to one who only tries
to understand just how the forces work
that I've implanted into the machine?
And then again what can I be to one
to whom I lovingly reveal my soul?
And it is owing to such thoughts as these
that the ideas stemming from the mystics
could open to me all their deeper meaning.
And thus I know, without initiation,
that in the sanctuaries souls of gods
reveal their essence lovingly to men.

KATHARINA RATSAM

The noble words that we have heard just now
from Dr. Strader on the sanctuaries
must be applauded by the many souls
who never could themselves approach the portal
through which initiates could freely pass
but still had made themselves acquainted well
with all that these initiates could teach.
That our ancestors tended to believe
the mystics hostile to the light,
is understandable. Their souls were sealed
against all hints of what the temples hold
concealed mysteriously within their walls.
This is no longer so. The mystics keep
their light but partly veiled. They tell the world
all that the non-initiates ought to know.
And many souls who have received this light
and have enlivened it within themselves
experienced this as an awakening

of forces in the soul that formerly,
shrouded in sleep, worked all unconsciously.

(*Three knocks are heard.*)

FELIX BALDE    The masters of this place are coming now,
and you will be allowed to hear their words.
But only those among you who are free
from prejudice will understand the words
and feel them working inwardly as light.
The power of the initiates will work
vigorously on open minds and hearts
if these have been prepared to sacrifice
illusions when the truth at last shines out.
But they will have no influence at all
where error has been hardened into will
and thus the sense for truth has been destroyed.

FERDINAND REINECKE
A man who seeks, through lengthy introspection,
to recognize himself within himself
may find the time to dwell on words like these.
But in our dealings with the mystic league
it would be better to recall the stories
preserved in records or in old traditions
about how secret brotherhoods behave.
These stories show that many able men
have let themselves be lured into the temples
when they were told, in veiled mysterious words,
that in these walls they could expect their souls,
starting from wisdom of a lower grade,
to move ahead to more advanced degrees
and in the end attain to spirit-sight.

Those who succumbed to such temptation
were in the lower grades shown signs and symbols
upon whose meaning they were told to brood.
They hoped, of course, that in the higher grades
the meaning of the signs would be revealed,
along with other wisdom. But they found,
when they were brought into the last degrees,
that lo! the masters also knew but little
about the signs, and that their revelations
were empty phrases, signifying nothing.
And then these men, if not bewitched by words
or overwhelmed by idle vanity,
would turn away from all such trickery.
At this time, I suggest, it would be prudent
to think of these historical reports
and not be swayed by edifying words.

(*Again three knocks are heard*)

*The Grand Master of the Secret Brotherhood, Hilary,
enters, followed by Magnus Bellicosus, the Second
Preceptor; Albert Torquatus, the First Master of
Ceremonies; and Frederick Trautman, the Second
Master of Ceremonies. The persons assembled group
themselves on each side of the hall.*

FREDERICK TRAUTMAN, *the Second Master of Ceremonies*
This moment is significant for you and us,
dear friends, because at last we are united
before our ancient holy temple's doors.
We sent our summons for the meeting here
because this was required by all the signs
that our revered Grand Master could perceive
in the great plan laid out to guide the earth.
In this plan it is clearly indicated

that now the time has come to bring together
the sacred wisdom of the sanctuary
and ordinary human common sense,
which seeks the truth far from the mystic paths.
But those same signs also revealed to him
that all this could not be accomplished till
a man should come who could express the knowledge
that has its base in reason and the senses
in forms that would enable normal men
really to comprehend the spirit-world.
This has occurred. Thomasius succeeded
in giving modern science a report
containing proofs for all the spiritual things
that up to now could be discovered only
on mystic paths and in the sanctuaries.
His book must be regarded as the bond
uniting you and us in spiritual life.
You will be able through this book to learn
how solid is the base of all our doctrines.
And this will make you willing to accept
from us the further knowledge that till now
could be acquired through mysticism only.
So we may hope a new life will arise,
blending the general sense of all mankind
with ancient customs of the mysteries.

MAGNUS BELLICOSUS, *the Second Preceptor*

My brother's words have made it clear to you
that we were moved by very earnest signs,
in sending you the summons to meet here.
Our master will soon add a few brief words
giving a deeper explanation of it.
My task is now to speak, so far as needed,

of that extraordinary man whose work
has brought us all together in this place.
Thomasius had devoted all his life
to painting, till he felt himself impelled
to scientific thinking, through some inner call.
Within the realm of art he could unfold
the glorious gifts with which he was endowed
only upon his entering those circles
that were devoted to true mysticism.
There he was made acquainted with the master,
who could display to him the early steps
of spirit-sight according to true wisdom.
And then, in spirit-heights experiencing
himself among creative powers and beings,
he painted pictures that could work like magic.
This would have driven any other artist
to keep himself within his chosen field,
while seeking ever higher peaks to climb.
To him, however, it was but a spur
to use his talents in the way that seemed
most apt to benefit mankind at large.
He came to see that spiritual science
can have a firm foundation only if
the sense for rigorous scientific thinking
is freed by art from its intense desire
for rigid forms and is enlivened so
that it can feel the world in all its glory.
And so Thomasius has sacrificed
his artist's work, which could have been his joy
to benefit his fellow men on earth.
If you, my friends, acknowledge this man's merits,
you'll understand the meaning of our summons
and hesitate no longer to respond.

HILARY, *the Grand Master*

In that spirit's name who has revealed himself
to many souls within this holy place,
we now appear before these persons who,
till now, were not allowed to hear the words
that here resound mysteriously.
The powers who guide our progress on the earth
could not, in the remotest days of yore,
reveal themselves in light to everyone.
For it was as with children; gradually
the forces had to be matured and strengthened
that were designed to carry on our knowing.
So was it that mankind in general
had slowly to unfold in course of time.
In darkness lived at first those impulses
that later came to show themselves as worthy
to see the spirit-light from higher worlds.
In those remotest days when earth began,
great spirits were sent down from higher worlds
to be the wise and watchful guides of men.
They cultivated in the sanctuaries
those spirit-forces that could penetrate
mysteriously into the souls, who had
no conscious knowledge of their leaders.
And later the wise masters found that they
could choose, from out the ranks of men, disciples
who, through renunciations and fierce tests,
had proved mature enough to be initiated
into the sacred wisdom of the mysteries.
And when the pupils of the early masters
learned to protect the treasures worthily,
those mighty teachers took their way again
back to their own far-distant habitations.

The pupils in their turn selected men
who could succeed them in the watchful care
of spirit treasures, so it went on further
through generations numberless to us.
And to this day all genuine mystic schools
descend directly from that earliest one,
which was established by the higher spirits.
Humbly we cultivate within these walls
what has been left us by our ancestors.
Never will we assert that our own merits
deserve the offices that we now fill:
the lofty spirit-powers choose by grace
the feeble men they need as messengers,
and to them they entrust the precious treasures
that can unbind the spirit's light in souls.
And it is to these treasures, my dear friends,
that we must give you access at this time.
Auspicious are the signs that we can see
with spirit-sight in the world's destiny.

FERDINAND REINECKE

How far afield you go to find the reasons
that should persuade us to join hands with you
in vigorously promoting the great work
Thomasius has given to the world.
All that you say sounds very beautiful,
but in our simple minds it is outweighed
by the conviction that, if it contains
exactly what is needed by men's souls,
the book can make its own way in the world.
In our opinion it has won acclaim
by reason of the science it contains
and not because it's full of mysticism.

If this is so, how can it help the book
to have the hearty praise of all the mystics
rather than winning minds by its own virtues?

ALBERT TORQUATUS, *the First Master of Ceremonies*
The spirit-science, that Thomasius
has so convincingly presented there,
will neither gain nor lose by any praise
that we or you may publish to the world.
The point is that through it the way is found
by which men turn their minds to mysticism.
It will accomplish only half its task
if looked at as a goal and not a path.
And now it's up to you to understand
that finally the moment has arrived
for reason to combine with mysticism,
giving to modern spiritual life
a force that can effect real impact only
if loosed at just the proper time and place.

(*Curtain*)

# SCENE TWO

*The same hall as in Scene One. The persons who were at first assembled there have left, with the exception of Felix Balde and Doctor Strader. Present are: Hilary, the Grand Master; Magnus Bellicosus, the second Preceptor: Albert Torquatus, the first master of ceremonies; Frederick Trautman, the second master of ceremonies; Maria Johannes Thomasius.*

HILARY
My son, you have accomplished now what must
receive the seal of sacred and primeval knowledge,
besides the blessing of the cross of roses
adorning here our consecrated place.
What you have given to the world
shall be through us a spirit offering,
that it bear fruit in all domains of life
where powers of men can be
of service for the progress of the world.

MAGNUS BELLICOSUS
To give the world your work, you were obliged
to separate yourself for many years
from much that once had been most dear to you.
The spirit teacher standing at your side
left you in order that your soul
could then unfold its power fully.
Your cherished friend and close companion

36

left you, too; for you should find
what men may find if they can follow
the forces of the soul in their own self.
With courage you have overcome these trials.
For your own good you were deprived of all
that, for your good, is now restored to you.
You see your friend before you; in the temple
she'll welcome you, complying with our wish.
You soon will also greet your teacher.
United with us at our temple's threshold,
these friends receive you as the one who brings
to modern man the knowledge of the spirit.

FELIX BALDE (*to Thomasius*)

The mystic way of life, which strove till now
in inner contemplation toward the spirit light,
will through your act be opened up
to knowledge gained within the world of sense.

STRADER

You've also found for souls who search
for spirit knowledge, though life fetters them to
matter,
the paths which lead each one in his way to the light.

THOMASIUS

Exalted Master and you gentlemen,
you think you see a man before you
whose earnest striving and whose strength of spirit
was able to produce a work entitled to
your praise and kind protection.
You think that he will certainly succeed
in reconciling science, as esteemed today,
with ancient, sacred occultism.
Indeed, if faith in my accomplishment

could be conferred on me by any other means
than my own inner voice,
it only could be by such words as yours.

FREDERICK TRAUTMAN

Our master's words no doubt express
what you feel in yourself, and so
your inner voice therefore has not to be confirmed.

THOMASIUS    O were it so! Most humbly would I stand
imploring you to grant me here
the temple's blessing on my work.
I thought it would be so when first I heard
that you would give protection to my work
and let me pass the gate which otherwise
is opened to initiates alone.
But on my way to you
a world unlocked itself to me,
which surely, at this time, you had not meant
to lead me into: Ahriman
in his full grandeur stood before me,
and I could recognize in him the expert
in laws that govern our world-order.
What human beings think they know of him
is worthless. Only he who has beheld
his being in the spirit, understands him.
From him alone have I been able fully
to learn the truth about this work of mine.
He showed me how impressions of it, formed
by men who judge in terms of science and of logic,
are valueless in gauging its effects
upon world evolution. Only then
would their opinion count, if the creation –

disjoined from its creator – were set free
from him. For then it might pursue
its own course in the sphere of spiritual life.
However, since this work must always
remain bound up with me, it well could happen
that from the spirit realm I might transform
what I have done into its opposite, –
though its own nature in itself is good
and could bring good results.
From spirit realms I'll have continually
to influence all that results on earth
from my activity in sense existence.
If I let evil pour from spirit regions
and into these results, the truth will be
more damaging by far than would be error.
For men must follow truth, impelled
by their own insight. Error leaves them cold.
I shall most certainly in future turn to evil
the consequences of my work,
for Ahriman has shown me clearly
that these results must be his property.
While I was busy at this work, intent,
and full of joy because it led me safely
from stage to stage within the edifice of truth,
I only paid attention to that part of me
that concentrated on my research,
while all the rest I left unguarded.
Wild urges could develop, unrestrained,
which hitherto lay dormant in my soul
and now in silent strength matured to fruit.
I thought myself in highest spirit regions
and was in darkest night of soul.
Quite clearly Ahriman within his kingdom

could show me all the power of these urges.
So now I know what later my effect will be;
for these wild urges must in future
become a part of my own personality.
I had – before I started with my work –
already pledged myself to Lucifer, whose realm
I wished to learn to understand.
But only now I know what, lost completely
in my creative work, I did not realize:
that Lucifer, with most enticing pictures,
surrounded all my thinking,
while, at the same time, he created
wild urges in my soul which still are quiet
but surely will in future gain control of me.

TRAUTMAN       How can a man who's reached such spirit heights
and knows all this for certain, still believe
that he will not escape such evil?
You can behold what is so harmful to you;
therefore you must destroy it and with courage save
yourself and the results of your great work.
A spirit-pupil has the iron duty
to kill what hinders progress in himself.

THOMASIUS      I see you do not judge by cosmic laws.
What you demand is something I could do
at present and could tell myself right now
all this that you are telling me.
But though my karma could permit this at the moment
it will not tolerate it later on.
For things must come which will obscure
my spirit and direct me just as I described.
I shall then in world-evolution greedily

seize everything destructive in my work
and shall endeavour to embody it
within the spiritual life.
I then, in having to love Ahriman,
must joyfully hand over to his ownership
whatever came from me in earthly life.

(*A pause, while Thomasius ponders deeply.*)

If this concerned myself alone,
I'd bear it silently within my soul
and would await, completely tranquil,
what destiny holds waiting on my path.
But it concerns your Brotherhood as well as me.
The bad results that follow from my work
for me and other human beings
will all be balanced by the laws of karma.
That you, however, fell so deeply into error
is far more serious for our life on earth.
As leaders of this life, who should read rightly
in spirit worlds, you never should have failed
to realize this work had better be achieved
by someone else and not by me.
You should have known it must be put aside
for now and only later be produced
afresh by one who could direct
its consequences in a different way.
Your judgment has deprived the Brotherhood
of rights it ought to have if it
would rightly guide the sacred rituals.
Because this follows for you from my vision,
I come here to your threshold with this knowledge
which would have otherwise kept me away.
Now truly, on this work of mine,

whose end effects will be both good and damaging,
I cannot take your blessing.

HILARY  Dear brothers, what we have begun
cannot be carried further.
We must withdraw now to the place
at which the spirit lets us know its will.

*(All except Maria and Thomasius leave. The hall grows
dark. After a pause the three spirit figures, Philia,
Astrid and Luna appear in a cloud of light; by grouping
themselves, they hide at first Maria from sight. The
following is a spirit experience of Thomasius.)*

PHILIA  The soul is athirst
to drink of the light
that flows from those worlds
which an all-watchful will
keeps veiled for mankind.
The spirit is seeking
all eager to listen
to converse of gods,
which benevolent wisdom
conceals from the heart.
But dangers can threaten
those thoughts that are searching
in regions of soul
where far from the senses
the Hidden holds sway.

ASTRID  The souls are expanding
that follow the light
and penetrate worlds
which vision with courage

reveals to mankind.
The spirit is striving
enraptured to live
in regions of gods,
which radiant wisdom
proclaims to the seers.
The Hidden is beckoning
to daring that longs
for cosmic domains
which, far from men's thinking,
life's mysteries hide.

LUNA      The soul gains matureness
to form itself insight,
engendering forces
which kindle in man
a will that is fearless.
From primeval sources
the powers of redemption
gain magical strength,
concealed to the senses
by barriers of earth.
And traces are followed
by souls that are trying
to search out those portals
which gods have shut fast
to willing that errs.

VOICE OF CONSCIENCE (*invisible*)
Your thoughts are wavering
at being's abyss;
and what upheld them in firm support
is lost now to you;

and what shone on them as sun
is now obscured to you.
You go astray in cosmic depths
which men, lured on by longing,
desire to conquer.
You shudder at the spirit ground of growth
where of soul consolation
men must be deprived.

(*The last words are immediately followed by those of
Maria, who, concealed by the spirit figures, is still
invisible. At first she speaks with a spirit-like but
inward voice*).

MARIA    So turn your soul again
toward powers of love,
which once could permeate your hope
with warmth of life;
which once could shine into your will
with spirit light.
Deliver from loneliness
your heart's far-searching power,
and feel the nearness of your friend
in striving's darkest hour.

(*The spirit figures disappear, with them the cloud of
light. Maria becomes visible in her former place, Maria
and Thomasius facing each other. The experience changes
to the physical plane.*)

THOMASIUS (*out of deep pondering*)
Where was I now? The forces of my soul
showed me the chaos of my inner life.
The conscience of the world disclosed to me
what I have lost.

44

And then, as blessing, sounded
the voice of love, within the realm of darkness.

MARIA   Johannes, the companion of your soul
may once again stand at your side,
and she may follow you to cosmic depths
in which souls fight their way to a true feeling
of gods through all-destroying victories,
that boldly from destruction wrench new life.
And I must lead my friend into the empty,
unmelting fields of ice, where now bursts free
from bonds the light that must be formed by spirits
when the force of life is lamed by darkness.
My friend, you now confront that threshold of your life
where one must lose what once has been acquired.
You have gazed often toward the realm of spirit
and have gained strength from it,
enabling you to work creatively.
It seems to you that now that work is lost.
Do not demand that this be otherwise
for such desire would rob you of all strength
to journey further into spirit realms.
Whether you walk this path in truth or error
you can keep ever clear the view ahead
so that your soul is able to pursue its way.
For this you must with courage bear necessities
stemming from the nature of the spirit realm.
This is the law of the discipleship of spirit.
As long as you still nurture the desire
that what has happened might be otherwise,
you'll lack the strength with which you must
sustain yourself in spirit-regions.
That you have lost what you've already gained –

let this provide for you the knowledge
for further journeys on the spirit's rightful path.
Henceforth you can rely no longer
upon that insight which, before, you used
in judging your own actions,
if now with certainty you look on it as lost.
Therefore your being must become completely silent
and wait in silence for the spirit's grace. –
You only can take counsel with yourself again
when you have gained yourself anew.
The solemn Guardian you have often met,
who keeps an unrelenting watch upon the threshold
that severs spirit life from worlds of sense;
but you have never penetrated past him.
At sight of him each time you turned away
and from the outside looked at everything.
Since you have never been within that inner world
which widens out as spirit actuality
beyond you, so be ready now for what reveals itself,
when at my side you can not only enter
but also pass beyond the Threshold.
(*curtain*)

# SCENE THREE

*Lucifer's Kingdom: a space not enclosed by artificial walls but by plant- and animal-like shapes and other forms of fantasy. At the left, the throne of Lucifer. At first the souls of Capesius and Maria are present; somewhat later Lucifer appears, and then Benedictus, Thomasius with his etheric counterpart (The Double); finally, Theodora.*

MARIA      You, known to me in sense existence
as Capesius, how is it that you are
the being I encounter first
in Lucifer's domain? There's danger
in breathing in the spirit of this place.

CAPESIUS      O do not speak to me about Capesius,
who in the realm of earth existence
has battled through a life he long has recognized
as dream. While there, he turned his mind
towards things that happen in the stream of time;
and so he thought he could discover
those powers which bring about the spiritual life
and its effect upon mankind. His soul
strove to hold fast his knowledge of these powers.
From this domain one can perceive
the knowledge that he cultivated.
He thought the pictures that he had were true
and able to reveal to him reality;

47

but, viewed from here, they clearly are but airy dreams
the spirits weave into weak men on earth,
who are too feeble to endure reality.
Benumbed and frightened would they be,
if they should learn how spirits guide
the course of life according to their plans.

MARIA       You speak as I have only heard those speak
who never had a life upon the Earth.
They claim the Earth is not significant,
that its effects within the universe
are small. But he who has belonged to realms of Earth
and owes to it his better powers
must have indeed a different opinion.
He finds significant the many threads
of destiny, that bind earth life
with cosmic life. And Lucifer himself,
who works with power here, looks towards the
        Earth.
He seeks to guide men's deeds in such a way
that they bear fruits of service to his spirit.
He knows that he would fall a prey to darkness
if on the earth he could not find his victims.
And so his fate is bound up, too, 'with
        Earth.
It is the same for other cosmic beings.
And when the human soul can see in picture form
the cosmic aims that Lucifer aspires to
and can compare them with the purposes
of all those powers who have him as their enemy,
the soul will know it can defeat him
by victories in conquering itself.

48

CAPESIUS     The man who here is speaking with you dreads
             those times that force him to put on
             a body, still alive, that keeps its earthly form
             although the spirit can no longer master it.
             At just such times this spirit feels
             the worlds he treasures are collapsing.
             It seems to him as if a narrow dungeon,
             bounded by nothingness, enclosed him cruelly.
             The memory of all that is pure life to him
             seems then extinguished for this spirit.
             And often, too, he senses human beings
             but cannot understand what they are saying.
             Words only that are special can be grasped,
             that lift themselves out of the general talk
             and bring remembrance of the beauty
             he is allowed to see in spirit realms.
             He's in his body then, – and he is not.
             He lives in it a life which he must fear
             when he beholds it from this region.
             And he is thirsting for the time to come
             when from the body he will be set free.

MARIA        The body which belongs to earthly souls
             bears in itself the means to recreate
             the divinely beautiful in noble pictures.
             And though these pictures only live as shadows
             in human souls, they are the seeds which later
             must flower and bear fruit in world-evolving.
             So through his body man can serve the gods.
             And the true meaning of his life of soul
             can only show itself to him when in his body
             the strength of the essential 'I' confirms
                  itself.

CAPESIUS O do not speak that word so near the being
which has appeared to you in spirit realms
and which is living as Capesius on earth.
It wants to flee whenever that word sounds,
a word which here can burn it fiercely.

MARIA Do you so hate
what raises man to his true being?
How can you live then in this realm
if you can find this word so frightful?
– for no one reaches this domain at all
who has not faced this word's essential
  nature.

CAPESIUS The one you see before you often stood
in front of Lucifer, who rules this realm.
And Lucifer revealed to him
that human souls who consciously use forces
out of their earthly bodies
bring only harm to this domain,
in which his will holds sway.
But other souls who in unconsciousness
live on within their bodies, yet possess
already powers of seership, these only *learn*
in Lucifer's domain and cannot cause it harm.

MARIA I know that in these realms of spirit
one does not learn by words, one learns by
  sight.
What in these moments I have here perceived,
because you have appeared to me,
will prove itself within my soul as progress
in my discipleship of spirit.

CAPESIUS          One gathers here not only teachings,
                  but duties also are revealed.
                  You have conversed with that soul-being
                  that calls itself Capesius in the body.
                  The spirit insight you have gained
                  into a former life shows that you owe
                  Capesius much through your own karma.
                  Therefore you should beg Lucifer that he,
                  the great light-bearer, let you give
                  protection to Capesius on earth.
                  Through your own wisdom you will know
                  what you can do for him, so that he may
                  be led to you in later earthly lives, –
                  and so through you the debt may then be cancelled.

MARIA             Must I allow this duty, which to me is sacred,
                  to be fulfilled through power of Lucifer?

CAPESIUS          This duty you must surely wish to do,
                  and this can only be with help of Lucifer.
                  But look! he comes himself, the Spirit of the Light.

                  (*Exit Capesius. Lucifer appears and, during his first
                  speech, Benedictus*)

LUCIFER           Maria, at my throne you are requesting
                  self-knowledge for the human soul
                  to whom you are attached in earthly life.
                  He shall, by the beholding of my being,
                  first learn to know himself in his reality!
                  He will arrive at this without your aid.
                  How can you think that I would grant to you
                  what you wish to accomplish for your friend?
                  You follow Benedictus as your guide,

who is my strong opponent on the earth,
devoting all his forces to my foes.
He has been able to tear much away from me.
Johannes has renounced his leadership
and now has given himself instead to me.
Not yet can he behold my real being
because he lacks full power of seership;
he will attain it later on through me
and then be mine completely.
But I command you not to speak a word
which might in any way refer to him
as long as you are standing at my throne.
Such words would burn me, spoken here.
At this place words are deeds
and further deeds must follow them.
But what would follow from your words,
that may not be.

BENEDICTUS                 You are obliged to hear her.
For where the word possesses action's force,
it comes as the result of former deeds. The deed
compelling Lucifer already has been done.
Maria is my own true pupil in the spirit,
and I have guided her to that maturity
through which she recognized the highest spirit task.
This certainly she will fulfil.
Fulfilment of her duty will not fail
to form the healing forces in Johannes
that will release him from your realm.
Maria carries in her soul
a holy, solemn vow that will arouse
these healing forces for the progress of the world.
You soon will hear it spoken forth in words.

Your aura's brilliant light gives you
the magic power of opposition
and power to gain by force all selfhood.
If you, with strength of thought, will
    dim your brilliance,
the healing rays that shine out of Maria's vow
perhaps will be perceptible to you.
These rays will shine in future with such force
that their strong love will draw Johannes to their
    realm.

MARIA        Johannes will come here, but side by side with him,
who has the form of earthly souls, will also be
that being whom a man bears hidden
within him as a much more potent double.
Were now Johannes to perceive you only
as you can show yourself to him on earth,
it would not give him all that he has need of
for the right progress of his soul.
You now shall give his double
what he requires upon those spirit paths
on which in future I shall guide his steps.

LUCIFER     So must Johannes then appear to me!
Well do I feel the power that you both exert.
It has opposed me since the earth began.

*(There enter at the same time, but from different sides,
Johannes Thomasius and his etheric Double.)*

THOMASIUS  O my own double-image, up to now
you've only shown yourself to me so that
I might be frightened at myself.

I know but little of you, still I recognize
that it is you who guides my soul.
You are a hindrance therefore to my free existence,
the reason also that I cannot grasp
what in reality I am. In front
of Lucifer I have to hear you speak,
to see what I in future shall achieve.

## The Double of Thomasius

I could indeed come often to Johannes
and bring him recognition of himself.
Yet I was active only in those depths of soul
which still are hidden from his consciousness.
My life within his inmost soul
has long since undergone important change.
Maria stood beside him years ago;
he thought that he was joined with her in spirit.
I showed him that his instincts and his passions
were actually the pilots of his soul.
He understood this only as reproach.
But you, exalted Bearer of the Light,
have shown his sensuousness the way
it best may serve the spirit. From Maria
Johannes had to separate his life.
Since then he gave his efforts to strict thinking,
and this has power to purify men's souls.
What streamed forth from his purity of thought
flowed over into me. I was transformed,
for now I also feel his purity in me.
He does not have to be afraid of me,
if he feels drawn back to Maria's side.
But he belongs as yet to your domain,
and at this moment I demand him back,

for he shall now experience my being
without your interference.
He needs me so that now into his thinking
soul warmth and forces of the heart, as well,
are mightily enkindled from my being.
He shall once more regain himself as man.

LUCIFER     Your striving in itself is good, – and yet
I cannot let you do what you desire.
For should I give you back now to Johannes
in the same being's shape as you appeared
before his soul-perception years ago,
he would from now on only give his love
to thinking and cold knowledge.
All warmth of selfhood would appear to him
unfeeling, void of essence, as if dead.
I cannot use my powers to make him this.
Through me he must discover in himself
his personality, the being that's his own.
I must transform you, that the right step now
is made for his own good and for his progress.
Long since have I prepared what at this time
must clearly show itself in you:
henceforth you shall appear as a quite other being.
Johannes will no longer love Maria
as he has loved her in the past,
but he will love another with the passion
and all the strength with which he once loved her.

BENEDICTUS     The noble work, in which we have succeeded,
you wish now to transform to your own use.
You bound Johannes once by his heart's force
to you, but now you'll see

that you must make the fetters stronger still
if you would hold his being in your power.
Indeed, his heart is longing to submit itself
completely to the spirit; and if he comes to this,
the deed which he accomplished for the sake
of higher knowledge, on the earth,
will in the future fall into the hands
of powers you oppose since earth's beginning.
If you succeed in changing, cunningly,
the love felt by Johannes for Maria
into the passion you have need of now
for your own aims, he will, from spirit worlds,
transform the good he has achieved to evil.

MARIA  Is rescue then still possible, – Johannes,
not destined to fall victim to those powers
who want to capture for themselves his deed?

BENEDICTUS  It would take place, if all the forces stay
as until now they have been able to develop.
But if at the right hour you will allow
your vow to take effect within your soul,
those forces must in future change their course.

LUCIFER  So work, compelling powers,
and feel, you elemental spirits,
the forces of your master;
then pave the way
that from the realms of earth
there can come forth
to Lucifer's domain
what my desires demand,
what shall obey my will.

THEODORA     Who calls me into realms so strange to me?
             I love it only when the worlds of gods
             are willing lovingly to show themselves, –
             and warmth in blissful weaving round my heart
             draws spirit words out of my inmost soul.

THE DOUBLE OF THOMASIUS
             Oh! how you transform my whole existence!
             You have appeared, and now I am a being
             who only can work on, made one with you.
             Through me Johannes shall belong to you.
             He shall from now on give to you the love
             which once rose in his heart so fearfully
             and warmly for Maria.
             He saw you years ago but did not feel
             what even then was secretly engendered
             as warmth of love in deepest grounds of soul.
             Now it will rise and fill his being with the strength
             to turn his every thought to you alone.

BENEDICTUS   The crucial moment now is very near.
             His strongest force has Lucifer unfolded.
             Maria, your discipleship of soul
             must take a stand against him, mightily.

MARIA        You Bearer of the Light which would restrict
             man's love to the advantage only of himself,
             you gave, at Earth's beginning, knowledge
             too soon to feeble human beings.
             For they were destined by the gods
             to follow not their own but spirit will,
             unconsciously at first.
             And since that time the souls of all mankind

57

have been the place where you combat the gods.
The times are fast approaching which must bring
destruction to yourself and your domain.
A thinker boldly could set science free
from gifts you had bestowed, so that
it can be offered to the gods
that guide mankind. And yet you try once more
yourself to take the forces destined for the gods.
Because Johannes through his deed released
out of your grasp that fruit of knowledge
with which you first seduced mankind,
you wish now to seduce him with a love
that he, according to his destiny,
should never feel for Theodora.
You wish to battle wisdom now with love,
as once you battled love through wisdom,
but know that in the heart
with which Maria now confronts you,
discipleship of spirit has enkindled forces
enabling her to keep self-love apart
forever from all knowledge. I never shall
in future let myself be overcome by bliss
such as men feel whenever thoughts of theirs grow
   ripe.
I will prepare my heart for sacrifice
so that my spirit only uses thinking power
in order to bring forth the fruits
of knowledge as an offering to the gods.
Cognition will become for me a consecration.
And what I bring about so actively within myself
shall stream forth strongly to Johannes.
Then when in future often in his heart
the words resound which come to him from you,

'His human nature shall discover it is love
that gives his personality its strength,'
my heart will answer you with might:
you once were listened to at Earth's beginning
when you revealed the fruits of wisdom.
The fruits of love shall only be received by man
when they spring forth out of the realms of gods.

LUCIFER          I mean to fight.

BENEDICTUS       And fighting serve the gods.

                 (*Thunder as the curtain falls.*)

# SCENE FOUR

*A room in rose-red tones in the home of Strader and his wife Theodora.*
*One notices by the arrangement of the room that they use it together, each for*
*his own work. On Strader's work-table there are models of mechanisms; on*
*Theodora's, things to do with mystic studies. The two are holding a conversa-*
*tion that shows them contemplating their seventh wedding anniversary.*

STRADER        On this day, seven years have passed
since you became the dear companion of my life,
became as well the source of light for me,
that shone on an existence until then
ever threatened by the darkness.
In spirit I was poor, a starving man,
when you came to my side and gave me everything
the world had, up to then, withheld from me.
For many years I'd striven earnestly
with scientific research in its strictest sense
to find the values and the goals of life.
I had to recognize one day, quite clearly,
that all my striving was in vain.
For I could learn from you how spirit
reveals itself in man, concerned with things
that had escaped my knowledge and my thought.
I saw you at that time within the circle
where Benedictus was the leader. I had
the privilege of listening to your revelation.

Then later, in Thomasius, I could perceive
how spirit training
works mightily within a human soul.
What I experienced through this
deprived me of my faith in reason and in science.
And yet it showed me nothing then
which could seem understandable to me.
I turned away from any kind of thinking
and only wished to go on living aimlessly,
now that life seemed so utterly bereft of value.
I hoped that purely technical work,
to which I gave myself completely,
would bring benumbed forgetfulness;
I lived a life of torment
until I once again met you
and we became good friends.

THEODORA    Well can I understand why just today
remembrance brings those times
so vividly before your soul again.
In my own heart I also feel the need
to look back on those days
when we were drawn together for our life.
I felt the constant strengthening at that time
of forces opening my soul
to knowledge from the spirit worlds.
And under Felix Balde's worthy guidance
these forces reached the height that they
were able to achieve just seven years ago.
About that time I met Capesius one day
in Felix' woodland solitude.
Long years he'd had of studious research

and now had fought his way
towards spirit training.
He felt he should become familiar
with my way of gazing on the spirit world.
I visited him often later on,
and it was in his house that meeting you
I was allowed to bring
some healing to your agonies of mind.

STRADER        And then the true light shone into my soul
that long had only looked into the darkness.
Now I could see what spirit is in truth.
You let me know what was revealed to you
from higher worlds in such a way
that every doubt could swiftly disappear.
All this affected me so much
that first I merely saw in you
the mediator for the spirit.
It took some time before I recognized
that not alone my spirit
was listening to your words,
as they unveiled its true abode,
but that my heart was taken captive, too,
and could no longer do without the speaker.

THEODORA      When you confided to me how you felt,
so strangely did you put it into words:
as if not even with a single thought
could you conceive of the fulfilment
of the longing living in your heart.
Your words seemed only seeking
for good advice from a dear friend.
You spoke of help of which you were in need

and of the strengthening of powers of soul
that they might steady you in times of trial.

STRADER     That she who heralded the spirit could
            be destined also as my life-companion
            was something far removed from all my thought,
            when I confided in you, seeking help.

THEODORA    And how the words, released
            from heart to heart, revealed
            that this would be our path.
            It is the heart that often points out destiny.

STRADER     And when your heart spoke out the word of destiny,
            great waves of life streamed through my soul;
            such waves I could not quickly feel or know,
            but when they later rose in memory
            out of soul-depths, they then
            could be experienced as radiant light.
            And so because I had that memory,
            yet could not grasp it consciously as long
            as it was happening, I realized
            how much still separated me
            from actual perception of the spirit.
            It was the first time that I recognized
            the spirit present in my soul.
            It never has recurred; and yet
            it could in truth give certainty to me
            which radiates its light on my whole life.
            And so these seven blessed years have passed.
            I've been allowed to feel how all my work,
            technology itself, can be enriched by those
            whose attitude toward the spirit world is right.

Through the enlivining spirit power that you bestowed
on me, I could observe the energies
of natural forces with such penetration
that, suddenly, as if inspired, there stood created
before my spirit that new and promising machine.
Within your light my soul has felt
the full maturing of those forces
which would have perished had I lived alone.
This certainty of life that I had won
helped hold me upright even when Thomasius
condemned before the Rose Cross Brotherhood
so startlingly his scientific work
and disavowed himself with a harsh judgment
the very hour that should have lifted him
to his life's peak.
When all the outside world appeared to show
almost too many contradictions,
this inner certainty sustained me, –
and you alone could give me this.
The spirit revelation I received through you
at first brought me the knowledge I had striven for;
and when the revelation came no more,
you stayed my strength-bestowing light of soul.

THEODORA (*deeply pondering, in a broken sentence*)
    And when the revelation came no more – – –

STRADER    That often gravely worried me.
    I wondered if great pain would not result
    for you from loss of seership,
    and whether you, to spare me, bore it silently.
    But by your equanimity I saw
    that you in calmness bore your fate.

However, recently a change has taken place:
your cheerfulness no longer shines around you
and in your eyes the glowing light has dimmed.

THEODORA  It could not truly pain me
that spirit revelation disappeared.
Through destiny my path had changed;
and this I could accept with calmness.
But now the revelation is renewed,
most painfully.

STRADER  This is the first time in these seven years
that I can hardly follow you.
For each experience of spirit used to be
a source of inner happiness for you.

THEODORA  Quite different is the revelation now.
At first, as earlier, I feel impelled
to blot out my own thinking. In former times,
when I achieved this inward emptiness,
a soft light would then weave around my soul
and spirit-pictures wished to form themselves.
But now there rises a repulsive feeling,
invisibly, – and I can tell quite clearly
the power that I feel comes from outside, –
and fear comes pouring then into my soul.
I cannot banish it; it takes control of me.
I long for flight from that dread Being
that is invisible, yet most abhorrent.
Filled with desire, it wants to move itself towards me
and I can only hate what is revealed.

STRADER  For Theodora this must be impossible.
They say, such an experience is usually

the working of the forces of one's soul, in
mirror-image.
But your soul could not show such things as this.

THEODORA (*reflecting, slowly and painfully*)
I know quite well this point of view.
Therefore with all the strength
still left within my soul, I let myself
sink fervently into the world of spirit
and prayed that all those beings who so often once
inclined themselves towards me would graciously reveal
how I could find the cause of all my pain.
And then . . . the radiant light . . . appeared . . .
as formerly . . . it shaped itself . . .
into the image . . . of an earthly man . . .
it was . . . Thomasius.

STRADER (*deeply afflicted, overcome by the quick inrush of feelings*)
. . . Thomasius . . .
The man in whom I always wanted to believe . . .
— — — — — — — — — — — — — — —
(*pause, then painfully reflecting*)

When I bring up before my inner being
how he, confronted by the occult brotherhood . . .
spoke there of Ahriman and of himself . . .

(*Theodora is lost in contemplation and stares into space as
if her spirit were absent.*)

O Theodora . . . what are you beholding . . . now? . . .

(*Curtain*)

## SCENE FIVE

*A room in the cottage shown in 'The Soul's Probation' as Balde's home.*
*Felicia, Felix, Capesius, Strader; later, The Soul of Theodora.*

FELICIA　　　　　We shall be able to perceive her being,
　　　　　　　　so radiantly lovely, only
　　　　　　　　when we ourselves set foot within the world
　　　　　　　　which took her from us all too soon.
　　　　　　　　A few short weeks ago we had the privilege
　　　　　　　　here in our home still to experience
　　　　　　　　how gentleness with warmth streamed through her
　　　　　　　　　　words.

FELIX　　　　　　We both, Felicia and I, loved her
　　　　　　　　from depths of inmost soul,
　　　　　　　　and so we, too, can understand your grief.

STRADER　　　　My own dear Theodora, – in her last hours
　　　　　　　　she spoke indeed of Felix and Felicia.
　　　　　　　　She was familiar with everything
　　　　　　　　about your daily life up here.
　　　　　　　　– – – – – – – – – – – – – – – –

　　　　　　　　Now I must grope my further path alone.
　　　　　　　　She was the substance and the meaning of my life.
　　　　　　　　What she has given me will never die,
　　　　　　　　and yet – she is not here.

| FELIX | With you, we shall send lovingly our thoughts |
| --- | --- |
| | to her in spirit worlds and be united still |
| | with her in times to come. |
| | But I must say, it was a shock to us |
| | to hear that she had met her earthly end. |
| | During the course of years an inner sight |
| | has grown in me that, quite unsought, |
| | reveals at certain moments |
| | a person's inward force of life. |
| | In her case has this inner sight deceived me. |
| | I truly took for granted, Theodora |
| | would be allowed for a long time to come |
| | to spread on earth that love through which |
| | she helped so many in their joy and sorrow. |

| STRADER | It is most strange, the way it came to pass. |
| --- | --- |
| | As long as I have known her, she has shown |
| | a sound and even disposition. |
| | But since the time she first became aware |
| | of something strange, unknown, that threatened her |
| | and tried to enter and oppress her mind, |
| | she grew immersed in gloomy thoughts, |
| | and sorrow poured itself through her whole being. |
| | One could observe then how some inner struggle |
| | consumed her body's strength. |
| | When often in my worry, I pressed her with my |
| | questions, |
| | she said she felt herself exposed to thoughts |
| | which frightened her, affecting her like fire. |
| | And what she further spoke – is terrible . . . |
| | In rallying her powers of thought, she strove |
| | to see what caused the suffering she felt: |
| | there always came before her spirit eye . . . |

Thomasius . . . he whom we both esteemed.
And yet from this impression there remained always
in her the strongest feeling, telling her
that she had cause to fear Thomasius . . .

CAPESIUS    Thomasius and Theodora must,
according to the strict decree of destiny,
never meet in earthly passion.
They would oppose the cosmic laws if either
should feel, about the other,
what is not founded purely in the spirit.
Thomasius violates within his heart
the stern decree of destiny's high powers:
he should not, in his soul, direct towards Theodora
thoughts that could cause her harm.
And yet he feels what he should never feel.
His disobedience has formed already
the forces which in future can deliver
his life to powers of darkness.
When Theodora had been forced to come
to Lucifer's domain, she sensed unconsciously
that, through the Spirit of the Light, Thomasius
was filled with sensual passion for herself.
Within that region hostile to the gods, there came
both Theodora and Maria, she
to whom by powers of destiny
Thomasius was entrusted in the spirit.
But there Maria was to be first severed from
Thomasius and he then bound to Lucifer
in future, through the strength of this false love.
What Theodora thus experienced
grew into a consuming fire in her soul
and working further, caused her all the pain.

| | |
|---|---|
| STRADER | Tell me, Felix, the meaning of all this. |
| | Capesius speaks so strangely |
| | of things that are incomprehensible, |
| | yet frightening and cruel to my soul. |
| | |
| FELIX | Capesius has been compelled to journey |
| | along the paths of soul which have, increasingly, |
| | from time to time led him perforce |
| | into this most unusual spirit mood. |
| | His spirit lives in higher worlds |
| | and passes by unnoticed all those things |
| | which through the senses whisper to man's soul. |
| | It seems by habit only he does all the things |
| | he used to do in daily life. |
| | He regularly visits his old friends |
| | and whiles away long hours with them, |
| | though even at their side he only seems |
| | to be turned in upon himself. |
| | Yet what he sees in spirit has been always right, |
| | as far as my own inner research |
| | could test it for its truth. |
| | Therefore I do believe in this case, too, |
| | that on his spirit path he could receive |
| | into his inmost soul |
| | the truth of Theodora's destiny. |
| | |
| FELICIA | It is so strange, he takes no notice |
| | of any conversations going on |
| | around him. It would seem as if his soul, |
| | freed from the body, gazes only into spirit worlds; |
| | and yet some word will often bring him back, |
| | out of his strange absorption, and from spirit realms |
| | he tells of things which somehow seem connected |
| | with what has just been said. |

At other times, whatever one may say
will pass him by as if his mind were absent.

STRADER        How frightful if he spoke the truth, how cruel . . .

(*Theodora's soul appears*)

THEODORA'S SOUL
               Capesius has been granted knowledge
               of my existence in the spirit land,
               and he proclaims the truth to you.
               We must not let Thomasius succumb.
               Maria has already set alight the sacrifice
               made to the might of love by her strong heart,
               and Theodora from the spirit heights
               will send out rays of blessing from the power of love.

(*Theodora makes the gesture of blessing.*)

FELIX          You must be silent now, dear Strader.
               She wants to speak to you. I understand
               the signs she gives to us; so listen.

THEODORA (*who has made a gesture of her hand toward Strader*)
               Thomasius has powers of seership, and he
               will also find me in the spirit realms.
               This must not come about until he searches for me,
               set wholly free from his dark passion.
               In future he will also need your help,
               and it is for this help I ask you now.

STRADER        O my Theodora, you are willing still
               to turn to me in love: now say
               what you desire. It shall be done.

(*Theodora makes a sign towards Capesius.*)

71

FELIX          She indicates she can no longer speak.
               She wants us now to listen to Capesius.

               (*Theodora's soul disappears.*)


CAPESIUS       Thomasius can use his spirit sight
               to gaze on Theodora. Therefore
               her death will not destroy in him
               the passion which is so destructive.
               He only must conduct himself quite differently
               from earlier times, when Theodora
               still lived within an earthly body.
               He'll strive with passion for the light
               that is revealed to her from spirit heights,
               although she has no longer earth-bound
                    knowledge.
               Thomasius is supposed to win this light,
               so that, through him, it is received by Lucifer.
               For Lucifer could use the light of gods
               to keep within his realm for evermore
               the science that Thomasius
               has gained through earthly forces.
               Since earth-beginning Lucifer has sought
               for men who through their false desires
               were able to acquire the wisdom of the gods.
               And now he wishes to unite pure spirit vision
               with human knowledge, in this way
               transforming into evil what is good.
               Thomasius, however, will be turned
               with certainty away from evil paths,
               if Strader gives himself to aims that in the future
               can change all human knowledge in a spiritual way
               to bring it closer to the knowledge of the gods.

In order that these aims can be revealed to him,
he must, as pupil, turn to Benedictus.

(*A pause.*)

STRADER      O Father Felix, give me your advice.
Was this in truth entrusted to Capesius
by Theodora, so that he could utter it to me?

FELIX      I often have of late held earnest converse
with my own inmost self about this man,
that I might clarify my thoughts.
I'll gladly pass this knowledge on to you.
Capesius is undergoing genuine
discipleship of spirit, though it seems
quite different now, if judged by his appearance.
His destiny has preordained that he
accomplish much in spiritual life.
He only can fulfil such lofty tasks
for which his soul has been selected,
if now his spirit can prepare itself for them.
And yet his inmost nature did not always choose
to seek the light on spirit paths,
preferring to devote itself to the false science
that blinds so many souls today.
The mighty guardian at the solemn threshold,
which separates the world of sense from spirit
    worlds,
had special obligations, strong and strict,
when he should find Capesius at the gate.
He had to open to the earnest seeker
but then to close the gate at once behind him, –
because the way he earlier had acquired his forces
in sense existence, now prevented him

from penetrating further into spirit realms.
He now can best prepare for the high service
he is to render in the future to mankind,
when he unheedingly ignores our presence.

FELICIA     There's only one thing he still notices
and that's the fairy tales I used to tell him
so often in those earlier days. Through them,
whenever he felt emptied out and stale,
his thinking was refreshed and fructified.

CAPESIUS    Such stories travel also to the spirit land,
if you can tell them only in the spirit.

FELICIA     So then, if I collect myself enough
to speak my tales in silence to myself,
I'll think of you with love – so that they may
be audible to you, as well, in spirit land.

(*The curtain falls.*)

# SCENE SIX

*A space not confined by artificial walls, but closed in by inter twining plants and forms which spread themselves and send out shoots towards the interior. The whole is in violent motion, caused by phenomena of nature, and at times filled with storms. Capesius and Maria are on the stage when the curtain opens. Later appear Benedictus, Philia, Astrid, Luna, The Other Philia, Lucifer and Ahriman, and Beings which move in a form of dance, representing thoughts; finally the soul of Felicia Balde.*

BENEDICTUS (*audible but not yet visible*)
               Within your thinking cosmic thoughts hold
               sway.

CAPESIUS       That is the solemn voice of Benedictus;
               his words are sounding forth in spirit here.
               They are the same that in the Book of Life
               are written for his pupils,
               and that, for earthly souls, are hard to grasp
               and even harder to experience.
               What region of the spirit land is this
               where words, which test men's souls on earth,
               can sound?

MARIA          You've been so long now in the spirit realms
               in such a way that much has been revealed,
               and still this place remains unknown to you?

75

CAPESIUS       What lives here in its deepest self
               can easily be grasped
               by souls accustomed to the spirit.
               Each thing explains itself through something else.
               The whole is full of light, although the part,
               seen by itself, is often dark.
               But when some spiritual essence must unite
               with earthly being for creative work,
               the soul begins to lose all comprehension.
               Then not alone the part: it is the whole
               that shrouds itself in darkness.
               Why, at this place, do words re-echo
               that can be found inscribed
               in Benedictus' book for men on earth?
               This turns to riddles all that happens here.


BENEDICTUS (*still invisible*)
               Within your feeling cosmic powers weave.


CAPESIUS       Again such words as are confided
               by Benedictus to his pupils on the earth,
               and here brought into being by his voice.
               Arousing powers of the dark, they stream
               throughout unending reaches of this realm.


MARIA          I feel already what I should experience
               within the boundless reaches of this place;
               and Benedictus is approaching me.
               He wants me to behold within this region
               what on the earth the soul can never understand
               while dwelling in a body, sense-endowed,
               even with the discipleship of spirit gained.
               My soul must follow him, the teacher, into regions

where words cannot be coined in human speech
as symbols only, of the beings here;
but where, in cosmic happenings, he calls forth
the script which offers to the soul
a breadth of meaning of all worlds.
I will, condensing forces of my soul,
detach my inner self from earth-existence
and so await what will emerge for me
as revelation of wide regions of the spirit
when I turn back to life on earth.
It will be thought which then in meditation
will shine as knowledge in my inner soul.

BENEDICTUS (*appears in the background*)

Gain your self in cosmic power of thought,
and lose your self through life in cosmic forces;
then you will find earth-goals that can
reflect themselves in cosmic light through your
own being.

CAPESIUS

Is Benedictus here himself in spirit
and not alone his words re-echoing?
The spirit teacher carries earthly knowledge then
to active life in regions of the spirit?
What do these words here signify,
to which on earth he gives a different turn?

BENEDICTUS

Capesius, you entered in your times
on earth my sphere of life
though you were never consciously my pupil.

CAPESIUS

Capesius is not here at this place.
His soul does not desire to hear of him.

BENEDICTUS    You do not wish to feel your self
within Capesius and yet you must,
remembering him, behold him spiritually.
For you, the strongly active force of thinking
has unlocked spirit-actuality
in your soul body. Your soul life freed itself
from all the dreaming play of thought
in your earth body. Yet it has felt itself
too weak to wander forth with it
from cosmic distances into soul depths; it felt
too strong to see with it the light
of spirit heights through darknesses of earth
      alone.
I must bear company with everyone who has received
the spirit light from me on earth,
if he with knowledge, or unconsciously,
has come to me as student of the spirit.
And I must guide him further on the paths
on which he has set out through me.
You have, through soul-sight, learned how to approach
the spirit knowingly in cosmic spaces,
for you can follow it, freed from your body.
But, not yet freed from thought, you cannot see
your own true being in the spirit sphere.
You can well lay aside your sense-bound body,
but not the fine corporeal web of thought.
You'll only see the world as fully real
when nothing of your personality remains
to dim the clearness of your vision.
He only who has learned to see his thinking
outside himself – just as the powers of seership
behold the body as a thing apart –
can penetrate to spirit-actualities.

Behold now thoughts in image form – in order that
   the image
be changed through your seer-forces into
   knowledge; –
such thoughts that shape themselves in space as
   beings
change then to forms that mirror human thinking.

(*A friendly subdued light; Philia, Astrid and Luna
appear in a glimmering cloud; Capesius and Maria
leave the stage.*)


VOICES (PHILIA, ASTRID *and* LUNA, *speaking in chorus*)


Now thoughts hover near
like weaving of dreams,
arising as beings
essential to souls;
self-quickening will,
self-wakening feeling,
self-mastering thinking
emerge for the dreamer.

(*As this resounds, Lucifer enters from one side, Ahriman
from the other, taking their places on either side of the
stage.*)


LUCIFER (*in a strong measured tone, emphasizing every word*)
   Within your willing cosmic beings work.

(*From Lucifer's side Beings, representing thoughts, draw
near. They carry out movements in a dance-like manner,
representing thought-forms corresponding to the words of
Lucifer.*)

79

AHRIMAN (*also in a strong measured tone, but roughly*)
        The cosmic beings are confusing you.

        (*In accord with these words, thought beings from the side of Ahriman move and carry out dance movements corresponding in forms to his words. After this the motions of both groups are performed in unison.*)

LUCIFER        Within your feeling cosmic forces weave.

        (*The thought beings on Lucifer's side repeat their movements.*)

AHRIMAN        The cosmic forces are misleading you.

        (*The thought beings on Ahriman's side repeat their movements; then both groups move again in unison.*)

LUCIFER        Within your thinking cosmic thoughts hold sway.

        (*Repetition of the motions by Lucifer's group.*)

AHRIMAN        The cosmic thoughts are disconcerting you.

        (*Repetition of the motions by Ahriman's group. Then four times a repetition of the movements of each group by itself, and three times in unison.*)

        (*The Thought Beings disappear left and right; Lucifer and Ahriman remain; Philia, Astrid and Luna come forward again out of the background and speak the words spoken before with the following alteration.*)

        So thoughts hovered near
        like weaving of dreams,
        arising as beings

essential to souls;
self-quickening will,
self-wakening feeling,
self-mastering thinking
emerged for the dreamer.

*(Philia, Astrid and Luna disappear; Capesius enters again and, after he has spoken a few words, Maria approaches, remaining at first invisible to him.)*

CAPESIUS      The soul lives out its life within itself,
believing that it thinks because it cannot
see thoughts spread out in front of it in space
believing that it feels, because the feelings
do not flash forth out of the clouds like lightning;
it sees the realms of space, and it perceives
the clouds above it . . .; and were this not so:
if lightnings were to flash, and no eye looked on
        them . . .
it would believe the lightnings must be in itself.
It sees not Lucifer from whom
thoughts spring to life, and from whom feelings flow.
Thus it believes it is alone with them.
Why does it give itself to such illusion?
O soul, give answer to yourself . . . yet . . . from
        where?
Out of yourself? O do not dare . . . perhaps
the answer too . . . is not from you . . . from
        Lucifer . . .

MARIA         And if it were: why then should you not seek?
Descend into the depths to find it there . . .

CAPESIUS      A being who is able to hear souls?

MARIA  The souls here are indeed not separate.
      That happens only when they use a body.
      Here each one hears himself in others' words.
      And thus you say it to yourself when I say this:
      search for the answer in the depths.

CAPESIUS  O, in the depths . . . there threatens darkest . . . fear.

MARIA  Yes, truly, it is there; yet ask yourself,
      since you have forced yourself into its realm,
      if clearly it reveals itself to you?
      And ask of Lucifer, whom you are facing,
      if he is pouring fear into your weakness.

LUCIFER  All those who flee from me, love me as well.
      The children of the earth have always loved me.
      They think, however, they should hate me.
      And yet they seek me for my deeds. They would
      have pined away in bounds of frigid truth
      throughout the earth's becoming,
      if I had not sent down into their souls
      beauty as life's adornment.
      I fill the artist's soul with my creative power.
      Wherever men perceive the beautiful,
      it has its archetype within my realm.
      Now ask yourself, should you fear me?

MARIA  In Lucifer's domains in truth
      fear is not in its rightful place.
      The gifts he sends into men's souls
      are the desires, but certainly not fear.
      Fear comes from quite another sphere of
        power.

AHRIMAN      In rank I was once equal to the gods.
But they curtailed perforce my ancient rights.
I wished to mould the human beings so
for Brother Lucifer and for his realm
that each should bear his own world in himself.
For Lucifer could only show himself
in spirit realms as equal among equals,
a model only, never
a ruler over beings.
I wanted therefore to give strength to man
to prove himself to Lucifer as equal.
And had I stayed within the realms of gods
this would have happened in primeval times.
The gods, however, willed to be the rulers upon
    earth;
they had to ban my power
out of their realm into the deep abyss
that I should not empower men too strongly.
Now only from this region am I able
to send my mighty power towards the earth.
It turns, however, on the way to . . . fear.

*(With Ahriman's last words Benedictus appears.)*

CAPESIUS      He who has heard what these two mighty ones
spoke from their places, sounding through the
    cosmos,
has hereby learned the way to search and find
both fear and hate in their own realms.

BENEDICTUS    In cosmic words now recognize yourself,
and feel yourself in cosmic powers of thought.
Since you could see outside yourself
what you were dreaming as your selfhood,

so find yourself and shudder not in future
to hear this word that rightfully resounds
and should confirm to you your own existence.

CAPESIUS      I may belong in future to myself again.
Now I will seek myself, because I dare,
beholding myself in cosmic thought, to live.

BENEDICTUS      And bind what you have won to everything
you formerly achieved, for world enrichment.

*(In the background Felicia Balde appears at Benedictus'
side in her ordinary garb.)*

FELICIA *(in a thoughtful voice, suitable for fairy tales)*
Once upon a time there lived
a light-filled child of gods.
It was akin to beings who with foresight weave
in spirit realms the web of wisdom.
Cared for by Father Truth, the child grew up
within its world to primal power.
And when it felt the ripened will
bestir itself creatively within its limbs of light,
it often looked with pity toward the earth
where human souls were longing for the truth.
Then spoke the child of light to Father Truth:
'Men thirst, O Father, for the drink
which you can offer them out of your springs.'
And Father Truth with earnestness replied:
'The springs which I must guard
let light stream forth from spirit suns;
and only those may drink the light
who never need to thirst for air to breathe.
On light, therefore, I have brought up the child

who feels compassion for the souls on earth
and can engender light in breathing beings.
So go, my child, and wend your way to men
and lead the light within them, spirit-kindled,
confidently forth to meet my light.'
Thereon the bright light-being made its way
to souls who feel their life by breathing.
It found good men in numbers on the earth
who offered it soul lodging joyously.
In faithful love it turned their gaze
unto the Father at the springs of light.
Now when this being heard from human lips
and happy human minds *Imagination*
as magic word, it felt itself
received with joy by friendly human hearts.
One day, however, there approached this being
a man who cast on it quite strange and chilling looks.
'I turn on earth the souls of men
toward Father Truth who tends the springs of light,'
thus spoke this being to the unknown man.
Then spoke the man: 'You weave wild dreams
in human spirits and deceive their souls.'
And since that day which saw this come to pass,
right many a man heaps slander on this being
that can bring light into the souls that breathe.

(*Philia, Astrid and Luna, and The Other Philia appear
in a cloud of light.*)

PHILIA          Let the soul find itself,
                by drinking the light,
                in cosmic expanses
                awakened to power.

ASTRID         Let the spirit, by knowing
no fear, feel itself
in cosmic unfoldment
arising with power.

LUNA          Let him who aspires
to reach to the heights
in life's firm foundations
sustain himself strongly.

THE OTHER PHILIA

Let man struggle on
to the bearer of light
who unlocks for him worlds
that liven and quicken
glad senses in man.
Inspired admiring
will lead on the spirit
to regions of gods
that waken a radiant
beauty in souls.
Achievement consoles
those feelings that dare
to step towards the thresholds
which strictly are guarded
from souls that feel fear.
And energy finds
a will that grows ripe
to face without fear
the powers creative
sustaining the worlds.

(*The curtain falls while all who were in the scene remain standing in their places.*)

# SCENE SEVEN

*A landscape of fantastic forms. Majestic in its composition of whirling masses of water, forming themselves into shapes, on one side; of blazing whirls of fire on the other. In the centre a chasm out of which fire blazes forth, towering up to form a kind of portal. Behind it mountain-like contours formed of fire and water. The Guardian, Thomasius, Maria; later Lucifer; then The Other Philia.*

THE GUARDIAN

What violent desires are here resounding!
So rage men's souls, that are approaching me
before achieving full serenity.
Such beings are impelled by strong desires,
not by the power which dares to speak
creatively because it could
create itself in silence.
The souls which show themselves in such a way
I must send back to earth,
for in the spirit regions they provoke
confusion only, and disturb the deeds
which cosmic powers wisely preordain.
To their own being also they do damage.
They breed destructive urges in themselves,
which they mistake then for creative power,
for they must take illusion for the truth,

when earthly darkness shelters them no
    more.

*(Thomasius and Maria appear.)*

THOMASIUS    You see, upon your threshold, not the soul
who came here often as Thomasius,
the spirit pupil of Benedictus,
although it still must call
Thomasius' form on earth its own.
He came to you, filled with a thirst for knowledge.
He could not bear your presence . . .
He wrapped himself, perceiving you,
into his selfhood; thus he often gazed
into such worlds as seemed to show to him
the origin of all existence
and the significance of life.
He found in them the blissfulness of knowledge,
found also forces that inspired the artist
to follow with his heart and hand
these traces of creation;
they led him to the firm belief
that cosmic powers were unsealed to him,
their actions caught in what he painted.
He did not know that nothing rose before him
in what he could creatively imagine,
except the content of his own soul-being.
And like the spider that will spin itself
into its web, he moulded his own self
and felt himself to be a universe.
Once he believed it was in truth Maria
confronting him in spirit; yet he saw
the picture only she had first engraved
into his soul, which showed itself as spirit.

88

And when he was allowed for fleeting moments
a glimpse of his own being as it really was,
he gladly would have fled away from self.
He thought himself to be in spirit, but he found
his inmost nature was united with his blood.
He learned to know the power of this blood;
this was reality, the rest imagination.
His blood alone gave him true spirit vision.
It was his real teacher. It revealed to him
who had, in long past times on earth
once been his father, been his sister.
His blood led him to blood relationships.
He knew then how the human soul
must greatly be deceived by the desire
to lift itself in vanity from matter to the spirit.
Such striving binds the soul, in truth, more firmly
to matter than a daily life, in which
men dreamingly, half conscious, spend their days.
And when Thomasius could view all this
as his own state, he gave himself
with vigour to that power which could not
deceive him, even though it showed itself
as semblance. For he realized
that Lucifer remains a real being, even
though he can only show himself in image-form.
The gods alone approach man in reality,
but Lucifer remains himself, regardless
of whether he is seen in truth or error.
Therefore I also recognize that I indeed
can sense reality when I believe
that I must find the soul which Lucifer
attached to me while in his kingdom.

Armed with the strength
bestowed on me by Lucifer, I mean
to force my way past you to Theodora.
She is, I know, within the realm
beyond this threshold.

THE GUARDIAN

Thomasius, reflect on what you know.
What is to be perceived beyond this threshold
is quite unknown to you; and yet you are
familiar with all I must demand
before you can set foot into this realm.
You must first separate yourself from many forces
you have acquired within your earthly body.
You can retain of them that force alone
which you achieved through pure and spiritual striving
and which has kept its purity.
But this you have yourself cast off from you
and rendered as his own to Ahriman.
What still belongs to you
is spoiled for spirit worlds by Lucifer.
I must deprive you of it here,
if you would cross this threshold rightfully.
Thus you have nothing left; – a being you will be,
without being, when you find yourself in spirit.

THOMASIUS

Yet I shall be, and then find Theodora.
She has to be the source to me of perfect light
that always can reveal itself so richly
without an earth-bound knowledge to her soul.
That is enough.
You will in vain oppose me, even though
the power I acquired on the earth

may not conform to the opinion
you once formed of the goodness of my spirit.

MARIA     It is well known to you, who's had to guard
the threshold of this realm since earth's beginning,
just what the beings of your kind and time
must have, in order to pass through;
and also men, who here encounter you,
have to turn back to life on earth
if they are bringing but themselves alone
and cannot offer genuine spirit substance.
But now Johannes was allowed to bring with him
to you and to your threshold here this other soul
who is so closely bound to him by destiny.
You are ordained by highest spirit powers
to bar the way for many human beings
who, drawing near the portal of this realm,
would only bring destruction to themselves
if they would pass beyond the threshold.
But you may open wide the gate for those
who turn their inmost self to purest love
and permeate themselves with it completely.
Such love your gods had preordained for them
before the battle Lucifer began to wage.
My heart has vowed, before the throne of Lucifer,
to render service to this love
so that no harm may come to it
in future times on earth, from the cognition
that streams from Lucifer into men's souls.
And human beings always must be found
who listen to what gods reveal to them
of purest love, as once they listened to the words
of Lucifer about cognition.

Johannes in his earthly body
no longer listens to my voice as once
he listened in our earthly lives long past.
I could reveal to him what was entrusted
to me within Hibernia's hallowed places
about the God who dwells in man
and who has conquered powers of death
because He brought to life within Himself
love's very essence.
My friend will hear again in spirit realms
out of my soul the word
for which his earthly hearing has been deafened
by Lucifer and his deluding powers.


THOMASIUS (*as one who spiritually beholds a being*)

Maria, do you see, dressed in long robes
that dignified old man, with solemn face,
his forehead noble, radiant his glance?
He walks through narrow, crowded streets
and everyone in reverence makes way
for him, so that he may pursue his path
in quiet, and his train of thought
not rudely be disturbed. For one can see
him musing, powerful in inward thought
upon essential things.
Maria, do you see him?


MARIA

Yes, I can see him
when I behold him with your eyes of soul.
He wishes at this moment
to show himself to you alone
in images of deep significance.

THOMASIUS    I now can look into his very soul;
             something of great importance lives within its
                 depths,
             a memory of what he just has heard.
             A teacher filled with wisdom stands before his
                 eyes.
             And through his soul flow words he's heard
             from this great teacher, from whom he just
             has come. His thoughts touch on
             the sources of all being:
             that men on earth once had true spirit vision,
             although their inner life was as a dream.
             The old man's soul is following trains of thought
             that he's received from the exalted teacher.
             And now he disappears from inner sight;
             O could I but behold him further!
             – – – – – – – – – – – – – – – – –
             Among the crowd I see some men conversing;
             I hear their words, –
             they speak of the old man with reverence.
             – – – – – – – – – – – – – – – – –
             He was in earlier years a valiant warrior,
             whose soul was burning with ambition
             and desire; he wished to count
             as foremost fighter in the ranks.
             He had committed countless cruelties
             while he bore arms; his one wish was to shine.
             There were some periods in his life
             in which he caused much blood to flow.
             At last there came the time when in the field
             his fortune suddenly deserted him.
             He rode from combat in disgrace and shame,
             back to his homeland. Scorn and ridicule

                             93

were heaped on him, and from that time
wild hatred filled his soul, which had not lost
its pride nor its ambition.
He saw in his own people only enemies,
to be destroyed at the first chance.
But soon, since his proud soul had to confess
that he could not wreak vengeance on his foes
within his lifetime, he controlled himself.
He overcame all pride and lust for fame.
Although he now was old, he still resolved
to join a little group of students
that at that time was forming in his city.
The teacher of this group possessed
within his soul the love and wisdom
which by the masters of primeval times
were handed down to the initiates.
All this I hear from men among the crowd.
— — — — — — — — — — — — — — — — —
I feel the warmest love when I direct
my inner sight toward this old man,
who first gained victories through love of fame
and then achieved the greatest victory men can:
the conquest of *himself*. —
Why do I, in this place, behold the man
to whom I wholly give myself,
although he only stands there as a vision?
The feelings that are mastering me
do not arise out of this single moment.
Through many lives long past I must be bound
to this soul-being whom I love like this.
I have not merely at this moment
aroused within myself this love I feel,
that is so powerful.

It must be a remembrance of ancient times;
though thoughts can hardly grasp these feelings yet,
my memory calls them up for me.
I must have been the pupil of this man,
and full of awe looked up to him.
Oh! at this moment how I long to find
the earthly soul again
that called this body once its own,
find it on earth or else in other realms.
I'll prove to it how strong my love still is.
It can renew in me good powers only,
which worthily once shaped such human bonds.

MARIA  And are you also sure, Johannes,
that this soul if it now draws near to you
will show itself upon the same bright peak
on which it stood in those far distant times
that rise in image form before your soul?
Perhaps it is now fettered by emotions
not worthy of the one it used to be.
Many a human being walks the earth
who would behold with bitter shame
how little in his present life there is
that corresponds to what he did before.
Perhaps this man is moved now by wild passions,
and lust – and you would see him only
with grief and consternation.

THOMASIUS  Why do you say all this, Maria?
I cannot understand what prompts you;
do thoughts move here in ways quite different
from those in places known to men?

THE GUARDIAN

Johannes, what reveals itself here at this place
is a probation of your soul.
Look down into the deepest layers of your being, –
this you have not in consciousness desired to do
and yet you well are able to. What in your depths
hid from you while you lived in inner blindness

(*Lucifer appears.*)

will now appear before you and will rob you
of the protecting darkness that you dwelt in.
So recognize what human soul it is
for whom you long with such a feverish love,
who lived within the body that you saw.
Perceive to whom you give your strongest love.

LUCIFER

Immerse yourself in depths of being
and recognize the strongest powers of your soul.
Now learn to know how strength of love
can hold you·upright in the progress of the
    world.

THOMASIUS

Yes, I can sense indeed the soul
that wished to show itself to me – Theodora –
She it was, who wanted to reveal herself to me.
She came to me because I shall behold her
when soon this portal will be opened up to me.
I am allowed to love her; that her soul
confronted me within the other body's form
proves it is she that I must love.
In you alone I now will rediscover
myself, and conquer, in your strength, my future.

THE GUARDIAN

> I cannot keep you back from what you have to do.
> As vision you already saw that soul
> which you love best; you shall behold it once again
> when you have passed beyond the threshold.
> Perceive it, and find out
> if it remains for you as beneficial
> as now you dream that it will be.

THE OTHER PHILIA

> O do not listen to the solemn Guardian;
> he leads you into desert spheres of life
> and robs you of your warmth of soul.
> He can behold but spirit beings
> and knows not human suffering,
> which souls can only bear
> if earthly love protects them from
> the cold of cosmic reaches.
> Austerity belongs to him,
> and gentleness escapes him.
> The powers of desire
> he has detested
> since earth's beginning.

> (*Curtain*)

# SCENE EIGHT

*Ahriman's kingdom. A dark gorge enclosed by mountains that tower up in fantastic forms out of black rock-masses. Skeletons appear everywhere as though crystallized, whitely, out of the rocks. Ahriman stands on a rocky slope. Hilary and Frederick Trautman enter; then Strader and the twelve persons gathered in Scene One; later Thomasius and Maria, the Guardian, and finally the Double of Thomasius.*

FREDERICK TRAUTMAN

How often now I've visited this realm –
and yet how horrible it always seems
that we should come down here to get advice
for enterprises that our Brotherhood
considers of importance for our goals.

HILARY

But every seed must first succumb to death
before the life can spring from it again;
in this place everything is to be found
that has been used up in the life on earth.
It is transformed down here to something
    new.
And if our Brotherhood will plant such seeds
as ripen into deeds in future times,
then it must fetch them from the realm of
    death.

FREDERICK TRAUTMAN

The lord who rules this place seems sinister;
and if it were not written in our books,
which are the greatest treasure of our temple,
that the being we encounter here is good,
one might suspect that he was evil.

HILARY       Not books alone; my spirit-vision, too,
tells me that what he can reveal is good.

AHRIMAN (*in a disguised voice*)

I know just why you two have come again.
You want to learn from me just how you can direct
the soul that many times has stood upon your
    threshold.
Since you regard Thomasius as lost,
you think that Strader now will be the man
to serve you for the mystic Brotherhood.
All he has mastered of the nature-forces
and given to the progress of mankind,
he owes to me, for I am in command
where forces that are useful in mechanics
receive their power from creative sources.
Thus all that he may still invent for man
will come back in the end to my account.
But this time I myself will take in charge the thing
that must be done for Strader in the future,
for in Thomasius' case your work
brought only loss to me and my designs.
If you desire to serve the spirit-powers,
why, first you still have to acquire
what you allowed in this case to be lacking.

(*Ahriman becomes invisible.*)

99

FREDERICK TRAUTMAN (*after a pause, during which he withdraws into himself*)

Respected master, I am greatly troubled.
I've tried a long time to suppress my worry,
because the strict rules of our Brotherhood
demanded I should treat it thus;
but many things I notice in our Order
make my soul-struggle difficult for me.
I wanted always to subordinate,
thankfully, my own darkness to the light
that you could give by virtue of your powers.
But when I saw, as frequently I did,
that you were really utterly deceived,
and that your words were proved by the events
gravely in error from the very outset,
I felt as though a dreadful nightmare
were pressing painfully upon my soul.
And now again your words fall into error,
for you believed that here we certainly
would hear some good things from this spirit.

HILARY

The cosmic ways are hard to understand.
Dear brother, it behooves us now to wait
until the spirit shows us the direction
that is in keeping with our whole endeavour.

(*Exeunt Hilary and Trautman.*)

AHRIMAN (*who has re-appeared*)

They see me, but they do not recognize me;
for if they knew who is the ruler here,
they never would have come here for advice.
And persons who were known to visit me
they would condemn to suffer in hell-fire.

*The group of people enter who, in Scene One, were assembled in the anteroom of the Brotherhood, but it is made plain that they are blind when they enter the realm of Ahriman. What they say is what lives in each soul, although they are unaware of it. They are experiencing in sleep unconscious dreams, which become audible in Ahriman's realm. Strader, however, who enters at the same time, is half aware of what is happening to him, so that he is able to recall it later.*

STRADER    The hints that Benedictus gave to me –
that I should cultivate my power of thought –
have led me to this kingdom of the dead.
I hoped, when lifted to the spirit, to receive
the truth from radiant worlds of wisdom!

AHRIMAN    The wisdom you can learn in this domain
will be sufficient for a long, long time, –
· if you conduct yourself accordingly.

STRADER    What spirit is my soul confronting now?

AHRIMAN    You'll know him later, when your memory
brings back to mind what you experience here.

STRADER    And then why do I find these people here
in your dark realm?

AHRIMAN    They only come as souls
into this place, and they know nothing in the least
about themselves, for all this time they can
be found submerged in deepest sleep at home.
But all that lives within their souls will be
revealed quite clearly here, though they themselves

are scarce aware of it when they're awake.
Also, they cannot hear what we are saying.

LOUISE FUERCHTEGOTT
      The soul should not believe, in blind devotion,
      that it can raise itself in prideful power
      up to the light, unfolding its full essence.
      I will acknowledge only what I know.

AHRIMAN (*audible only to Strader*)
      You do not know how blindly you are leading
      yourself, with prideful power, into darkness.
      She'll serve you, Strader, right well in the work
      that you'll achieve in future with my forces.
      For this she does not need belief in spirit,
      a thing unsuited to her haughtiness.

FREDERICK GEIST
      Alluring are the ways the mystics follow;
      I will in future never lack in zeal,
      but will devote myself to all the wisdom
      that can be gathered from the temple's words.

MICHAEL EDELMANN
      My soul's demand for truth is guiding me
      toward the spirit's light. The noble teachings
      that so illuminate our human life
      will surely find in me the best of pupils.

GEORGE WAHRMUND
      I'm always deeply moved by everything
      that is revealed to me from varied sources
      about the spirit-treasures of the mystics;
      with all my heart I will continue striving.

AHRIMAN (*audible only to Strader*)

> They mean it well, but all their striving sits
> in superficial layers of their souls.
> And so I will be able to employ
> for many years still all the treasures lying
> unconscious in their spiritual depths.
> They also will be useful to my goal:
> that Strader's work develop brilliantly
> within the life of men upon the earth.

MARIA TREUFELS

> A healthy view of life will of itself
> produce the fruits of spirit in the soul,
> if men unite a reverence for the world
> with sharp-eyed sense for all reality.

AHRIMAN (*audible only to Strader*)

> She speaks in dreams about reality;
> she dreams so much the better when awake.
> Thus she will serve me badly now, although
> in her next life perhaps she'll do much better.
> She will then be an occultist
> and on request describe for all and sundry
> their lives since the beginning of the earth.
> But loyalty's not in her; in one life
> on earth she scolded Strader viciously,
> while now she praises him; that's how things go.
> She will give Lucifer more cause for joy.

FRANCESCA DEMUT

> I think that mysticism, sought in earnest,
> will reshape human nature to a whole,

if thoughts allow the feelings proper scope
and feelings let themselves be led by thoughts.

KATHARINA RATSAM
I must admit men strive to see the light,
but do it often in the strangest way.
First they extinguish it, and then they wonder
why they can nowhere find it in the dark.

AHRIMAN (*audible only to Strader*)
These are the souls in whom a well-turned phrase
provokes the feeling that the world goes well,
but firmness is entirely lacking in them.
They're really inaccessible to me,
but in the future they'll do many things
that can be very fruitful for my ends.
They are by no means what they think they are.

BERNARD REDLICH
If caution's lacking in the search for knowledge,
our fancy brings in castles in the air
as answers to the riddles of the world,
though rigorous thinking is what they demand.

HERMINE HAUSER
Things in the world must be in ceaseless flux
if life's potential's fully realized;
if you would keep things as they've always been,
you lack the strength for understanding life.

CASPAR STUERMER
To live in fantasies can only be
to rob the soul of just the forces needed

to give it strength to render, here on earth,
the service needed by itself and others.

MARIE KUEHNE

A soul that is content to drift along
will let itself be shaped by outer forces;
a man becomes a personality
by working out what's hidden in his soul.

AHRIMAN (*audible only to Strader*)

What's hidden in their souls is only human;
one cannot tell what they may yet achieve.
I'll leave them to the wiles of Lucifer;
for he can make them actually believe
that they have mighty forces in their souls,
and thus perhaps they're not pure loss for him.

FERDINAND REINECKE

The one who wants to fathom cosmic riddles
should wait till understanding and good sense
develop in him of their own accord.
And he who wants to find his way in life
must seize what profits him and gives him joy.
To value wisdom above earthly things
and preach of lofty goals to feeble men
leads absolutely nowhere on this earth.

AHRIMAN (*audible only to Strader*)

This fellow is a born philosopher,
and really will be one in his next life.
With this one the account is balanced out.
Of twelve I must have seven for myself,
and five I'll give to Brother Lucifer.

From time to time I take a look at men
and study how they are, what they can do.
And when I once have picked out twelve of them,
I need not go on searching any more,
for when I come to thirteen in my count,
the last is clearly equal to the first.
So if I can lure twelve into my kingdom,
with all their different kinds of soul,
others will surely follow after them.

(*To himself, holding his hands over Strader's ears to keep
him from hearing.*)

I must confess I have not yet succeeded;
the earth would not surrender to my will.
But I will strive on through eternity
until – perhaps – I gain the victory.
One must make use of all that is not lost.

(*The following is again audible to Strader.*)

You see I do not speak in pretty words;
I'm never anxious to please anyone.
If you would like, by elegant orations,
to stir enthusiasm for your aims,
you'd best betake yourself to other worlds.
But if with reason and a sense for truth
you see the things that happen here through me,
then you will know that here are to be found
the forces without which the sons of men
must lose themselves in life upon the earth.
Even the world of gods has need of me,
for gods seduce the souls away from me
only when I have worked within their depths.
And if my adversaries then succeed

, making men believe that my existence
can be dispensed with in the universe,
then souls will dream indeed of higher worlds,
but genuine force will die away on earth.

STRADER      You see in me a soul who might be able
to follow you and give its strength to you.
What I have seen and heard here seems to show
that only lack of common sense and reason
lets men become your adversaries.
You surely did not speak in pretty words;
you seemed well pleased almost to mock these
     people,
as you described their future destinies.

— — — — — — — — — — — — — — —

I must confess that what you want to give
to human souls appears to me as good.
They'll gain in strength through you if they are good;
and if instead they should become more evil,
it will be only when the evil's there already.
Your mocking even could be well applied
by men to their own weaknesses with profit,
if they could only better know themselves.

— — — — — — — — — — — — — — —

But what is this that's bursting out of me?
The words that I have spoken would destroy me
if on the earth I found them all correct.

— — — — — — — — — — — — — — —

You *must* think thus, and I can only find
all that you said just now to be the truth;
but only in this place is it the truth,
and for the earthly world it is all error,
if there it proves to be what here it seems.

107

I may not here go further with my human thinking . . .
for it is at its end.

— — — — — — — — — — — — — — — — —

In your rough words there is the sound of pain
in you; and they cause pain in me as well.

— — — — — — — — — — — — — — — —

I must lament – beholding you – can only weep.

(*Exit quickly. Maria and Thomasius enter. Both are
fully conscious, so that they can hear all that happens and
can speak consciously.*)

THOMASIUS Maria, fear is flashing out all round me;
it's closing in and presses hard upon me.
Where will I find the strength to fight against it?

MARIA My holy solemn vow radiates strength.
If you will feel its healing influence,
your soul can soon endure the pressure.

AHRIMAN (*to himself*)
They have been sent to me by Benedictus.
He guided them so that they'll recognize me
when in my realm they come to feel my presence.

(*He speaks what follows in such a way that Thomasius and
Maria can hear him.*)

Thomasius, the Guardian had to guide
into my kingdom here the first steps that you made
to find the light within the depths of your own
  nature.
And I can give you truth, although with pain, –
pain, such as I too suffer for long ages;

because, although the truth can find me here,
it first must separate itself from joy,
before it dares to venture through my portals.

THOMASIUS     Then I will have to see without delight
              the soul I ardently desire to see.

AHRIMAN       Wishes content you only when soul-warmth
              can nourish them, but here they freeze
              and have to live in coldness evermore.

MARIA         And I must lead my friend into the empty,
              unmelting fields of ice, where now bursts free
              from bonds the light that must be formed
              by spirits, when the force of life is lamed
              by darkness. Now, Thomasius, feel your strength.

              (*The Guardian appears on the threshold.*)

AHRIMAN       The Guardian himself must bring the light
              that you have been so ardently desiring.

THOMASIUS     I shall be able to see Theodora!

THE GUARDIAN
              The soul that on my threshold stood before you
              within that body's sheath, that once it wore
              upon the earth so many years ago,
              has in this solemn hour of your life
              enkindled in your deepest soul-foundations
              the strongest love, concealed within you. –
              While you still stood outside the realm I guard
              and first requested that I grant admission,

that soul appeared to you in picture-form.
And pictures are illusions only if
they're born of wish. Now you shall see in truth
the soul that in a long-past life
once dwelt in that old man you saw.

THOMASIUS    Again I see him, dressed in the long robe,
that grave old man with earnest countenance.
O soul that lived once in this earthly sheath,
why do you hide yourself so long from me?
It must – it can – be only Theodora.
Now the reality is taking shape
out of distorted images – Theo . . . myself.

(*At the syllables Theo . . . the Double enters.*)

THE DOUBLE (*coming quite close to Thomasius*)
    Know what I am . . . behold yourself in me.

MARIA    And I may follow you to cosmic depths,
in which souls fight their way to a true feelin;
of gods through all-destroying victories,
that boldly from destruction wrench new life.

(*Rolls of thunder and increasing darkness.*)

# SCENE NINE

*A pleasant, sunny morning landscape, in the background a city with many factories. Capesius, Benedictus, Strader, Maria, Thomasius engage freely in conversation while walking back and forth.*

CAPESIUS (*alone*) Here is the place where Benedictus
　　　　　　so often, in the morning sunlight,
　　　　　　gives his time generously to his students,
　　　　　　and they may, in a mood of consecration,
　　　　　　receive his words of wisdom.
　　　　　　Far off there lies what cruelly must sever
　　　　　　the souls of men from all the glorious beauty
　　　　　　displayed by God-created Nature as a blessing.
　　　　　　In the vast stony desert of that city
　　　　　　is Benedictus always occupied
　　　　　　in healing sorrow by his deeds of love.
　　　　　　But when he speaks in words of wisdom
　　　　　　about the world of spirit to his students,
　　　　　　he wishes to find hearts, unlocked
　　　　　　by the free powers of creation here in nature,
　　　　　　which like the sun reveal themselves, awakening
　　　　　　　　souls. –
　　　　　　I, too, am now allowed to share the happiness
　　　　　　his words can bring to all who hear them.
　　　　　　He lovingly took on the spirit burden
　　　　　　of guiding me into the spirit world.
　　　　　　And so I feel, when I am near him
　　　　　　that I have been returned to my own self.

III

BENEDICTUS (*joins Capesius*)

> There shall, through your free deed in future
> and deeds of others in the circle of my students,
> a knot be loosened formed by threads
> that karma spins in earth-becoming.
> All you experienced must serve this loosening.
> In human hearts which follow with devotion
> the spirit guidance that I serve, myself,
> your strength can find the helpers, joined
> with whom you will complete the work
> for which you were prepared in spirit.

CAPESIUS

> I've learned to know you and I'll follow you.
> When I had been allowed to hear your words
> as beings in the spirit worlds,
> and you had brought me to myself again,
> I held communion with my soul.
> Then I perceived within the spirit light
> the goals toward which in progress of the earth
> my future lives shall be devoted.
> I am convinced by now, you chose
> to show to me the paths that I should take.

BENEDICTUS

> United with you, Strader and Thomasius
> in future will be able to accomplish much
> for the right progress and the good of men.
> The forces of the soul which they possess
> have been prepared since earth's beginning
> in such a way that in the cosmic course
> they can unite now with your spirit
> to form a triad filled with strength.

CAPESIUS

> So I must thank my destiny's stern powers
> which had to be at first incomprehensible,
> that they at the right moment showed me clearly
> the aims that make my life now meaningful.

*(He pauses, pondering.)*

How wondrous was your guidance.
It seemed at first as if I strove in vain
to enter with my spirit consciously
those worlds your words had put before my soul
in concept-form. When in your books I laboured deeply
for many years I could find only thoughts.
And then quite suddenly, I had around me
the spirit world in its reality –
I hardly knew then how to find myself aright
in my accustomed, earlier world.

BENEDICTUS  Through its effective power, this former world
would always have concealed from you the life of
    spirit,
unless the stronger nature of this spirit life
had not subdued the world of sense
into a thin and shadow-like existence.
You therefore with full spirit vision must perceive
yourself upon the threshold which
for others opens first the eyes of soul.

*(During the last words of Capesius, Strader joins them; the three go away together, and after a short time Benedictus returns with Strader.)*

STRADER  Deep pain I felt within my inner being
mounting like heavy pressure on the soul
when, on awakening,
I recognized myself again within
the body from which your words had guided me.
I was tormented first by my half-conscious
soul-life, yet it was more than torment,
for it brought forth the memory of all
I had lived through before I saw, with terror,
what I just learned from Ahriman:

all thinking must come to a standstill there.
And then I had to ask myself:
why did the words of Benedictus take me
into that realm where souls are merely counted
and where each soul is valued for its help
towards that Power's aims to shape
to his own purposes what I have done?
He in his wisdom wanted to select
from the full count of men, twelve for his work.

BENEDICTUS    You surely know quite well why all these souls,
displayed by Ahriman, drew near to you
when he by force intruded in their destinies?

STRADER    This, too, my pain made very clear to me.
It showed how in an earthly life, long past,
I was connected with an Order
which now has formed the Occult Brotherhood.
It showed too my relationship to all
those people who revealed their actual selves.
And I could feel that Ahriman intends
to use these ties which in our future lives
must firmly bind their souls to mine.

BENEDICTUS    The cosmic powers guide their deeds so that
in strict accord with measure and with number
they follow wisely cosmic progress.
The outer token of this ordering
shows itself clearly to the earthly senses
when they observe the sun upon the course
it takes through the twelve stellar constellations.
The way that it relates itself to these
reveals how on the earth things come to pass
in the successive periods of time.
So Ahriman desired to use those souls
who are united with you, for energies

from which your work can radiate forth.
He wished by measure and by number
to bind your own soul fast to theirs.

STRADER     Since I have learned to understand the meaning
            of number and of measure, I'll succeed
            in rescuing my work from Ahriman's domain
            and offering its results to gods of earth.

BENEDICTUS  You've had to recognize the sense of number
            within the universe, through power of Ahriman;
            this way was necessary for your soul.
            Your spirit training led you to this realm,
            which you must recognize,
            if your creative power shall rightly blossom forth.

            (*The two walk away; from the other side Maria and
            Thomasius enter.*)

MARIA       Johannes, you have conquered and brought knowledge
            out of the icy realms of truth.
            And you'll no longer weave in images
            as souls live them like dreams within their bodies.
            For far from cosmic progress are the thoughts
            that merely self-begotten come to life.

THOMASIUS   And that they do so, springs from love of self,
            pretending to be thirst for knowledge.

MARIA       Whoever wants to dedicate himself
            to human progress and perform such works
            as prove essential forces in the course of time,
            must first entrust himself to just those powers
            which bring, in deep realities, measure and number
            into the battle between order and confusion.
            Knowledge, in truth, will only come to life

and manifest itself within the soul
if it can bring to men, in earthly bodies,
the memory of life in spirit realms.

THOMASIUS    My course of life is then marked out for me.
All that I am, I have to feel as double nature.
Through Benedictus and your help
I am a being that exists apart,
whose forces do not yet belong
to my own nature stirring still within me.
What both of you have given me
is for itself a human being
who must give willingly to other men
what has been granted him through spirit training.
He shall devote himself now to the world
as best he can; but with this new man in him
nothing of the other one must mingle,
the one who senses that he only is
at the beginning of a true self-knowledge.
Contained in his own world, he will go on, –
if his own strength and if your help enable him
to shape in future his own destiny.

MARIA    Whether you walk your path in truth or error
you can keep ever clear the view ahead
so that your soul is able to pursue its way.
For this you must with courage bear necessities
stemming from the nature of the spirit realm.

(*Curtain*)

# SCENE TEN

*The temple of the Occult Brotherhood that appeared in Scenes One and Two.*
*Standing in the East are Benedictus and Hilary; in the South, Bellicosus*
*and Torquatus; in the West, Trautman; then enter Thomasius, Capesius,*
*Strader, Maria, Felix and Felicia Balde; later, the Soul of Theodora; and*
*finally the four Soul Forces.*

BENEDICTUS    My pupils have unlocked their souls, each
in his own way, in order to receive
the spirit light according to his destiny.
What they have conquered for themselves
each one shall render fruitful for the others.
But this can only happen if their powers,
in harmony of measure and of number,
form willingly a higher unity
together at this sacred place. This unity
alone can waken to true life what otherwise
could merely stay as single bare existences.
They stand upon the threshold of this temple.
So may their separate souls now join themselves
to sound in unison, attesting to the principle
recorded in the book of cosmic destiny:
that harmony of spirits may achieve
what each alone could never bring about.
These will bring something new to what is old
and has so nobly ruled since earliest times.
To you, dear brothers, I present these pupils, who
have had to take their paths through worlds of spirit

and through their soul probations to this place.
They'll honour reverently the ancient customs
and ancient, holy, mystic rites, which here
are manifest as power of spirit light.
To you who have so long and faithfully
discharged your solemn duties to the spirit
will other work be given in the future.
Now sons of men are called by cosmic destiny
into the sacred temples for a certain time,
and it will summon them to other tasks
when, in this service, they exhaust their strength.
The temple, even, faced its own probation
when in a cosmic moment fraught with destiny,
the error of one man had to protect
this guardian of the light against the darkness.
Thomasius recognized, by way of knowledge
that lives unconsciously in human souls:
his journey to this sacred temple
could never carry him beyond its threshold
before he stepped across that other one,
of which this portal here is but a symbol.
So voluntarily he shut the door
which you in kindness would have opened wide.
He now returns transformed to you,
in worthy manner to receive your consecration.

HILARY        Our souls give humbly to the spirit here
what will bear fruit within men's inmost being.
We strive to let our own will be
the revelation of the spirit will.
The temple's guidance is the cosmic wisdom
which resolutely leads us to the future.
You point out the direction you could read
within the book of cosmic destiny,
as your disciples passed through their probation.

So let them enter now this sacred place
that they may join their work with ours.

(*After Hilary knocks three times, there enter the
temple: Thomasius, Capesius, Strader, Maria, Felix
and Felicia Balde; Trautman and Torquatus lead
them in, so that Thomasius takes his place in front
of Benedictus and Hilary, Capesius in front of Bellicosus
and Torquatus, Strader in front of Trautman; Maria,
Felix and Felicia Balde take their places in the centre.*)

HILARY (*to Thomasius*)

My son, the words one utters at this place give rise –
if truth alone does not direct the speaker –
to spirit guilt, which rends the spirit worlds with
    cries.
As great the guilt, as great also the forces
arising from the guilt, that will strike down
the speaker who's unworthy of this office.
Aware of the effect of temple words,
the one who stands before you did his best,
to the last limit of his strength, to serve
the spirit, at this holy symbol of the light
that shines out of the East upon the earth.
It is the will of destiny that you
shall henceforth hold this place in spirit service.
The one who has the obligation to ordain you
and hand to you the key of his high office
gives you with this his blessing; may it prove
for you of service in so far as he himself
has served the sacred customs worthily.


THOMASIUS

Exalted Master, it would be presumptuous
of the frail mortal now permitted
to stand before you bodily, to wish

he might succeed you in your office
within this age-old consecrated place.
He is indeed not worthy to set foot
upon the threshold of this sanctuary.
But what he could not wish for, for himself,
must be accepted with humility,
since powers of fate out of necessity desired
to send the summons to his soul.
Not I, the one I am in life, who saw himself
in spirit recently as fully worthless,
dare to approach this place.
But Benedictus and my friend have fashioned
for this man visible before you
a second being, whom the first unworthy one
must serve in future only as a bearer.
Discipleship of spirit now has given me
a self that can prove strongly able
to unfold its full, creative power
even while this bearer knows himself to be
still far removed from highest aims of soul.
If, in this situation, duty tells him
to offer to the progress of the earth
his second self awakening in him,
there must as beacon for his spirit eye
at all times stand before him
the strictest rule of life:
that nothing of his lower self must cause disturbance
within the work his second self,
not he himself, has to perform.
He will work actively, withdrawn within himself,
in order later to achieve the goal
of his own being, which he knows to lie
in the far distant future.
His own anxieties he'll take with him
through life, locked fast within his inmost soul.
That with my ordinary human nature

I am not capable of entering the temple,
I had to tell you, when at first you summoned me.
The one, who as a second self has come to him
in trust, perceives that destiny has laid
on him the duty and the task of watching over
the consequences of his work, as long
as he is ordered in this by the spirit.

TORQUATUS (*to Capesius*)
Capesius, henceforth you will perform
the service of our consecrated temple,
where into wisdom love should stream with warmth,
as the sun's power streams warmly forth at noon.
The one who wants to serve the spirit
with sacrifice, as is the way with mystic works,
must be aware of dangers. Lucifer
can stealthily draw near to him who serves
the spirit and imprint upon his words
the seal of the opponent of the gods.
You stood before this adversary's throne
and saw the consequences of his deeds;
hence for this office you are well prepared.

CAPESIUS
When one has seen the adversary's realm,
as powers of destiny have granted me to do,
he knows that good and evil are but words
almost incomprehensible to men.
Whoever says that Lucifer is only evil
might also say that fire is evil, too,
because its power can do away with life;
he might call water evil, since a man
might easily be drowned in it.

TORQUATUS
So Lucifer appears to you as evil
through other things, but not
through what he, in his being, signifies.

CAPESIUS       The cosmic spirit, who at earth's beginning
could bring the light to human souls,
must render service to the universe.
That spirit's work is neither good nor bad,
when spirits view it who have learned
to see what stern necessity reveals.
Good turns to evil if an evil mind,
destructive in itself, makes use of it.
And what seems evil may be changed to good
if some good being offers it its guidance.

TORQUATUS    You know what your continuing need will be
in standing at this place.
Not by mere reasoning does love evaluate
the forces that the universe reveals.
It treasures them, however they spring forth
and asks how it may use what is so able
to bring itself to life out of world depths.

BENEDICTUS   Yet love speaks often with a gentle voice
and needs support within the depths of soul.
It should unite with everything
that will devote itself in noble threefoldness
here at this place in harmony with cosmic law.
Maria will unite her work with yours.
The vow she took in Lucifer's domain
shall radiate for you its strength.

MARIA         The words Capesius spoke were of such depth
that only when they spring forth from the spirit
which guides mankind in progress of the earth
towards love, do they reveal the truth.
These words, however, will heap error upon error
when they're distorted by a vicious mind
and change to evil then in souls of men.

For Lucifer, in truth, reveals himself
as bearer of the light to eyes of soul
that turn themselves toward spirit distances.
But man's soul-being wishes ever to arouse
within its inmost depths, as well,
what it should only gaze on and admire.
It should behold the beauty that is Lucifer's
but never fall beneath his sway
by letting him work actively within.
He, Bearer of the Light, rays wisdom forth;
he fills the worlds with proudest sense of self
and brilliantly projects into all beings
himself as model of courageous selfhood;
then may the inward life of men,
rejoicing in the senses, shine out like Lucifer
and, filled with happy wisdom, radiate
the life of *Self* and love of *Self* in life.
But more than any other spirit, man has need
of that one God Who does not merely ask
for admiration, when He manifests Himself
within the glory of the outer world,
but Who rays forth His highest power only
when He Himself dwells in man's inmost being
and, in His love, transforms death into life.
A man may turn toward Lucifer
and warmly feel inspired by his bright glory;
he may in that way well experience himself
but he should not take Lucifer into his *will*.
A man, however, when he rightly understands
himself, will call out to that other Spirit:
this is the goal of love for earthly souls,
'Not I, but Christ lives in my life and being'.

BENEDICTUS (*turning to Maria*)

When now her soul turns to the spirit
as she has vowed before the throne of Lucifer,

then through her strength the temple shall gain light
to show the paths of earth-salvation,
and Christ will warmingly shine forth
a spirit sense of love in wisdom's hallowed place.
What she can offer to the world
is bound to her own course of life
by one of many knots of destiny
which karma forms in human lives on earth.
In a long past existence, she estranged
the son from his own father; and now back
to him again she leads the son.
The soul that lives within Thomasius
was in that former life by ties of blood,
as son, bound to the soul
which feels itself now in Capesius.
The father will not any longer through the might
of Lucifer demand the debt Maria owes,
for through the power of Christ she has annulled it.

MAGNUS BELLICOSUS (*speaking to Hilary and Benedictus, and often
turning to Felix and Felicia Balde*)
Into the sacred places shines that light
which powerfully flows from spirit heights
if souls are worthy to receive it.
But those high powers of wisdom
who thus reveal themselves in occult temples,
have chosen also other paths to souls.
The signs of our own time proclaim distinctly
that all the paths should now be joined in one.
The temple must unite itself with souls
who've reached the spirit light in other ways,
yet are, in truth, illumined inwardly.
In Felix and Felicia there enter
this sacred place two human beings now
who can bring light to it in rich abundance.

FELICIA

I can but tell the fairy tales
which form themselves to images within.
I only know of their true spirit sources
from what Capesius has often told me.
In all humility I must believe
what he has said about my gift of soul;
and so I will accept what you have said
as to the reason why the temple summoned me.

FELIX BALDE

I followed not alone the outward call
the guardian of this temple sent to me.
True to the goal of my own spirit path,
I have obeyed that inner power
in the direction it has always counselled me
to turn my steps, so that I best fulfil
what by the spirit has been preordained for me.
This time I was directed clearly
to just that path in spirit life
which Benedictus now has shown his pupils.
Before I came, a premonition showed me
the signs that now I find here in the temple.
For many times my soul descended into depths,
and all the personal in me was cast away,
and strength and patience could maintain
    themselves,
despite the fearful loneliness that comes
before I am allowed to sense the spirit light:
then all the universe seemed one with me.
I found myself within that world
which manifests the sources of existence.
During such spirit journeys I was often
within a temple which it seems to me
relates to this one here, apparent to the senses,
as sounds of spoken words relate to written script.

TRAUTMAN (*to Strader*)

> Dear Strader, at this place your task will be
> to speak the words which, when compared
> to what Thomasius has to proclaim,
> are as the setting sun to morning's hopeful rays.
> These words, within their meaning, will seize
> with keenness on the working of that power
> which showed itself to you at your probation.
> You had to step into the spirit realm
> that brings all thinking sternly to a standstill.
> Just as your hand would have to swing the hammer
> into the void, and your own strength
> could never become conscious of itself,
> unless the blow struck down upon an anvil,
> so thinking could not fathom its own nature
> if Ahriman would not oppose himself to it.
> Throughout your life, your thinking cast you up
> on rocks of opposition which have caused
> within your soul grave doubts and sufferings.
> You learned on them to know yourself in thinking,
> just as the light can only see itself
> with its own power of radiance, through its
>    reflection.
> The words of him who serves the temple at this place
> show life's reflection thus in picture-form.

STRADER

> Indeed, the light of thought for a long time
> shone into my existence only through reflection.
> But then for seven years the spirit
> revealed itself to me in all its splendour
> and showed me worlds before which, earlier, my thinking
> stood still in torment and in doubt.
> Within my soul this light must grow so deep
> that it shall last through all eternity,
> am I to find the path to spirit goals,
> and blessing is to flow from my creative work.

THEODORA (*becoming visible as a spirit being at Strader's side*)
Because your strength was striving toward my light,
I was allowed to gain the light for you
as soon as your right time had been fulfilled.

STRADER    Your light, my spirit messenger, shall radiate
on all the words which at this place
are wrung out of my soul.
For Theodora's self now too, with mine,
is consecrated to the temple's holy service.

(*Philia, Astrid, Luna and The Other Philia appear in glowing cloud of light.*)

THE OTHER PHILIA
Thoughts are arising
from altars as offerings
to primal world sources.
What in souls is alive,
what in spirits is shining
soars up from worlds of form;
and cosmic mights incline themselves
in grace to human beings,
to kindle
in powers of soul
the spirit light.

PHILIA    I will entreat the cosmic spirits
that their true being's light
sustain the sense of soul
and that the sounding of their words
set free the spirit ear;
that never be extinguished
what here has been awakened
on paths of soul
in human lives.

ASTRID        I will direct the streams of love
that fill the world with warmth
toward spirit realms
for those who here are consecrated,
so that the mood of consecration
continue steadfast
in human hearts.

LUNA        I will implore from primal powers
courage and strength
and let them help
self-sacrifice to grow,
so that what is perceived
as temporal
can be transformed
to seeds of spirit
for all eternity.

*(The curtain closes while everyone is still in the temple.)*

# THE SOULS' AWAKENING

SOUL AND SPIRIT EVENTS

IN DRAMATIC SCENES

*by*

RUDOLF STEINER

translated by Ruth and Hans Pusch

## THOUGHTS ON THE SEAL

When the eye rests for the first time on the design as a whole, it is most intrigued and impressed by the picture of the snake, forming the outer circle, as it were, in a protecting gesture. It brings to mind the situation in Goethe's Tale of 'The Green Snake and the Beautiful Lily' when the green snake formed a wide circle around the lifeless body of the Youth, and, 'seizing the end of her tail between her teeth, she lay quite still'.

But the picture, as it presents itself here, wants to tell us much more. Is it not puzzling that the mouth of the snake is open and that the tail does not touch it? It 'breathes' a mystery which unravels gradually when one tries to forget for a moment the complete design, and begins with the so obtrusive ring in the centre. One can identify oneself with it by feeling the smallness and within-oneself-secluded day-reality of Self. The person one is in this present incarnation has his own limited horizon; he lives in a world which he is shaping into his own world of soul. It is a decisive step when one tries to reach out to what is around and about one, what goes beyond this ring-existence.

3

In the drawing, this step is made by the twelve lines of radii in the direction towards the periphery. Three of them, on the left side, show a zig-zag form, reminding one of the dynamics of lightning. With this twelvefold direction one is already aware of a world outside oneself; one may call it a world oriented to the cosmos.

What one next meets in the design is a complete surprise. Letters, forming words, are displayed in a circle. One may remember that the spirit-researcher speaks of illumining guidelines which can be seen and read in the 'astral light' of the cosmos. Something similar is expressed here. Where the zig-zag lines have attracted our attention, we begin to read:

ICH ERKENNET S ... up to here the circle is complete. We grasp the meaning, and read on by adding the next three letters which overlap: ICH. 'ICH ERKENNET SICH.' In English, a not quite satisfying equivalent would be SELF KNOWS ITS (ELF). It can be taken as a cosmic script, expressing the task of man's repeated lives on earth: that the I recognizes itself.*

It is worth the effort to dwell on this mantric line with the awareness of its cognitive character. It speaks to one's mind as a challenge to thinking. Then one is prepared to appreciate the next step in the drawing: the thought transforms itself into a picture. Now one has arrived at the image of the snake, forming a circle by turning its tail towards itself. Moreover, the three zig-zag lines point in the direction of the letters T S I and from there to the tail, approaching the open mouth, and the opened, watchful eye of the snake. The mystery that 'breathes' there is the awakening of the higher self in man. It becomes aware of the task to let live and weave and breathe in itself the Spirit in the Paulinean sense of the word. The ancient symbol of the snake that 'seizes the end of her tail between her teeth' is a pre-Christian one. With the design for the 'Awakening of Souls', something is brought into the picture which is deeply connected with Theodora's prophetic vision in the First Scene of

*In the design, the 'J' is the curved form of 'I'.

4

*The Portal of Initiation*: 'Not I, but Christ lives in my life and being.'

There is still another riddle left to be solved in the fact that the three zig-zag lines, the letters TSI and the tail and face of the serpent are placed at the left side of the circular drawing. There is a certain orientation evident, which could be connected with the four main directions in which the altars of the Sun Temple as initiation center are oriented, the Eastern altar in the zenith, the others clockwise, so that the Northern altar stands at the left side. The design for the fourth play emphasises this Northern aspect. It has to do with the encounter of the forces of evil, in our time predominantly the ahrimanic forces. It makes sense that the three letters TSI in their sequence are part of the mantric line, described above. Read backwards, IST, they express as 'IS' a state of mere existence without the I's activity, the ahrimanic aim in earth evolution.

The most decisive moment in the struggle with Ahriman is the time between lives when the souls of men prepare themselves in the spirit world for the shaping of a new earthly body, during the so-called cosmic midnight. It is portrayed in Scenes Five and Six of this fourth play. One can assume then that the North must play a vital part. Looking at the composition of the design with its emphasis on the dynamics of the left side, the words of the Guardian of the Threshold toward the end of Scene Six verify the significance of the North:

> So shall the lightning melt now into naught,
> having shone dazzlingly on *what must be*
> when wakeful souls live through the Cosmic North.
> Thunder shall lose its rumbling, rolling tone
> of warning at the cosmic midnight hour.'

After having gone through the process of developing the design step by step, from the centre to the periphery, the eye looks again at that tiny ring, expressing the limits of our Self. Now it grows to something stronger, a condensed mirror-image of the circumference, not shrunk to a point, but a spheric microcosmic, living image of its macrocosmic origin.

HANS PUSCH

# THE SOULS' AWAKENING
## SOUL AND SPIRITUAL EVENTS
## IN DRAMATIC SCENES

BY

RUDOLF STEINER

The occurrences of a spiritual and soul character portrayed in 'The Souls' Awakening' are to be considered as following at about a year's interval those described in the preceding play, 'The Guardian of the Threshold'.

*Persons, Spiritual Figures and Happenings*

I. THE BEARERS OF THE SPIRITUAL ELEMENT:

1. Benedictus: The personality whom a number of his students consider the discerner of profound spirit happenings. In the preceding soul portrayals, *The Portal of Initiation, The Soul's Probation,* he is represented as the leader of the Sun Temple. In *The Guardian of the Threshold* there is expressed in him that spiritual current which wishes to replace traditional spirituality, protected by the mystic brotherhood, by a modern, alive spiritual life. In *The Souls' Awakening* Benedictus should not be considered as merely standing above his students, but as interwoven with his own soul destiny in the inner experiences of his students

2. Hilary Gottgetroy: The knower of a traditional

7

spiritual life which is connected with his own spirit experiences. He is the same individuality who appears in *The Soul's Probation* as Grand Master of an occult brotherhood.

3. The Business Manager of Hilary Gottgetroy.
4. The Secretary of Hilary Gottgetroy, the same personality as Frederick Geist in *The Guardian of the Threshold*.

II. THE BEARERS OF THE ELEMENT OF DEVOTION:

1. Magnus Bellicosus, called Gairman in *The Portal of Initiation*. In *The Soul's Probation* and in *The Guardian of the Threshold* he is the Preceptor of an occult brotherhood.
2. Albert Torquatus, called Theodosius in *The Portal of Initiation*. The same individuality appears as the First Master of Ceremonies of the occult brotherhood in *The Soul's Probation*.
3. Professor Capesius: His individuality appears in *The Soul's Probation* as First Preceptor.
4. Felix Balde: As the bearer of a certain Nature-Mysticism in *The Portal of Initiation*; here in *The Souls' Awakening* as the bearer of subjective mysticism. His individuality appears as Joseph Kean in *The Soul's Probation*.

III. THE BEARERS OF THE ELEMENT OF WILL:

1. Romanus: Here re-introduced under the name used for him in *The Portal of Initiation*; this is in accordance with the core of his being which he has been endeavoring to reach in the years lying between the first and the fourth play. Frederick Trautman is his name in the physical world, used when his inner

8

life has very little to do with the occurring events. His individuality appears in *The Soul's Probation* as Second Master of Ceremonies of the medieval occult brotherhood.

2. Dr. Strader: His individuality appears in *The Soul's Probation* as Simon, the Jew.

3. The Nurse of Dr. Strader: The same personality as Maria Troyfels in *The Guardian of the Threshold*. In *The Portal of Initiation* she is known as The Other Maria because the imaginative cognition of Johannes Thomasius forms the imagination of certain powers of Nature in her image. Her individuality appears as Bertha, Kean's daughter, in *The Soul's Probation*.

4. Felicia Balde: Her individuality appears in *The Soul's Probation* as Dame Kean.

IV. THE BEARERS OF THE ELEMENT OF SOUL:

1. Maria: Her individuality appears in *The Soul's Probation* as the Monk.

2. Johannes Thomasius: His individuality appears in *The Soul's Probation* as Thomas.

3. The Wife of Hilary Gottgetroy.

V. ENTITIES OF THE SPIRIT WORLD:

1. Lucifer.

2. Ahriman.

3. Gnomes.

4. Sylphs.

VI. ENTITIES OF THE HUMAN SPIRITUAL ELEMENT:

1. Philia ⎫ The spiritual entities who further the
2. Astrid ⎬ uniting of human soul powers with the
3. Luna ⎭ cosmos.

4. The Other Philia: The bearer of the element of love in that world to which the personality belongs.
5. The Soul of Theodora: Her individuality appears in *The Soul's Probation* as Celia, the foster daughter of Kean and sister of Thomas.
6. The Guardian of the Threshold.
7. The Double of Johannes Thomasius.
8. The Soul of Ferdinand Fox in Ahriman's realm (Scene Twelve): He appears as Ferdinand Fox only in *The Guardian of the Threshold*.
9. The Spirit of Johannes' Youth.

VII.

The personalities of Benedictus and Maria also appear as thought experiences; in Scene Two as those of Johannes Thomasius; in Scene Three as those of Strader. In Scene Ten Maria appears as thought experience of Johannes Thomasius.

VIII.

The individualities of Benedictus, Hilary Gottgetroy, Magnus Bellicosus, Albert Torquatus, Strader, Capesius, Felix Balde, Felicia, Romanus, Maria, Johannes Thomasius, Theodora appear in the spirit region of Scenes Five and Six as souls; in the temple of Scenes Seven and Eight as personalities living in a far distant past.

In regard to 'The Souls' Awakening', a remark may be added similar to that made about the preceding soul portrayals. Neither the spiritual and soul events nor the spirit beings are intended to be mere symbols or allegories. To anyone interpreting them as such, the real character and being of the spirit world will remain closed.

Even in the appearance of personalities as thought experiences

(Scenes Two, Three and Ten) nothing merely symbolical is portrayed; they are genuine experiences of the soul as real for the one who enters the spirit world as are persons or events in the sense world. For such a person this Awakening presents a completely realistic soul portrayal. Had it been a question of symbols or allegories, I should certainly have left these scenes unwritten.

In response to various questions, I considered adding a few supplementary remarks in explanation of this whole Soul Portrayal; but again, as on former occasions, I suppress the attempt. I am averse to adding material of this kind to a portrayal intended to speak for itself. Such abstractions do not play any part in the conception and elaboration of the portrayal. They would only have a disturbing effect. The spirit reality here depicted presents itself to the soul as convincingly as the objects of physical observation. It lies in the nature of such a portrayal that a sound spirit vision relates the images of spirit perception to beings and events quite differently than the perceptions of the physical world relate to the physical beings and events. On the other hand, it must be said that the manner in which spirit events present themselves to the inner perception contains implicitly the character, disposition and composition of such a portrayal.

Munich, August, 1913                                          R. Steiner

# SYNOPSIS

Hilary has offered to Benedictus and his students a factory and business he owns in mountainous surroundings. It includes, as we can assume, a complex of buildings, a sawmill and a factory for producing wooden articles and furniture. The idea is to let Strader be the guiding hand for the technical tasks ahead, with Thomasius as his artistic adviser, while the others will create a centre for spiritual science. The first difficulty that arises is the unexpected opposition of the Business Manager, a close and loyal associate of Hilary. We witness a sharp confrontation he has with Hilary and Strader, ending with the words of Strader:

'. . . that will come which has to come about.'

The next three scenes have as their background a mountainous landscape, still untouched by modern civilization. Elemental beings are part of it, and soul- and spirit-entities reveal themselves to those whose inner training has made them sensitive and receptive to the supersensible realities around and about them. The three main characters of the drama, Johannes, Capesius and Strader, experience, each in his own way, a crisis which is decisive for their individual development. – *Johannes* feels the 'young artist' is reawakened in him. Maria guides this introverted tendency of his towards a realization of his soul qualities as the result of elemental and cosmic forces from outside. He encounters the 'Spirit of his Youth', a karmically enchanted part of his being that he has to liberate from its spellbound existence. – *Capesius* is, through an unexpected clairvoyant experience, thrown back upon himself and seeks complete solitude, shunning the duties which the new project had in store for him. – *Strader* goes through the severest test; he meets his own 'abyss'. This is a situation which everyone has to face who connects himself, first in meditative thoughts, then in unfolding imaginations, with the dominant power of opposition to spirit development: Ahriman. – Interwoven with these trials are conversations among Hilary and his friends, reflecting the conflict aroused through their doubts of Strader's ability. These doubts are obstructively voiced by the Business Manager.

Scene Four ends with an event that is purely supersensible in character. It is the beginning of a retrospect by Maria into the time before birth, the decisive time when the preparation of a new earthly incarnation begins. – The next two scenes reveal certain culminating moments in the life between death and a new birth. The soul spheres of most of the individualities portrayed in the drama, touch each other first of all in the *Sun* sphere. Then a few of the characters prove mature enough to experience an awakening at the actual cosmic midnight hour within the *Saturn* sphere (Scene Six).

It lies now in the current of these retrospects that a most decisive moment in an earthly incarnation in the distant past can emerge: an act of initiation at the time of ancient Egypt, in which all are involved (Scenes Seven and Eight). This is, however, only accessible in full consciousness to the souls of Maria and Johannes, under the guidance of Benedictus. The original title of the fourth play was 'Maria's and Johannes' Awakening of the Soul'. It referred specifically to the fact that they are the only ones who penetrate consciously to the karmic secrets emanating from this Eygptian initiation scene: Maria as the neophyte, Johannes as the woman who is guilty of taking part in the temple rites by putting herself in a trancelike state. The Spirit of Johannes' Youth has its origin in this situation. – Capesius' overpowering longing for solitude, but also his intensive reaction to Benedictus' guidance here find their explanations in his courageous attitude as Egyptian High Priest.

Both of the following meditation scenes, Scenes Nine and Ten, with their atmosphere of quiet after the stormy finale of the Egyptian happening, bring to light the fact that the true awakening happens only in Maria and Johannes.

With Scene Eleven, the tragedy in which Strader becomes more and more involved, gains momentum. Scene Twelve reveals the spirit background, through the gigantic figure of Ahriman and his machinations. This scene, although conditioned by the plot of the play, reveals the characteristics of the ahrimanic intrigues in our time, an increasing use of power over the human mind.

In Scene Thirteen, Hilary's conversation with Romanus already shows the effects of Ahriman's interference. They have heard that Strader grows uncertain of the feasibility of his recently invented machine. Romanus hints that such a crisis must be met with the courage and insight that springs from initiation wisdom. He quotes mantric words which he himself once spoke at the Western altar of the Sun Temple (*The Soul's Probation*, Scene Thirteen).

In the remaining scenes (Fourteen and Fifteen), the tragedy leads to Strader's inner victory over doubt and defeat, although it is a victory he has to pay for with death. His leaving the physical body strengthens his spirit influence on his friends. This shows itself in the inspiration Capesius receives, which will help to liberate him from his tendency towards an introverted mysticism. It shows itself in the warm enthusiasm through which the wife of Hilary lets us feel Strader's spirit presence.

The last lines of the play, spoken by Benedictus, have become the last ones of the Mystery Dramas, because a fifth play, planned for 1914, never could materialize. The lines ending the fourth play, written in August 1913, today sound prophetic: 'Strader's light shall shine . . .

at such times too,
when, over full-awakened spirit light,
the fierce, dark Ahriman, suppressing wisdom,
attempts to spread chaos' gloomy night.'

# SCENE ONE

*Hilary's office; a not too modern interior. He is the owner of a factory which produces wooden articles.*

SECRETARY   And all our friends in Georgetown make it plain
            that even they are losing patience with our firm.

MANAGER     These, too, now. It's indeed deplorable –
            and always the same reasons. You can see
            how painful our friends find it to decide
            that they must take their leave of Hilary.

SECRETARY   It's that we're lacking punctuality,
            and that our merchandise cannot compete
            with other firms in the same field,
            is what they write; the same complaints
            I hear now more and more upon my trips.
            The good name of this house, as it came down
            from Hilary's forebears to us
            and which we added to, is disappearing.
            The opinion is that Hilary, bemused
            by dreamers and false visionaries,
            in his obsession has quite lost
            the conscientiousness which up to now
            has given all our products world-renown.
            As numerous as our admirers were,
            as many now are critics of our work.

MANAGER     For quite a while it has been clear that he

15

is influenced and led astray by those
who strive for very special spirit powers.
He's always had such tendencies of soul
but until now he's kept them separate
from all the work of daily life.

(*Enter Hilary*)

MANAGER (*to the Secretary*)
I think it necessary now to speak
with Hilary in private, briefly.

(*Exit the Secretary*)

My deep concern is prompting me to take the
chance to ask you for a serious talk.

HILARY       What is of such concern to my adviser?

MANAGER      So much is happening that shows me
how our production slackens more and more
and how we're failing in our obligations.
Too many are complaining that our products
are growing worse in quality and so
the other firms are starting to outdo us.
Our well-known punctuality is lacking,
as many customers have rightly claimed.
Soon all the best friends that the firm has made
will find themselves no longer satisfied.

HILARY       A long time now I've been aware of this,
and yet it leaves me wholly unconcerned.
However, I should like to talk it over
with you, for you not only gave me help
in service to my company but stood

beside me as a faithful friend.
Therefore you now shall hear directly
what I have often hinted at before.
The one who wishes to create the *new*
with calmness must be able to perceive
how first the *old* must die away.
No longer will I carry on the work
as up to now it took its course.
It seems to me degrading when a business –
remaining in the narrowest range –
throws thoughtlessly the work itself
upon the market of our earthly life,
completely unconcerned with what becomes of it.
This view I've gained since I have realised
the noble form that labour can assume
if men of spirit put their stamp on it.
Thomasius, the artist, shall now direct
the workshops that I build here, near to us.
The products made by our machines will first
be formed artistically by his creative spirit
and so supply for daily human needs
the useful moulded into noble beauty.
Thus craftsmanship will be combined with art
and daily life imbued with taste.
So I would add unto the dead sense-body –
for this is how I see our work today –
the *soul* that gives it its true meaning.

MANAGER (*after some reflection*)
The plan for such miraculous creations
is not in keeping with the spirit of our time.
Today production must be narrowed down
and specialized minutely to achieve perfection.

The forces which in life impersonally
allow the part to work into the whole
give to each part without a thought
the value with which no wisdom can endow them.
And even if this fact were not a hindrance,
all you intend would nonetheless be futile:
that you can find the man to carry out
the project you've devised so splendidly
is something inconceivable to me.

HILARY     My friend, you know I do not follow dreams.
I could not aim at such high goals
unless good fortune had brought to me the man
who will accomplish all I'm striving for.
I am astonished that you do not see
that *Strader* is, in fact, this very man.
The one who knows the essence of his spirit
and has a sense for highest obligations
should not be called a dreamer
when he conceives it as his duty
to find a field of action for this man.

MANAGER (*showing his surprise*)
What? is Strader then the man?
Is it not clearly evident in him
how a man's mind is apt to blind itself
when lacking common sense for true reality?
He owes the mechanism he invented,
without a doubt, to intuition's light.
And if some day it can materialize,
then from it countless blessings will flow forth,
which Strader has believed were very near.
But it will long remain experimental

because the forces still are inaccessible
which alone can bring it to reality.
It saddens me that you can think
it would do good if you entrust your work
to such a man who's suffered shipwreck
with his so daringly conceived creation.
In truth, this led his spirit to those heights
which always will entice the human soul
but will be scaled and conquered only then
when rightful forces shall have been acquired.

HILARY      Now see! you praise the spirit of the man
while seeking for the reasons to reject him,
and this significantly proves his worth.
You have implied that it was not his fault
that his invention did not meet success.
Then here within our circle is most certainly
his place – for here no outer hindrances
can come into his spirit's way.

MANAGER    And even if – with inner opposition
to all that has been said – I tried
to put myself into your way of thinking,
there's something else that drives me to dissent.
Who will appreciate your products then
and show sufficient understanding
to make the proper use of them?
Your capital will soon be eaten up
before the work has actually begun
and then it can't be carried any further.

HILARY      It is quite clear to me that all my plans
will prove impossible, unless at first

there is aroused in people understanding
for ways of working that are new.
What Strader, what Thomasius will achieve
must be perfected here where I establish
a place to foster knowledge of the spirit.
What Benedictus, what Capesius,
and what Maria will communicate
shall show to every human mind the path,
so that it feels the need to permeate
our life of sense with spirit revelation.

MANAGER
So you will then endow this little clique
to live, self-centred, from the world apart.
You'll separate yourselves from real life.
In truth, you wish to wipe out egotism
in such a place, – but you will simply nurture it.

HILARY
You seem to think that I am dreamily
and thoughtlessly belying the experience
that life has brought me. This would certainly
be true if for one moment I would seek
results that are successful in *your* sense.
What seems to me of value may go wrong,
but even if the world despises it
and, on account of that, it falls to pieces,
it would at least have been embodied once
by souls of men on earth, as an example.
In spirit it will work its way in life
although it disappears from sense existence.
It will contribute part of that great power
which in the end must lead to the uniting
of spiritual goals and earthly deeds.
The science of the spirit affirms this fact.

20

MANAGER     I wanted to discuss these things at first
            according to my duty to the firm.
            And now your frankness has encouraged me
            to speak more openly, as friend to friend.
            At work with you I have for many years
            felt urged to look for knowledge of the sort
            to which you sacrifice your strength devotedly.
            My guidance I could find alone in books,
            wherein this spirit knowledge was revealed.
            Although the worlds to which I was directed
            seem inaccessible to me,
            perceptively I can imagine mind
            and mood of people, who with greatest faith
            devote themselves to all such spirit paths.
            What several experts in this field of study
            describe as tendency of soul in those
            who find themselves at home in spirit realms,
            I've found confirmed by my own searching
                 thought.
            Above all else, it seems to me important
            that souls like this cannot distinguish,
            despite their care, *illusions* from reality
            at times when they must naturally return
            from spirit heights to earth existence.
            Then in the spirit worlds, in which they are,
            spectres will rise, preventing them
            from clarity of sight in realms of sense, –
            confusing, too, the certain powers of judgment
            that men must have for living on the earth.

HILARY      What you are telling me as your objection
            is reassuring, for it proves to me
            that I can count on you in times to come

                            21

with those who stand beside me in my
plans.
How could I ever guess that you
are well acquainted with the kind of men
who willingly will join me in my work?
You know the dangers that can threaten them;
so will their actions make it clear to you
that they know well the ways that give protection.
You soon will get to know the situation
and I will still in future have from you
the wise advice I could not do without.

MANAGER    I cannot lend my strength to any work
whose ways and methods are not plain to me.
The friends in whom you wish to put your trust
seem caught in just those same illusions
of which I spoke. And others, hearing them,
can also be misled by such illusions –
and thus they drown the voice of conscious
thought.
You'll find me at your side, advising you,
as long indeed as you intend to base
activities on firmly grounded reasons.
*But not for me is your new kind of work.*

HILARY    By your refusal you will jeopardize
a work which is to serve true spirit goals.
Without your counsel I shall be disabled.
Consider how responsibility
must grow when destiny has given us here
such hints as I can clearly recognize:
that all my friends have found their way
together.

22

MANAGER     The more you speak like this, you prove to me
            quite clearly that you do not realize
            how you yourself are caught in sad illusion.
            Although you think to serve humanity,
            you really only serve the little circle
            which can devote itself a short time longer
            to spirit dreams, because of your support.
            Great efforts soon will be in progress here,
            ordained, no doubt, by spirit for *these* souls,
            and yet they'll seem to us as phantom efforts,
            devouring all the harvest of our work.

HILARY      If you now cannot offer me your hand,
            the future stands before me wrapped in gloom.

            (*Strader enters from the right*)

HILARY      Dear Strader, I have been expecting you.
            As things are now, it seems advisable
            to spend the present hour in serious talk
            and at a later time make the inspection.
            My old friend here has just confessed to me
            that he cannot approve what we have planned.
            . . . So let us listen to the man himself
            who promises his spirit to our work.
            Much now depends on how men find each other,
            who each to each seem like a separate world
            and yet united could accomplish much.

STRADER     So Hilary's good helper has no desire
            to take upon himself the hopeful work
            our friend's discernment has made feasible?
            The plan indeed can only be successful

when your well-proven skills in daily life
unite themselves in wisdom with our aims.

MANAGER     Not only will I hold myself aloof,
            but I should also like to show my friend
            the hopelessness I see in such a venture.

STRADER     It can't surprise me that for you a plan
            which stems from Strader is foredoomed to fail.
            Important work of mine was forfeited
            because today those forces are still hidden
            which could materialize a well-thought out idea.
            One knows I owe to spirit intuition
            what in itself proved true
            and yet could not be brought to life.
            This testifies against my power of judgment,
            against, too, my belief that spirit harbours
            the source of true creation on the earth.
            It also will be difficult to prove
            that an experience like this gives me the power
            to escape from error for the second time.
            I had to go astray that now this time
            I might avoid the dangers that rim the heights
                of truth.
            It's clear that men will question this.
            Your kind of mind, especially, must conclude
            our way of working promises but little.
            I've heard you praised for your participation
            with sensitivity in all our cultural life,
            and for the time and strength you give to it.
            But it is also said you wish to keep
            the work on earth severely separate
            from spirit aims that out of their own force

24

would work creatively within the inner
    life.
You would consider them appropriate
for times not occupied by daily work.
The goal, however, of that spirit stream
in which I see quite clearly life's direction
is this: to join what spirit in itself can do
to earthly labour in the world of sense.

MANAGER     As long as spirit only gives to spirit
what it accomplishes in free creating,
will souls be raised to human dignity.
This will endow their earthly life with meaning.
But when the spirit wants to find within itself
reality as well and even wants
to take command of other spheres of life,
it then approaches regions where illusions
can often become dangerous to truth.
It was this knowledge, shown to me through
    efforts
I made in spirit study – it was not
the inclination of my heartfelt feelings
(as you assumed from what you heard of me) –
that was decisive in my attitude today.

STRADER     It is an error then in spirit knowledge
that makes you hostile to the views I hold.
Through this the difficulties will increase.
No doubt it's easy for the spirit-researcher
to work in partnership with other men
who have already let themselves be taught
by life and Nature what existence means.
But when the thoughts that claim to spring

from spirit sources join reluctantly
with others flowing from the self-same source,
one can but seldom hope for harmony.
– – – – – – – – – – – – – – – –

– – – – – – – – – – – – – – – –

(*after musing quietly*)

And yet will come what *has* to come about.
Renewed examination of my plans . . .
*perhaps* may let you change the view which you
on first consideration had to take.

(*The curtain falls, while all three stand, deep in
thought.*)

# SCENE TWO

*A mountain landscape; in the distance the house of Hilary near the work-shops which are not visible. There is a waterfall on the right side. Johannes is present; also Capesius, who is not visible to Johannes.*

JOHANNES      The piled-up, towering forms whose silent life
         fills widths of space with sculptured riddles
         can never pain with questions, never deaden him
         who wishes – not to think – but, blessedly alive,
         to look upon the sense world's revelation.
         Around the rocky masses here:
         what weaving streams of light!
         And there: the mute existence of bare walls;
         woods that dimly fade from green to blue;
         this is the world in which Johannes' soul
         would like to linger, weaving images of
             things-to-be.
         – – – – – – – – – – – – – – –
         Johannes' soul should draw into itself
         and feel the depth, the wideness of this world.
         Creative forces should unloose from out his soul
         the power by which in art-transfigured radiance
         the world's spellbinding glory moves men's
             hearts.
         – – – – – – – – – – – – – – –
         But this Johannes never could accomplish

27

had not Maria lovingly aroused
his inner forces with her gentle warmth.
I praise my destiny's wise guidance
that brought me near to her.
How short the time that we have been together;
how close the bond uniting, within weeks,
Johannes' soul with hers!
She lives in me as spirit, even when afar;
She thinks within my thinking when I call forth
before my soul the goals of my own willing.

(*Maria appears as a thought of Johannes*)

Maria here with me? how strange she is! . . .
she should not show herself to me like this;
her face so spiritually stern – her dignity –
it chills my earthly feeling – Johannes
will not, can not see her coming near like this –
it cannot be Maria whom wise powers
once brought through destiny's kind providence
    to me.

(*Maria disappears from Johannes' vision*)

But she who loved Johannes before she changed
his soul and led it to the coldness
of spirit heights, O where is she?

– – – – – – – – – – – – – – – –

Where is Johannes too who loved Maria –
where is he now –? he was just here.
I cannot see Johannes who with joy
was giving me myself back to myself – the past
so cruelly can not, must not rob him from myself.

(*Maria becomes again visible for Johannes*)

28

| | |
|---|---|
| MARIA | Maria, as you desire to see her |
| | does not exist in worlds where truth is |
| | radiant. |
| | Johannes' spirit weaves in regions of deceit |
| | enticed by soul-illusions; – free yourself |
| | from these desires and their alluring power. |
| | I feel your storm of soul in me. |
| | It robs me of the calmness which I need. |
| | The one who sends such storms into my soul |
| | is not Johannes; it is another being |
| | whom long ago he conquered in himself. |
| | As phantom now it roams through realms of |
| | spirit. |
| | O recognize it, |
| | for then it will dissolve to nothingness. |
| | |
| JOHANNES | This is Maria as she is in truth. |
| | She speaks about Johannes as he seems |
| | at present in reality to be. |
| | Long since, he rose to quite a different life |
| | than the illusionary play of dreams |
| | depicts it now, for I've allowed in laziness |
| | my soul to muse in twilight comfort. |
| | And yet this life does not hold fast my being. |
| | I still can flee from it – I'll do so now – |
| | it calls me often; it wants with all its power |
| | to win me for myself. |
| | But still I feel the urge to free myself. |
| | Long years ago it filled |
| | my soul depths with reality of spirit. |
| | And yet – I do not want |
| | to recognize it now in me. |

– – – – – – – – – – – – – – – –

You stranger being in Johannes' soul, leave
    me alone –
O give me back unto myself
as I once was before you worked
so actively within me.
I will behold Johannes freed from you. –

(*Benedictus appears at the side of Maria,
also as a thought of Johannes*)

BENEDICTUS    Johannes, heed the warning of your soul.
The one, who, kindling you with spirit, rises
within you as your being's primal power,
must faithfully hold sway beside you.
He must demand that you bring forth as man,
within your willing, forces of his being.
Hidden within you must he work, so that
you reach in future what you know to be
your being's distant goal.
Your cares and sorrows you must take through
    life,
locked fast within your inmost soul.
You'll gain your self if ever more you'll let
yourself be seized courageously by him.

MARIA    My holy, solemn vow rays forth new strength
to hold for you what you have gained.
And you will find me in cold fields of ice
where spirits must themselves create the light
when darknesses disable powers of life. – – –
Seek me in grounds of worlds where souls
must struggle to achieve their feelings for the
    gods,
victoriously wrestling being from the void.
But never seek me in the realm of shades

where worn-out soul experience gains by tricks
a fleeting life through self-illusion;
where phantom-images beguile the dreamer
because in pleasure he forgets himself
and looks on serious efforts with distaste.
(*Benedictus and Maria disappear*)

JOHANNES　She speaks about illusion – – – – – –
– – – – – and yet, how lovely this illusion is!
It is alive; Johannes feels himself in it;
He feels Maria's nearness in it too.
Johannes does not want to know how spirit
can solve the riddles in dark depths of soul.
But he will work, he will create as artist.
So let in him stay buried what only wants
to look at cosmic heights with consciousness.

(*He sinks into further musing. Capesius rises from
his seat, shaking himself awake as if out of deep
contemplation.*)

CAPESIUS　Have I not been aware quite clearly
what in Johannes, musing there in dream,
has shaped itself as image of his longing?
Thoughts flamed up within which did not come
from me – which only he could shape.
There lived in me the being of his soul. – –
I saw him young again as he perceived himself
through spirit error, and as he blamed with spite
the ripened fruits of his own spirit. –

– – – – – – – – – – – – – – – –

But wait. – Why am I now aware of this?
For seldom may the spirit searcher see
within himself the life of other souls.

– – – – – – – – – – – – – – – –

31

From Benedictus have I heard it said
that one alone can do this, for a while:
the man whom gracious destiny ordains
to be upraised one further step
upon the spirit path. – – – Can I interpret thus
the happening I experienced just now?
How seldom, truly, should this ever happen!
How dreadful for the seer to have to listen
at all times to the inward life of others!

– – – – – – – – – – – – – – – – –
– – – – – – – – – – – – – – – – –

Did I behold the truth? – – or did illusion
cause me to dream of other soul existence?
From Johannes must I beg the answer.

(*Capesius approaches Johannes, who notices
him for the first time*)

JOHANNES        Capesius . . . I thought you far away.

CAPESIUS        My soul, however, has felt close to you.

JOHANNES        Not close to me . . . just now . . . O surely not!

CAPESIUS        Why do you shudder at these words of mine?

JOHANNES        O no, not shudder . . .

                (*At this moment Maria joins them; this enables
                Johannes and Capesius each to speak to himself.*)

JOHANNES (*to himself*)
                . . . It is his glance
                that pierces to the bottom of my soul.

32

CAPESIUS (*to himself*)

His shudder shows me that I saw the truth.
(*he turns to Maria*) You come, Maria, at a fitting
    time.
Perhaps your word will help to solve the riddle
whose solemn weight is so oppressing me!

MARIA

I thought to find Johannes here, – not you.
Foreboding brought me first to him
to seek the riddle's weight. – But you I
    thought content
devoted to the enterprising plan
which Hilary is offering to us

CAPESIUS

This plan – for me it has no meaning –
it's disturbing.

MARIA

Disturbing? – were you not overjoyed
To think your hopes might now be realized?

CAPESIUS

What in this fateful hour I just lived through
Has fully changed the purpose of my soul.
Now every earth activity and work
would rob me of my wakened seer forces.

MARIA

The one allowed to tread the paths of spirit
finds many a hint to shape his destiny.
These hints he'll follow on his paths of soul.
And yet he could interpret them quite wrongly
should they disturb his duties here on earth.

(*Capesius sits down and falls into a short
contemplation while Maria experiences the
appearance of Lucifer*)

LUCIFER       Your urging will not yield to you much fruit.
              Forces are stirring there within his heart
              which open portals of his soul to me.
              Maria, – now direct your strength of vision
              into his depths of soul, – see how
              he frees himself on wings of spirit
              from earthly work of yours enwarmed by love.

              (*Lucifer remains in the landscape. Maria
              turns herself quite distinctly to Capesius
              to rouse him from his musing, but he seems
              at the same moment to shake himself out of it.*)

MARIA         That Johannes on the spirit path should feel
              tormented by his duties' earthly nature,
              would seem not justified – but understandable,
              for his creative mind must serve the outer work.
              But you should bring to others spirit knowledge
              without a step, thus, out of your soul orbit.

CAPESIUS      The power of spirit can waste itself in words
              far more than when it works in outward action.
              For words would have us grasp what we perceive,
              yet concepts are opposed to powers of vision.
              I had a spirit vision even now
              which could reveal another human soul
              only because – though we are close in friendship –
              my earthly nature never understood him.
              If this experience is real, no longer
              can I be bound to any earth activities.
              For I must feel that higher powers now
              have pointed out quite other aims for me
              than those that Hilary has in mind. –

              (*He confronts Johannes*)

34

Johannes, tell me frankly, did you not
just now when you were lost in quiet musing,
experience outlived desires of yours
as if they were your present self?

JOHANNES    My spirit's own confusion, can it form
an active life within another soul?
And can his vision make my error strong,
that it can find the way to world-becoming?

*(Johannes falls again into musing. Maria turns
her glance to Lucifer and hears him speak.)*

LUCIFER     Here too I find soul-portals opened wide.
I will not hesitate, will use my chance.
If in this soul, too, – spirit-wish arises,
then must the deed of love be forfeited
which threatens me, through Hilary, with
        danger.
Through this desire I can destroy Maria's
        strength;
then all that she achieves falls to my power.

*(Exit Lucifer. At this moment Capesius
straightens himself up with inner consciousness
of self and in the course of the following
speech acquires an ever more positive mood)*

CAPESIUS    There is no doubt that what I saw was true;
I was allowed to see Johannes' inner life.
Now it is clear: he could reveal his world
only because my own had no desire
to come near to his world with comprehension.
The spirit path demands its solitude. –

35

Only such men can work together
who face each other comprehendingly.
The soul remote from human beings reaches
The wide horizons of the worlds of light.

———————————————

I find in Father Felix an example;
he seeks on paths quite strange to others,
in proud seclusion, for the light of spirit.
His searching was rewarded with success, –
because he always kept himself aloof
from all in man that merely comprehends.
I'll strive now further on his path.
Your work that weighs down visionary force
     with earthiness
no longer will entice Capesius.    (*Exit*)

MARIA        This happens when a person's better self
sinks into spirit sleep, and powers of desire
can feed his nature till a new awakening
rays light into his spirit being.
It is the sleep that all men sleep before
the force of seership awakens them.
They notice nothing of this waking sleep –
they seem awake – because they always
     sleep.
The seer sleeps when he must bring himself
into this waking sleep out of his true existence.
Capesius will now forsake us.
It is no fleeting whim; his inner state
draws him away from us and from our
     goals.
It is not he who turns himself from us.
One sees the stern decree of destiny.

So must we others then re-dedicate
more strongly all our forces to the work.

JOHANNES      Maria, do not ask it of Johannes
that he prepare himself at such a time
for further goals. His soul needs, like Capesius,
the spirit sleep that it may bring
to full maturity its germinating powers.
I know that in the future I will dare
to work for spirit worlds, – but do not now
demand that I am active – ask not *now*.
Consider that I drove away Capesius. –
Were I now ready for the work, – he would be
    too.

MARIA      You drove away Capesius? – you? – you're
    dreaming.

JOHANNES      I dreamed while conscious, was awake while
    dreaming.
What would to cosmic powers seem illusion
has been to me a symbol of my growth.
I know that my desire was I myself;
my thinking only was another Self.
Johannes stood before my soul as he
once was before the spirit laid its hold
on him and filled him with the second self.
Johannes is not dead – – – his live desires
have made him the companion of my soul.
I may have numbed but have not conquered him.
His natural right to be, he claims whenever
that other self must sink in sleep. Always
to be awake – – – is far beyond his strength.

It was asleep, too, at the time in which
Capesius could experience in himself
this other self that tears me from myself.
To him my dreaming was a hint of destiny.
And so there works in me and not in him
a force that, driving him away, forbids us
to turn our minds to earth activities.

MARIA      The spirit powers are coming – summon them. –
To cosmic spirit sources turn your gaze,
and wait until the forces in those depths
perceive that part of your true self
which stirs in kinship to their being.
They'll conjure up before your inner eyes
the bond which grows from you to them.
Forswear your own mind's dissonance;
your spirit then will speak with spirit beings
and, listening, will heed this spirit speech.
It will convey you into spheres of light,
uniting you with spirit entities.
What dawns on you from times long past will
then grow clear to you, distinct, in cosmic light
and will not force you, for you can direct it.
Compare it with the elemental beings,
with shadows and with phantoms of all kinds;
confront it, too, with demons manifold
and so discover what it signifies.
But root yourself within the realm of spirits
who, binding primal source to primal source,
are close to cosmic germinating powers
and give direction to the thoughts of spheres.
Such vision of the worlds will give you strength
amid the surging spirit waves to join

this essence of existence with your soul's
core.

_ _ _ _ _ _ _ _ _ _ _ _ _ _ _

_ _ _ _ _ _ _ _ _ _ _ _ _ _ _

The spirit has commanded me
that I should make this known to you myself.
Hear now what you are conscious of
but have not yet united with your soul depths.

JOHANNES (*He collects himself for a determined effort*)
I *will* hear, – I'll dare to bid defiance to myself.

(*From both sides come elemental spirits. From the left,
gnomelike beings with steel-gray bodies, smaller than
men; they are nearly all head, but this is bent forward
and downward. Their limbs are long and mobile, deft
in gesturing but clumsy for walking.*
*From the right come sylphlike figures, slender and
almost headless; their feet and hands are something
between fins and wings. Some of them are blue-green,
others yellow-red. The yellow-red ones are
distinguished by sharper outlines; the blue-green
ones are less distinct. The words spoken by these
figures are accompanied by expressive gestures
developing into a dance.*)

CHORUS OF GNOME-SPIRITS
We harden, we strengthen
the earth-stuff's dusty glimmer.
We loosen, we powder
the stark, hard-crusted strata.
What's firm we quickly crumble.
What's loose we slowly harden
with bodies built of spirit,

39

spun out of stuff of intellect,
that were already clever
when human souls still sleeping
at earth's beginning lay a-dreaming.

CHORUS OF SYLPH-SPIRITS

We weave, we unravel
the web of air and water.
We sever, we scatter
the quickened sun-strength in the seed.
With skill we densen powers of light,
erase the rip'ning forces wisely
with bodies built of soul
out-flowing from the beams of feeling
which, ever-living, glimmer,
that human beings living,
enjoy the sense of earth's becoming.

CHORUS OF GNOME-SPIRITS

We chuckle, we snicker,
we banter, we grimace
when human senses stumbling
and human spirits tumbling
behold what we have fashioned,
and think they wisely understand
what spirits of our age's time
can conjure for their stupid staring.

CHORUS OF SYLPH-SPIRITS

We foster, we cherish,
we ripen, we hover,
when human children, dawning lifeward,

and aged grey-beards, weaving error,
consume what we have laboured
and childlike or grey-haired
within time's current dimly relish
what in eternity we ponder.

*(These spirit-beings collect in two irregular
groups in the backgeound and remain there visible.
From the left appear the three soul-forces: Philia,
Astrid and Luna, with The Other Philia.)*


PHILIA

They radiate brightness
as love-giving light rays
to blissful a-ripening;
so gently they warm
and so mightily heat
where growing is ready
to quicken to life;
that quickened enlivening
those souls will enchant
who surrender in love
to the radiant light.


ASTRID

They weave on the living,
as helpers creative
in up-welling beings.
They shatter the soil
and densify breezes
that change may be seen
in striving creating,
that striving creating
give joy to those spirits

who feel themselves weaving,
in life that's creating.

LUNA      They cumber with forethought
as active creators
the formative substance.
They sharpen the edges
and flatten the surface
to shape in wise measure
the uprising forms;
that uprising forms
enrapture willed purpose
to shape in wise measure
as active creators.

THE OTHER PHILIA
They gather the blossoms
as carefree availers
in spell-binding magic.
They dream of the true
and hold the delusion
that seeds, still asleep,
might waken to life;
and wakening dreaming
reveals to the souls
the enchanted weaving
of their own being.

(*The four soul-forces disappear towards the right
side. Johannes, who has been in deep meditation
during the preceding events, arises out of it.*)

JOHANNES     'And wakening dreaming
reveals to the souls

42

the enchanted weaving
of their own being.'
These are the words which sound still clearly
within my soul – while all that I beheld
before has in confusion disappeared.

– – – – – – – – – – – – – – – –

        When I consider:
The enchanted weaving
of my own being – – – what power stirs in me?

*(He falls again into meditation: there appears
before him as his own thought-form a group
consisting of the Spirit of Johannes' Youth,
Lucifer at its left side, the Soul of Theodora
at its right.)*

THE SPIRIT OF JOHANNES' YOUTH
        The life of your desires nourishes my life.
My breath drinks thirstily your youthful dreams.
I am alive as long as you refuse
to enter worlds which I can never find.
But should you lose me in yourself, I would
in pain do evil service to grim shadows – –
Preserver of my being, – – – do not forsake
        me.

LUCIFER
        Forsake you he will not. – I can perceive
desires for light within his depths, desires
which cannot take the path Maria takes.
If his desires with self-engendered glory
turn their full light on his creative soul,
the fruit they bear he will not wish to waste

43

within the realm where love holds sway,
but love deprived of beauty.
His self no more will seem of worth to him
should it, by setting too much store by
      knowledge,
throw all his better forces to the shades.
When wisdom lightens up in his desires,
their value will be gloriously revealed;
as long as these desires remain in darkness,
will they appear to him of little worth.
Until they can attain the light of wisdom
I will be your protector through the light
that I can find innate in souls of men.

— — — — — — — — — — — — — — —

Till now he lacks compassion for your pain;
he lets you sink into the realm of shades
while lifting up himself to heights of
      light.
And then he can forget that you, his child,
must lead a woeful, spellbound life.
But henceforth at your side you will have *me*
when you are chilled, as shadow, by his guilt.
I will exert the rights, which Lucifer

(*at the word 'Lucifer', the Spirit of Johannes'
Youth quivers*)

holds for himself by law of ancient worlds,
to capture from Johannes' depths whatever
he leaves unguarded in his spirit flight.
I'll bring you then this treasure that it eases
the dismal solitude of realms of shade.
But only then will you be freed from spell
when he can join himself again with you.

He can delay it, – – – but prevent it, never!
for Lucifer will safeguard Lucifer's rights.

THEODORA    You spirit child, you live Johannes' youth
in dismal realms of shades. – The soul that guards
Johannes bends down lovingly to you
from realms imbued with love and filled with
      light.
She will from spellbound regions set you free
if, from her feelings, you will take enough
to gain existence in pure blessedness.
I will ally you with the elementals
which work unconsciously in world-wide space
and ever shun the wakening of souls.
With spirits of the earth you'll fashion forms
and with the fire-souls will you ray out power,
if you will sacrifice your conscious life
unto that Will which without human wisdom
sends forth its light-filled strength. And so shall you
preserve the knowledge that is half your own
from Lucifer, and to Johannes give
the services that are of worth to him.
Out of his soul life I will bring to you
what makes him crave for your existence
and offers him requickening spirit sleep.

LUCIFER    She never will bestow upon you beauty,
for I will pluck it daringly from her.

THEODORA    I will from noble feeling bring forth beauty,
maturing it by sacrificial deeds.

LUCIFER    She will from free will tear you and will yield you
to spirits holding sway in darknesses.

THEODORA    I will awaken vision filled with spirit,
            which is at last set free from Lucifer.

            (*Lucifer, Theodora and the Spirit of Johannes' Youth
            disappear. Johannes, awakening out of his musing,
            sees The Other Philia approaching him*)

THE OTHER PHILIA
            And wakening dreaming
            reveals to the souls
            the enchanted weaving
            of their own being.

JOHANNES     You mysterious spirit, – through your words
            I stepped into this world! – – And only one
            of all its wonders – – is important to my soul:
            the shade who sought to show himself to me
            with Theodora and with Lucifer,
            is he in spirit realms a living being?

THE OTHER PHILIA
            He lives – awakened to a seeming life
            through you. As mirrors show in image form
            what light allows to cast upon their surfaces
            so must be mirrored livingly
            in realms of half-awakened shadow-spirits
            all you behold in spirit realms, before
            maturity gives you the right to it.

JOHANNES     Only an image is mirrored thus through me?

THE OTHER PHILIA
            Yet one that lives and keeps its hold on life
            as long as you preserve within yourself

a lived-out life which you indeed can numb
but which, as yet, you cannot overthrow.
Johannes, your awakening will be delusion
until you liberate, yourself, the shadow being
on whom your guilt bestows a spellbound life.

JOHANNES    What thanks I owe this spirit, who brings truth
and counsel to my soul! – – I must obey.

*(The curtain falls slowly while The Other Philia
and Johannes remain standing quietly.)*

# SCENE THREE

*The same landscape as in Scene Two. Magnus Bellicosus, Romanus, Tor-
quatus and Hilary enter from the right. They continue a conversation which
they have been conducting on their walk. Its content becomes so important
that they stand still.*

BELLICOSUS     And if his stubborn mind remains unchanged,
how can the work succeed, which Hilary
would dedicate in loving service to mankind?

ROMANUS     The reasons which our friend's associate
has given for his opposition
have weight not just for those who form
opinions based on outer facts. Do they
not also correspond to occult truths?

BELLICOSUS     And yet they do not lie within the aims
of those who firmly guard our spirit goals.
We were succeeded in our occult work
by Benedictus' students. Hilary will
create for them a field of action, where
their fruits of spirit can mature.
Wise powers of destiny united them
with us within the temple, and Hilary
is answering the consecrated orders
revealed to us as spirit obligations.

| ROMANUS | Are you so sure that you interpret rightly |
|---|---|
| | this spirit order? More convincing seems |
| | the thought that Benedictus with his students |
| | whom he in his way guided to the spirit |
| | should stay within the temple's innermost, – |
| | that they should not yet tread the rugged road |
| | to which friend Hilary would lead them. |
| | There spirit vision changes all too quickly |
| | into a dream-filled sleepiness of soul. |

| BELLICOSUS | I had not hoped to hear such words from |
|---|---|
| | you. |
| | They might be said by Hilary's co-worker, |
| | Who gains his knowledge out of books |
| | alone, a knowledge that's indeed of little |
| | value. |
| | But you are bound to recognize the signs |
| | which are begotten on the occult path. |
| | How Benedictus' pupils were impelled |
| | to come to us speaks clearly to our souls. |
| | They're joined with us so that we can obey |
| | the revelations of their seership. |

| TORQUATUS | Another sign, however, seems to show |
|---|---|
| | that spirit powers have not only poured |
| | abundant blessings on this work |
| | as it was offered to us in the temple. |
| | Capesius has withdrawn from Benedictus |
| | and from the circle of his friends. The fact |
| | that he can in its fulness not yet feel |
| | the inner wakefulness, which Benedictus |
| | expects of him, now casts obscuring shadows, too, |
| | upon the teacher's own assurance. |

BELLICOSUS   The gifts of seership lie far from me.
             But often I can feel how some event
             evokes foreboding in my soul. When first
             I saw Capesius at our sacred place,
             the thought arose oppressively that fate
             had placed him near and also far from us.

ROMANUS      In this foreboding I can understand you.
             But in that moment I could sense that Strader
             was joined with us by power of destiny
             more closely than the other occult friends.
             This kind of premonition is for me
             a sign that guides my soul into directions
             in which I then can search with reasoning.
             And when I turn toward action, I abolish
             the premonitions surging through my thinking.
             For me strict occult rules are here my guide.
             Indeed, in spirit realms I feel close ties
             to Benedictus' students. But if I have
             to find my way out of the inner circle
             back into daily life on earth, I'd dare
             to take that way at Strader's side alone.

             (*during the following speech Ahriman appears in the
             background and slowly crosses the stage*)

TORQUATUS    The loyal friend of Hilary does not
             see Strader as the sturdy spirit able
             effectively to serve the outer life.
             When I allow my inner voice to speak,
             it's clear to me that Strader lacks completely
             the genuine mood of soul for mysticism.
             What outer signs can prove to him, and what
             his reasoning can grasp of spirit life

can stimulate in him the urge for research.
He stands far off from inward life of spirit.
What else could this man's spirit-work consist of
but mystically dark dream-fabrications?


ROMANUS  And still he has not yet progressed so far
upon the spirit pathways of his friends
as to ally himself with inner foes,
who are so dangerous to many mystics
when they pursue him into sense-existence.


BELLICOSUS  If you believe him safe from such attacks
no hindrance should prevent your work for Strader
in order that the project is successful
which Hilary would carry out through him.
For when our friend's co-worker comes to hear
how you revere the man he rates so low,
his firm decision surely will be shaken,
and only you can gain him for our cause.
For well he knows that in your outer life
you have invariably achieved success
in everything you planned with prudent care.


ROMANUS  If you, dear Hilary, will give to Strader
a field of work with you and yet will keep
the other students Benedictus guides,
with no illusions outside your activities,
you will not stand alone. For I will offer,
besides the help that Bellicosus asks,
all earthly means in order to assist
effectively the splendid plan of Strader.

HILARY  How can you think that Strader at this time
from Benedictus' students would depart
to follow his own spirit goals alone?
His friends are just as close as he is to himself.

ROMANUS  They may be close to him as human beings.
But that part only of his soul which still
is wrapt in spirit sleep can well believe
that they in spirit, too, are one with him.
And yet I think that it will soon be clear
how this part too matures to waking life.

*(The four exeunt to the left. From the other side
appear Capesius, Strader, Felix Balde, and
Felicia Balde, pausing in their walk, because of the
significance of their words.)*

CAPESIUS  One task alone at present can I follow:
to seek the spirit on inner paths of soul.
Were I to load myself with outer work,
to bring to life the spirit in realms of sense,
I'd boldly have to try to grasp the truth
of earth existence in those worlds whose essence
to me has not yet come to full reality.
I can behold of cosmic life no more
than has already shaped itself to me.
How shall my work do good to other men
if I, creating, but enjoy *myself*?

STRADER  I think you mean, in each creative act
you imprint alone the stamp of your own self
and so impart through this in every deed
your self-will only to the outer world?

CAPESIUS     Till I, with my own inward world, encounter
             a being strange to me, then that is so.
             With pain I've had to realize how far
             I now can penetrate another soul,
             when for a while I wakened into clearness.

FELIX BALDE  You utter words I've never heard from you . . .
             but never have I understood . . . so well
             as now, when you are only speaking for yourself.
             There sounds within your words the mystic mood
             which I've austerely sought for many years.
             This mood alone is able to perceive
             the light in which man's spirit feels itself,
             with clearest sight, within the cosmic spirit.

CAPESIUS     Because I sensed how close I've come to you,
             did I take flight to you from all the turmoil
             that wanted to destroy my inner world.

STRADER      I often understood . . . what you are saying . . .
             I took it then for wisdom . . . but no word
             of what you say has meaning for me *now*.
             Capesius and Felix, both . . . to me . . .
             conceal dark meaning in transparent words . . .
             – – – – – – – – – – – – – – –
             I wonder if these words of yours are merely
             the outer cloak of forces . . . of soul forces
             that exile me from you into those worlds
             which lie remote from all your spirit paths? . . .
             to worlds for which I've no desire because
             deep in my soul I love that world of *yours*.
             It is not hard to bear the opposition
             which from outside is threatening my work.

53

Yes, even if my will were to be shattered
by opposition . . . still I'd uphold myself.
But I can never do without your world.

FELIX BALDE    A man cannot attain the spirit world.
by wanting to unlock it through his *seeking*.
Some time ago you gave me pleasure, when
you spoke to me about your mechanism, –
for it was found by true enlightenment
and not by reason set on finding it.
Then you were closer to the mystic mood.

– – – – – – – – – – – – – – –

To strive for nothing . . . wait in peaceful stillness,
one's inmost being filled with expectation . . .
that is the mystic mood. – When waked in man,
it leads his inmost soul to realms of light.
Our outer work cannot endure this mood.
If you through mysticism strive for this,
your own delusion will destroy its life.

STRADER    I am in need of you . . . but cannot find you . . .
The life uniting us . . . you do not value.
How can men come together for world-action
if mystics never lay aside self-interest?

FELIX BALDE    The fragile being of the inner sight
you cannot take into the world of action,
for it will fade as vision when you cross
the border of this world's absorbing life.
In piety, revering spirit-sway,
with spirit sight reposing in the heart:
thus mystics should approach the world of
            deeds.

54

| | |
|---|---|
| CAPESIUS | And if they *otherwise* would enter it, |
| | effects of error it would show to them |
| | but not the radiant being of true wisdom. |
| | Into another's soul just now I looked. – |
| | I knew my sight was not deceiving me, |
| | yet only that soul's error could I see. |
| | This was my fate for spoiling spirit sight |
| | by my desire for outer deeds on earth. |
| | |
| STRADER | So speaks Capesius, who has advanced |
| | beyond me far upon the paths of soul; – – |
| | but spirit vision rises in *me* only |
| | when I devote myself to thoughts of action. |
| | My soul is flooded then with living hope |
| | to build an earthly home for spirit deeds, |
| | a place in which the light shall be enkindled |
| | to radiate and warm the spirit worlds, |
| | the light which through men's sense-activity |
| | will seek anew a home in earthly life. |

– – – – – – – – – – – – – – – –

Am I the son of error . . . not your son,
you wisdom-filled and wide-flung spirit realms?

*(Strader turns away for a moment from the others.
He has the following spirit vision: Benedictus, Maria
and Ahriman appear, in real spirit communion,
though as his thought-forms; first Benedictus with
Ahriman, then Maria.)*

| | |
|---|---|
| BENEDICTUS | In wisdom-filled and wideflung spirit realms |
| | you sense approaching help for pains of doubt |
| | that age-long secrets of your inner life |
| | allow to weigh upon your earthly thinking. |

Now listen to the *answer*, through my voice,
which wide expanses of the spirit world
are willing to reveal from depths of soul.
But learn to understand what you believe
you know and often boldly put in words,
yet merely dream within your own soul being.
Give to your dreams the life which I can offer
while bound to you in spirit, but transform
to dream-existence what your thinking
draws forth for you from sense experience.
Capesius and Felix banish you
out of the spirit light which they behold.
They open the abyss between themselves and
    you.
Do not complain that they have done this thing,
but gaze into your own abyss.

AHRIMAN      Dare to gaze there!
And so perceive what seems to you most worthy
of human spirit in evolution's course.
Much better would it be if other spirits
could show you this while dull in your soul-sleep.
But Benedictus shows it while you're waking
and thus you kill the answer as you look.
Yes, dare to gaze there!

STRADER      I *will* dare. But what? . . .
The shapes confused? They're changing . . .
and they're tearing . . .
Each tearing at the other . . . like a battle . . .
The phantoms rush upon each other wildly . . .
Destruction reigns and generates fierce darkness . . .
Out of the darkness other shadow-beings.

Etheric brightness round them ... rose-red weaving;
one of the figures clearly frees itself
and comes to me . . . sent from the dark abyss.      •

(*Maria appears out of the abyss and comes forward.*)

MARIA  Demons you see . . . if you build up your strength
then they are not . . . to you they must appear
what they are not. If you can hold them fast
until their phantom being is illumined
before your soul life, they will show how high
their order is in world-becoming.
Your vision, though, may be extinguished in you
before they have revealed their shining might.
You can illumine them with your own light.
Where is your light? . . . You radiate fierce darkness.
Perceive your darkness, round about yourself . . .
you pour confusing darkness into light,
you feel it pouring forth through your *creating*,
yet you can never feel *what* you create.
Whereas you would forget creating's thirst,
unknown to you it dominates your being
because your cowardice holds back your light.
This light of yours you would enjoy, and yet,
yourself in it is what you will enjoy.
You seek yourself by seeking in forgetting:
dreaming you sink yourself into yourself.

AHRIMAN  Yes, listen to her . . . she can solve your riddles,
but her solutions will not help you solve them.
She gives you wisdom . . . so that you may turn
Your steps, with it, to foolishness.
She might be good for you . . . in future when
the spirit-day shines for you bright and clear.

57

|            | But when Maria speaks into your dreaming, |
|------------|-------------------------------------------|
|            | she kills your riddle's answer by her counsel. |
|            | Yes, listen to her. |

STRADER  What do these words desire to do,
Maria, are they born out of the light?
Out of my light? ... Or can it be my darkness
from which they sound? Speak, Benedictus,
who brought me counsel from the dark abyss?

BENEDICTUS  At your abyss she sought you out.
So spirits seek out men to shelter them
from beings who form *phantoms* for men's souls
and who confuse the cosmic spirit's rule
with darkness; then the souls can only see
reality within the web of self.
Gaze further into your abyss.

STRADER  What is alive there in the abyss' depths?

BENEDICTUS  Behold the shadows: on the right, the bluish-red
enticing Felix – look upon the others, –
at left, – red, gently brightening to yellow:
they press on hard to reach Capesius.
They both can feel the power of these shadows, –
and each in solitude creates the light
that halts such shadows which deceive men's souls.

AHRIMAN  He would do better if he showed to you
*your* shadows, – and yet he almost cannot do it, –
although he truly does not lack good will.
He does not notice where to seek these shades.
They stand behind you, dangerously near, –
and it is you yourself concealing them.

| STRADER | So here at the abyss I have to listen |
| --- | --- |
| | to words which I considered only foolish |
| | when Hilary's adviser uttered them! – – – |

| MARIA | While Felix tempers for himself the weapons |
| --- | --- |
| | which shield him against danger, – one who walks |
| | your paths of soul must use another kind. |
| | The sword Capesius forges for himself |
| | and bravely wields in battle with his foes |
| | must change for Strader to a shadow-sword |
| | were he to start with it that spirit war |
| | which powers of destiny ordain for souls |
| | who mightily must turn the spirit-being, |
| | matured for deeds, to earth activity. |
| | You cannot use their weapons for yourself, |
| | but you must know them so that you can forge |
| | your own from out soul-substance thoughtfully. |

*(The figures of Benedictus, Ahriman and Maria disappear, that is, from outward sight; Strader returns from his spirit vision; he looks around for Capesius, Felix Balde and Felicia, who again join him; he has seated himself on a rock.)*

| FELIX BALDE | Dear Strader, did the spirit not, just now, |
| --- | --- |
| | drive you away from us? – for so it seemed to me. |

*(He pauses in the expectation that Strader will reply, but since Strader remains silent, Felix continues.)* '

I did not want to banish you unkindly
from out our group to other ways of life.
I only wish to keep you back from yielding
to delusions that perplex you.

What spirit sees in spirit should be received
and taken up by souls in spirit only.
How foolish if Felicia should take
the magic creatures living in her soul,
which only want to be perceived in *souls*,
and let them dance upon a puppet stage!
Their magic charm would be completely lost.

FELICIA BALDE  I think that I've been silent long enough.
And speak I will if with your mystic mood
you even want to bless my fairy sprites.
They'd thank you kindly if their power were first
sucked out of them, and then with mystic pap
you'd try to nurse them back to life again.
With all respect to mysticism, it
should keep its nose out of my fairy realms.

CAPESIUS  Felicia, was it not your fairy tales
that set me first upon the spirit path?
The spirits of the air and of the water,
which you called up before my thirsting soul,
were messengers to me from out those worlds
to which at present I seek mystic entrance.

FELICIA  Yet, since you came with this new mystic mood
into our house, you've hardly asked to know
what all my lovely, magic beings want.
You've more or less allowed at times the ones
which show a dignified and solemn face;
but those who gaily dance and bounce with joy,
cause you quite mystical discomfort.

CAPESIUS  Undoubtedly someday I'll understand
the deeper meaning of these wondrous beings

60

who show their wisdom in such merry masks.
But now, my strength is not yet up to it.

FELIX

Felicia, you know how much I love
the fairy beings which reveal themselves to you.
But to imagine them mechanical,
embodied dolls – this goes against the grain.

FELICIA

I have not so presented them to you –
for that – *you* – stand – too high!
But I was glad
when I was told of Strader's plan, and heard
thomasius too intends to show how spirit
can enter into matter, sense-perceived.
I saw in spirit all my fairy princes,
my fire souls too, dance merrily on thousands
of puppet-stages, shaped with artistry.
And so, with inner happiness, I left them
to find their way to many, many children.
*Curtain*

## SCENE FOUR

*The same landscape as in Scene Two. Hilary's business manager and Romanus, pausing in their walk.*

MANAGER
You know the mystic friends of Hilary,
and I can see in you the prudent man
who heeds the power of careful judgment needed
in occult strivings or in daily life.
I value the opinion which you hold;
but how can I make sense of what you said?
You think it right for Strader's friends to stay
in realms of spirit and not use their power
of seership to work here in this world.
But is this not as dangerous for Strader?
His mode of spirit seems to me to prove
that nature demons always will delude him
when he attempts, impelled by strong desires,
to work in terms of outer, earthly deeds.
The prudent mystic knows that he at first
must strengthen forces from within
in order to resist these enemies.
But Strader's sight, it seems, is not yet ripe
to see such foes upon his spirit path.

ROMANUS
But those good spirit beings, guiding men
who stand as yet outside the spirit realms,

62

have still not left his side. They turn away
from mystics, though, who make a pact with beings
to serve their personal mood and way of spirit.
In Strader's bearing I distinctly feel
that nature spirits still endow his self
with fruits that spring from their good forces.

MANAGER  And nothing but your feelings forces you
to think good spirits work in Strader?
You offer little and demand so much!

Am I in future to consult these spirits,
if I would further work where for so long
I have been privileged to give to labour
its meaning and its genuine spirit to which
the father of Hilary was bound in loyalty?
I still can hear him speaking from his grave,
although his son no longer cares to listen.
What would the spirit of that gallant man
be saying if he saw these crazy minds
his son now tries to bring into this house?
I know that spirit who for ninety years
maintained himself in body and in soul.
He taught me the real secret of good work
in those old days when he could work himself
and while his son crept off to mystic temples.

ROMANUS  My friend, is it unknown to you how much
respect I have for such an attitude?
The old man whom you rightly chose as model
was surely its good servant all his life.
And I myself have striven, from my childhood
up to this very day, to serve this spirit.

63

But I too stole away to mystic temples.
I planted faithfully into my inner depths
what they were willing to bestow on me.
But when I left their doors, my reason swept
aside the temple's mood, for daily life.
I knew that in this way I best could carry
this mood's strong forces into earthly life.
From out the temple, nonetheless, I brought
my soul into my work. It's well that soul
stays undisturbed by earthly reasoning.

MANAGER    And do you think that Strader's mode of spirit
is but remotely similar to yours?
At your side I would always know myself
free from the spirit beings Strader brings.
I feel acutely, even in his random speech,
that elemental beings pour themselves
with quickening life into his words and being,
revealing things our senses cannot grasp.
And yet it's this I find in him repellent.

ROMANUS    This word, my friend, strikes deeply to my heart.
Since I drew near to Strader, I have had
to feel the thoughts which I receive from him
endowed with quite extraordinary powers.
They moved me just as if they were my own.
And one day I reflected: what if you
owe not to yourself but to him the power
which let you grow to full maturity?
This feeling soon was followed by a second:
what if, for all that makes me of some use
in life and work and service for mankind,
I am indebted to some past earth life?

| | |
|---|---|
| MANAGER | This is exactly what I feel about him. |
| | The closer one draws near him, the more strongly |
| | the spirit working in him moves one's soul. |
| | If your strong mind could thus succumb to him, |
| | how could I manage to protect my own |
| | if I unite with him in active work? |
| | |
| ROMANUS | It will be up to you alone to find |
| | the right relationship between you both. |
| | I think that Strader's power can not harm me |
| | since in my thought I have conceived the way |
| | in which he may have once obtained this |
| | power. |
| | |
| MANAGER | Obtained – – he – – power – – over you – – |
| | he, the dreamer, – – over you – – the man of |
| | action? |
| | |
| ROMANUS | If one might dare imagine that in Strader |
| | a spirit lives its active life who once |
| | could raise himself in some past life on earth |
| | to most unusual inner heights – – who knew |
| | then much of what the others of that time |
| | were not advanced enough to even dream – |
| | it would be possible that, from his spirit, |
| | thoughts once originated which could find |
| | their way into the common life of men, |
| | and that from this source people like myself |
| | could gain proficiency in work on earth. |
| | The thoughts which in my youth I seized upon |
| | and which I found in my environment |
| | could well have sprung from this, his |
| | spirit. |

MANAGER          And do you think it then permissible
                 to trace back thoughts, which are of general value
                 in life, to Strader in particular?

ROMANUS          I'd be a dreamer if I thought that way.
                 I do not spin ideas about life's conduct
                 with eyes shut tight. It never was my way
                 to dream along in thoughts that came to
                      me.
                 With open eyes I look at him and see
                 how Strader shows himself as entity,
                 what qualities he has and how he acts,
                 what's more, in how he fails – and I know clearly
                 I had to form my judgment of his gifts
                 as I have just presented it to you.
                 I see him present in my mind as if
                 this man had stood before my earthly eyes
                 already many hundred years ago.
                 And that I am awake I know full well.
                 I will work side by side with Hilary.
                 All that will come that has to come about. –
                 Do give some further thought to all his
                      plans.

MANAGER          For me it is of greater value now
                 to think about what you have been confiding.

                 (*Exeunt Manager and Romanus. Johannes comes
                 from another direction, deep in thought, and sits down
                 on a boulder. He is at first alone; afterwards appear
                 Johannes' Double, the Spirit of Johannes' Youth,
                 and finally the Guardian of the Threshold and
                 Ahriman.*)

                              66

JOHANNES       I was astonished when Capesius
disclosed to me how my soul's inward life
revealed itself unto his spirit sight.
Thus could a truth become obscured to me
which years ago stood out in clearest light. –
That everything which lives in human souls
works further in the outer realms of spirit:
I knew it long ago, – but could *forget* it.
When Benedictus pointed out the path
to my first seership, I could behold
Capesius and Strader quite distinctly
as spirit images, though changed in age.
I saw the forming power of their thinking
start circling waves that spread in world-expanses.
All this I know so well – and did not know it
when I beheld it through Capesius.
The knowing part within me was asleep.
And, too, that in a long-past life on earth
I was bound closely with Capesius:
this also for a long time I have known, –
I did not recognize it at that moment.
How can I guard my knowledge at all
     times?

(*A voice from the distance, that of Johannes' Double.*)

The enchanted weaving
of their own being.

JOHANNES      And wakening dreaming
reveals to the souls
the enchanted weaving
of their own being.

*(While Johannes is speaking these lines, his Double
approaches him. Johannes does not recognize him but
thinks The Other Philia is coming towards him.)*

JOHANNES

You come once more, O you mysterious spirit,
you, who brought true counsel to my soul.

DOUBLE

Johannes, your awakening remains illusion
till you yourself will liberate the shade
on whom your guilt bestows a spellbound life.

JOHANNES

This is the second time you speak these words.
I will obey them. – Point me out the way.

DOUBLE

Johannes, let live within the realm of shades
what has been lost to you in your own self,
but give him light out of your spirit light
so that he will not have to suffer pain.

JOHANNES

I may have only numbed the shadow being,
but not subdued him; he must therefore stay
a spellbound shade among the other shades
till I unite myself again with him.

DOUBLE

Then give to me what now you owe this being:
the power of love impelling you towards him;
the hope which he engendered in your heart;
the quickening life which is concealed in him;
the fruits of earth-lives in the distant past,
now lost to you along with his existence;
O give me them; I'll bring them faithfully to him.

JOHANNES

You know the way to him? – Show it to me.

68

DOUBLE         I could approach him in the realm of shades
               when you had raised yourself to spirit spheres.
               But since the powers of desire have lured you
               and to his being you have turned your mind,
               my strength must always fail me when I seek him.
               But if you will abide by my advice,
               my strength might then create itself anew.


JOHANNES       I've promised you that I would follow you.
               I will with all my strength of soul renew
               this vow, O spirit, you who are a riddle.
               But if you still can find the way to him,
               then in this fateful hour show it to me.


DOUBLE         I find him now, yet cannot guide you to him.
               I can alone show to your eye of soul
               the being whom your longing ever seeks.

               (*The Spirit of Johannes' Youth appears.*)


SPIRIT OF JOHANNES' YOUTH
               I shall be bound forever to the spirit
               who's opened now the eyes of soul for you,
               so that your inner sight will find me when,
               commanded by the spirit, I show myself
               to you in future. You should, though, know in
                    truth
               this spirit at whose side you see me now.

               (*The Spirit of Johannes' Youth disappears; and
               now Johannes recognizes his Double.*)


JOHANNES       Not that mysterious spirit – my other self?

DOUBLE          Now follow me – for you have made the vow –
                I must now lead you to my sovereign lord.

                *(The Guardian of the Threshold appears and
                places himself at the side of the Double)*


GUARDIAN        Johannes, if you wish to tear away
                this spirit shade from spellbound worlds of soul,
                destroy desires alluring you still further.
                The clues which you pursue lead you to naught
                as soon as you are driven by desires.
                They lure you past my threshold and elude it.
                But following here the will of higher beings,
                I can confuse the inward sight of those
                within whose spirit-glance live vain desires.
                Their sight must first encounter me before
                they can ascend to purest light of truth.
                I hold you, therefore, fast within your gaze
                as long as you approach me with desires.
                You see myself, too, in delusion's form
                while vain desires are joined to inner sight
                and spirit peacefulness as sheath of soul
                has not yet taken hold of your whole being.
                Make strong the words of power that you know:
                their spirit-strength will conquer your delusion.
                Then recognize me, freed from all desires,
                and you will see me as I really am.
                And then I need no longer hold you back
                from gazing freely into spirit realms.


JOHANNES        You, too, reveal yourself as my delusion? – – – –
                You, too – – whom I must see in truth as first
                of all the beings in the spirit realms.

                                  70

How shall I know the truth when I must find,
one truth alone confronts my further steps:
that I make my delusions ever denser.

AHRIMAN  Do not permit him to confuse you quite.
He guards the threshold faithfully indeed,
although he shows himself in borrowed clothes
which you have patched together in your mind
from odds and ends that look like melodrama.
You as an artist could, of course, avoid
producing him in such a wretched style,
though later you will surely do it better.
But even his distorted image serves.
It does not need too much of emphasis
to show you what his present stature is.
You should take note of how the Guardian speaks:
too mournful is his tone, too much of pathos. –
Forbid him this, and he will show to you
from whom today he borrows to excess.

JOHANNES  The content, even, of his words deceives?

DOUBLE  Do not ask this of Ahriman, who always
in contradictions finds his chief delight.

JOHANNES  Whom shall I ask?

DOUBLE  Why, ask your Self.
I will now strongly arm you with my power,
that wakefully you find that part of you
whence you can gaze without your burning wishes.
Give yourself strength.

JOHANNES      The enchanted weaving
of my own being.
Enchanted weaving of my own being,
reveal what is beyond my burning wishes.

*(The Guardian disappears. In his place*
*appear Benedictus and Maria.)*

MARIA        You see me, too, but in delusion's form,
while vain desires are joined to inner sight.

BENEDICTUS   And spirit peacefulness as your soul sheath
has not yet taken hold of your whole being.

*(The Double, Benedictus and Maria disappear.)*

JOHANNES      Benedictus, Maria, they – – – the Guardian!
How could they now appear to me as Guardian?
– – – – – – – – – – – – – –
Though I have been with you for many years, – –
yet I must seek you still: for so commands
the enchanted weaving of my own being.

*(Exit left. Strader, Benedictus and Maria*
*enter from the right.)*

STRADER     You gave, in close communion of spirit,
before the deep abyss of my own being,
wise counsel to my inner vision.
Though at this time I cannot comprehend it,
it will work on in me and surely solve
within myself the riddles of my life
which would impede me in my further strivings.
I feel in me the power that your endeavor
gives to the seeker on the spirit path.

Therefore I will be able now to give you
the service which you'll need for Hilary's
great work, planned for the good of all mankind.
Capesius will indeed be missed by us. –
The others' vigour never will replace
his part in the performance of his duties;
but that will come which *is* to come about.

BENEDICTUS    But that will come which is to come about.
These words express the grade of your maturing.
They do not find, however, in the souls
of all the other spirit-friends, an echo.
Thomasius is not prepared to carry
the power of spirit into sense existence.
He, too, withdraws from our activities.
Through him a sign of destiny is shown:
we all must now discover other tasks.

STRADER    And is Maria, – are not *you* still here?

BENEDICTUS    Maria, if she is to find the way
which leads her back in truth from spirit life
to realms of sense, must take Johannes with her.
The earnest Guardian has ordained it so;
he holds stern watch where both realms have
        their border.
She cannot lend her help to you as yet.
And this may serve you as a certain sign
that at this time you will not truly find
the way into the realm of earthly matter.

STRADER    So I am then alone now with my aims!
O loneliness, was it you that sought me out
when I stood there at Felix Balde's side?

73

BENEDICTUS    All that has lately happened in our circle
              has taught me, from your course of destiny,
              to read in spirit light a certain word
              which hitherto concealed itself from me.
              I saw you joined with special kinds of beings
              who would work evil if already now
              they would take hold of human spheres of action.
              Yet now they live as germs in certain souls
              to ripen for the earth in future times.
              I saw such germs alive within your soul.
              That they're unknown to you is for your good.
              They will first recognize themselves through
                      you.
              But as of now the road is barred for them
              which leads them into realms of earthly matter.

STRADER       Whatever else your words may say to me,
              they show that loneliness is seeking me. –
              This loneliness in truth will forge the sword. –
              Maria told me this at my abyss.

              (*Benedictus and Maria draw back; Strader is alone.
              The soul of Theodora appears.*)

SOUL OF THEODORA
              And Theodora will in realms of light,
              engender warmth so that your spirit-sword
              may strike with vigour enemies of soul.

              (*She disappears. Exit Strader. Benedictus and
              Maria come forward.*)

MARIA         O my wise teacher, I have never heard you
              speak in such tones the words of destiny

74

to students who have reached the stage of
    Strader.
Will his soul's course take on such speed that
these words' power will be of benefit to him?

BENEDICTUS    Fate ordered me, – and so it had to be.

MARIA    And if this power is not of use to him,
will not its ill effects touch you as well?

BENEDICTUS    Evil it will not be; I do not know
how it will manifest itself in him.
Although my vision reaches now those realms
where such a counsel shines into my soul,
I cannot see the picture of its effect.
And if I try to see, my vision dies.

MARIA    Your vision dies, beholding? My leader, yours?
Who then destroys the seer's trusted gaze?

BENEDICTUS    Johannes flees with it to cosmic reaches.
We must now follow him; I hear him call.

MARIA    He calls . . . his call rings out from spirit spaces.
Through it there radiates far distant fear.

BENEDICTUS    So sounds from ever empty fields of ice
the friend's entreating call in cosmic reaches.

MARIA    The cold of ice is burning in my Self,
enkindling tongues of flame in my soul depths;
the flames consume the power of my thinking.

BENEDICTUS    In depths of your own soul the fire blazes.
              Johannes kindles it in cosmic frost.

MARIA         The flames are fleeing . . . fleeing with my
                  thinking;
              – – – – – – – – – – – – – – – –
              And there at distant cosmic shores of soul
              a furious battle . . . my own thinking fights . . .
              at flowing nothingness – – cold spirit light . . .
              my thinking wavers, reels . . . cold light . . . it
              strikes out of my thinking flaming waves of
                  darkness . . .
              what now emerges from the fierce, dark heat? . . .
              in red flames storms my Self . . . into the light . . .
              into cold light . . . of cosmic fields of ice.
              *Curtain*

# SCENE FIVE

THE SPIRIT REALM. *The scene is set in floods of meaningful colour, reddish deepening into fiery red above, blue merging into dark blue and violet below. In the lower part a symbolically indicated earth-sphere. The figures that appear seem to blend into a complete whole with the colors. On the right, the group of gnomes as in Scene Two; in front of them Hilary, and in the immediate foreground the soul-forces. Behind Hilary and placed somewhat higher, Ahriman. In the left foreground Felix Balde's Soul. Lucifer somewhat in the background, to the right of and towering over Felix Balde's Soul. Strader's Soul at the right, at a distance from Felix. The soul forces are near Strader's Soul.*

FELIX BALDE'S SOUL (*Having the form of a penitent but arrayed in a light violet robe girdled with gold*)

> My thanks, wise spirit, ruler of the worlds,
> my liberator from dark solitudes.
> Your word awakens life and active work.
> I will make use of what you give to worlds,
> on which I may reflecting muse, when you
> allow my world to sink again to dullness.
> You'll carry to these worlds upon your rays
> what can create for me new-shaping powers.

LUCIFER (*Bluish-green, shining undergarment, reddish outer-garment, shaped like a mantle and gleaming brightly, which*

*extends into winglike shapes. This upper part is not*
*an aura, but he wears a mitre-like headdress, deep red*
*with wings; on his right wing a blue swordlike shape;*
*a yellow spheric shape is supported by his left wing.)*

My servant, such activity as yours
needs time within the Sun-sphere which we've
    entered.
The earth-star now receives but gloomy light.
This is the time when souls like yours
can best be working on themselves.
Out of my fount of light I let the seeds
of self-awareness brightly shine on you.
Go, gather them to make your ego strong.
In your earth life the seeds will come to flower.
Your soul will search for them as blossoms there
and take delight in its own self by planning
with wishful joy what it desires.

FELIX BALDE'S SOUL (*gazing at the group of gnomes*).

There, far away, a luminous life is fading;
it floats in misty forms into the depths
and, floating, wants to gather heaviness.

HILARY'S SOUL (*With the figure, though resembling a man's, of a*
*steel-blue-grey elemental spirit, the head less bowed*
*and the limbs more human*).

The mist of wishes is reflection only
thrown on the realms of spirit by the earth-star,
that star for which you weave within this world
a thinking life from substances of soul.
For you it is but fleeting misty weaving.
Yet these are beings, sensing density.

They work on earth with cosmic intellect
in ancient fiery depths that thirst for form.

FELIX BALDE'S SOUL

      I will not let their heaviness oppress me.
      It gives resistance to the urge to float.

AHRIMAN      Such splendid words! I'll seize them fast
      and hold them unspoiled for myself;
      you cannot further cherish them yourself,
      yet you would hate them on the earth.

STRADER'S SOUL (*Only his head is visible; it is in a yellowish-green*
          *aura with red and orange stars.*)

      Words audibly resounding – echoing?
      They carry meaning, but their meaning fades.
      Desire for life is seizing on the echo.
      Its tone – in which direction will it turn?

THE OTHER PHILIA (*Arrayed like a copy of Lucifer, though the*
          *radiance is lacking. Instead of the sword, she has a*
          *kind of dagger and, in place of the planet, a red*
          *ball like a fruit.*)

      It travels onward with desire for weight
      to reach that place where radiant being fades
      and enters depths in form of misty pictures.
      Uphold the meaning of that sound within
      your sphere; I'll take its force into the mist
      that you may rediscover it on earth.

PHILIA (*An angelic figure, yellow merging into white, with wings of a*
       *bright violet, a lighter shade than Maria has later.*)

I'll tend for you the mist-created beings
that they, unknowingly, may guide your will.
I will entrust your will to cosmic light
where they create the warmth your being needs.

ASTRID (*An angelic figure, robed in light violet, with blue wings.*)

I'll radiate the blissful life of stars
to them that they condense it into forms.
They will endow with strength your earthly body,
from knowledge far, yet near to heart's content.

LUNA (*An angelic figure, robed in blue-red, with orange wings.*)

The pond'rous substance formed from weightiness
I'll hide from you within your next sense-body
that you, in thinking, turn it not to evil
and thus unleash a storm in earth-existence.

STRADER'S SOUL

The three were speaking words here, sun-imbued.
I see them working actively around me,
creating forms and figures manifold.
I feel the urge to shape them into one,
endowed with strength of soul and filled with
    meaning. –
Awake in me, O royal solar power,
that I may dim you by the opposition
which my desire brings from the lunar sphere.
There stirs a golden glow, imbued with warmth,
and silver gleam that sparkles with cold thoughts.
Still glimmer, wishful urge of Mercury,
Unite for me the sundered cosmic life.

– – – – – – – – – – – – – – –

And now I sense: an image has again
been partly formed which I must work on here
to weave it out of cosmic spirit forces.

(*Exit Ahriman*)

CAPESIUS' SOUL (*Appears at the first lines of Strader; only his head
is visible, in a blue aura with red and yellow
stars.*)

On that far shore of soul a picture rises
that's never touched my being since I wrenched
myself away from former earth existence.
It rays forth grace, benignly, gently weaves.
The warming glow of wisdom flows from it
and grants my being clarifying light. –
If I could make this picture one with me,
I would obtain the bliss for which I thirst.
And yet I do not know what force could bring
the picture actively into my sphere.

LUNA            What in two earthly lives you've gained – feel
                now.
                The first flowed by, in ancient times long past,
                in solemn growth; the later one you lived
                made dark by selfish craving; fill it now
                with powers of grace the earlier life endows,
                and Jupiter's fire-souls will be revealed
                on the horizon of your spirit sight.
                By wisdom will you then be strengthened
                so that the picture you behold
                upon the far shore of your sphere of soul
                can ever closer move to you.

CAPESIUS' SOUL Am I indebted to that other soul
that now prepares for being while it shows
a warning vision in my sphere of soul?

ASTRID You are indebted, but the other soul
does not in your next earth-life ask redress.
The vision wants to give you powers of thought
that you as man may recognize that man
who shows you in a picture his earth future.

THE OTHER PHILIA
The picture may indeed move closer still
but cannot pierce the sphere of your own life.
Hold back, therefore, its urge towards your
    existence
that you may find yourself again on earth
before it flows into your inmost being.

CAPESIUS' SOUL I can foresee what I will owe the vision
if I should bring it closer to my sphere,
yet, free from it, keep firm within myself. –
From Philia's domain I can behold
in form of pictures, thought-imbued, those powers
which from its near approach I shall draw forth.

PHILIA When Saturn soon will shed its rays on you
of many-colored light, use well the hour.
The picture of the one akin to you
will plant the roots of thoughts through Saturn's
    power
into your own soul's sheaths. They will reveal
the meaning of life's course on earth for you
when once that star is carrying you again.

CAPESIUS' SOUL The counsel you have given shall be my guide,
as soon as Saturn shines its light on me.

82

LUCIFER         I wish still to awaken in these souls,
                before they leave behind this sphere of Sun
                with forces for their later life on earth,
                the sight of worlds whose light will cause
                    them pain.
                In grief they must be fructified with doubt.
                I will now conjure up those spheres of soul
                which they have not the strength to look upon.

                *(The souls of Benedictus and Maria appear in the*
                *center of the stage. Benedictus, in dress and in*
                *figure, is a microcosmic counterpart of the entire*
                *scenic effect. Below, his robe, becoming broader,*
                *shades into blue-green: around his head is an*
                *aura of red, yellow and blue: the blue blends*
                *into the blue-green of the entire robe. Maria is*
                *an angelic figure; yellow shading into gold, without*
                *feet and with light violet wings.)*

BENEDICTUS' SOUL
                You weigh down heavily my cosmic sphere
                with these condensed earth-laden spheres of yours.
                Should you let self-indulgence grow too strong,
                then you will find that in this spirit life
                my own sun-nature cannot shine within you.

MARIA'S SOUL    He was unknown to you when you wore last
                the garment woven out of earthly substance.
                And yet, the Sun-word's power with which
                    benignly
                he guided you in ancient times on earth
                continues to bear fruit in your soul-sheaths.
                O feel the deepest urge within your being,
                and you shall strongly sense that he is near.

83

FELIX BALDE'S SOUL

> Out of spheres strange to me are sounding words
> whose tones do not create enlightening life
> and so they are not fully real to me.

STRADER'S SOUL

> A radiant being there on spirit shores!
> Yet it is silent, though I struggle hard
> to hear the meaning of those luminous powers.

FELICIA BALDE'S SOUL (*Figure of a penitent; robe yellow-orange,
> with silver girdle. She appears quite close to Maria.*)

> You souls now conjured up by Lucifer,
> the penitent can hear your speech as tone,
> and yet alone the Sun-word gives him light;
> its noble splendour silences your voices.
> The other soul can see your starry light;
> the script of stars is still unknown to him.

CAPESIUS' SOUL The script of stars! This word . . . awakens
>   thoughts.
> It bears them on the waves of soul to me;
> those thoughts that in far distant days on earth
> revealed themselves to me so gloriously.
> _ _ _ _ _ _ _ _ _ _ _ _ _ _ _
> They radiate, but . . . vanish as they grow . . .
> forgetfulness spreads out its shadowy gloom.

THE GUARDIAN (*In symbolic robe, angel-like. Enters and moves
> near Benedictus' and Maria's souls.*)

> You souls that by command of Lucifer
> have now drawn near the spheres of other souls,
> in this domain you are within my power.

The souls whom you are seeking – seek you too. –
But at this cosmic hour, within their spheres
their being shall not touch you by mere thought.
Take heed and do not penetrate their orbits.
Yet if you dare, it will harm both you and them. –
I would be forced to take away from you
this starry light and banish you from them
to other spheric realms for cosmic ages.
*Curtain*

# SCENE SIX

*Spirit region, similar to that of Scene Five. The lighting is warm and diversified, but not too bright. On the left are the Sylphs, in front Philia, Astrid, Luna.*

CAPESIUS' SOUL (*On the right, near the centre of the stage.*)

> The vision shown me at the solar hour
> in radiant grace and kindly gentleness
> holds sway within my being even now
> when other light of wisdom shines upon
> this spirit region in many colored hues.
> But from the vision comes still stronger force;
> it wants me to draw forth for future times
> what in an earlier life a soul has given me –
> the one who shows himself significantly
> now to my sphere in picture form.
> And yet – no stream of feeling leads me on
> to this soul actively.

ROMANUS' SOUL (*A figure showing the upper part of the body down to the hips. He has mighty red wings, which extend around his head into a red aura, running into blue on its outer edge. He stands close to Capesius' soul; the souls of Bellicosus and Torquatus are near by.*)

> Arouse
> within yourself the image of the Jew,

who heard but hate and scorn on every side,
yet truly served the mystic brotherhood
of which you were a member once on earth.

CAPESIUS' SOUL  There now begin to dawn thought-pictures,
                wanting
to seize me with their overpowering strength.
There rises Simon's image to my sight
out of the surging sea of soul. Another
soul is joining him, a penitent . . .
Could I but keep him far from me!

    (*Felix Balde's Soul appears.*)

ROMANUS' SOUL  He can be active only at the sun-sphere's
cosmic hour; in solitude and shrouded
in darkness must he wend his way alone,
when Saturn shines upon this spirit land.

CAPESIUS' SOUL  O how this penitent bewilders me.
His rays of soul pierce burningly the sheaths
of my own soul. Thus souls are active by
beholding inmost depths of other souls.

FELIX BALDE'S SOUL  (*in a hollow, somewhat veiled voice.*)

    'My worthy Kean – faithful you have always
        proved . . .'

CAPESIUS' SOUL  Myself – my very words – from him –
as echo sounding forth in spirit realms –
This is the soul I am compelled to seek.
He knows me well; through him I'll find myself.

*(Capesius' Soul disappears. The Other Philia
appears from the left, with Theodora's soul;
behind her, Felicia Balde's soul.)*

ROMANUS' SOUL Two souls are drawing near the penitent,
            ahead of them the spirit whom through love
            the souls will always choose to be their guide.
            The first soul radiates a tender light
            that flows into the other, and she nears us
            robed, too, as penitent. The vision shines
            in beauty's glow, which lives as wisdom here.

TORQUATUS' SOUL *(A figure visible only down to the chest, with
            blue aura, green wings.)*

            You see the afterglow of longing's light
            that I ray forth from my soul sheaths into
            your sphere, pledged by true spirit brotherhood.
            The powers of destiny assigned to me
            the task of stirring gentleness in you.
            Thus souls serve other souls in spirit.
            Out of itself, your stern, unbending mind
            would never find the life-gift of compassion.

BELLICOSUS' SOUL *(A figure like Torquatus' soul, but with
            blue-violet aura and blue-green wings).*

            Make strong your power of spirit hearing –
                there speaks
            the soul that radiates the light of mildness
            and Saturn's glory draws from out these souls
            the shining glow of spirit blissfulness.

THEODORA'S SOUL *(An angelic figure, white with yellow wings
            and blue-yellow aura.)*

O you, my true companion in the spirit,
pour forth your soul-sheath's loving power to him
in gentle radiant light, that it may soothe
his solitude's consuming fire-force.
Direct to him rays of illumined thoughts
from yonder shadow-souls that at this time
are gathering forces in the spirit worlds
to fill their sheaths of soul with glimmering life.
Out of their glimmering creative glow
men's souls may draw new strength to quicken
     thus
the sense of growth, evolving in earth-life.

FELICIA'S SOUL  You spirit, garbed as penitent – feel me;
O sun-filled soul, receive the power of stars. –
Until your spirit sheath can struggle free
from Lucifer's dominion, I shall guide
you through your solitude and bring to you
the forces which I now will gather up
in cosmic journeying from star to star.

THEODORA      Earth-thoughts long past arise in glimmering light
on yonder shores of souls – a human image –
I saw its earthly form – it follows here –
what once I heard re-echoes here:
    'Out of the godhead rose the human soul.
    In death it can descend to depths of being.
    It will, in time, from death set free the spirit.'

(*During the last lines Lucifer appears, with the
soul of Johannes.*)

THE OTHER PHILIA
    This living, sounding image carries hither
    the active force of noble brother-love

you once in loyalty displayed on earth.
I will transform it into your soul power.
The glimmering light of yonder shadow-beings
receives the word that I direct to you.
They will arouse in you in earth existence
the thoughts on which they muse eternally. – –
And you, the penitent in spirit realms,
turn now your soul-steps onward towards the
    stars
where nature-spirits long to use your work
to kindle fantasy in human souls
and thus create the wings they'll need on earth.

FELICIA'S SOUL   I'll follow you, dear sister of my soul,
my Philia, who weaves and quickens love
from star to star, from spirit unto spirit.
I'll follow you aloft to starry worlds.
I'll bring your word to many a cosmic sphere.
By spirit deeds I'll shape myself anew
for my own future wanderings on earth.

*(Felix Balde's soul, led on by Felicia's soul,*
*disappears slowly. Theodora stands motionless,*
*looking at Johannes' soul; then she also disappears,*
*as does Lucifer with the soul of Johannes.)*

ROMANUS' SOUL

We have beheld within this spirit orb
the word of love and word of action join
themselves, and this will strengthen in our being
the seeds we'll need in future life on earth.

*(The souls of Romanus, Torquatus and Bellicosus*
*disappear. Benedictus' soul and Maria's soul at the*
*side of the Guardian of the Threshold appear.)*

THE GUARDIAN

>Perceive and know your cosmic midnight
>>hour.
>I hold you in the spell of ripened light,
>which Saturn shines on you until through power
>of this light your sheaths, illumining yourselves,
>can live in stronger wakefulness their colours.

MARIA'S SOUL   The cosmic midnight hour in souls'
>>awakening? – – –
>It was within the moon-time that the sun spoke
>the solemn word of destiny: those human souls
>who at the cosmic midnight hour are wakeful
>see lightnings dazzlingly illumine
>in such swift flashes things that *have to be*
>that spirit visions die on recognition,
>and dying shape themselves to scripts of fate
>forever actively engraved in souls.
>Such souls hear thunder-words reverberating
>in heavy rumbling through the cosmic grounds,
>that threaten soul-illusion as they roll.

>(*Lucifer reappears, with the soul of Johannes.*)

BENEDICTUS' SOUL

>From ever empty fields of ice there calls
>our spirit friend with voice of destiny.
>When we perceive the cosmic midnight hour,
>we'll reach the spirit orbit of this soul.

MARIA'S SOUL   The flames are nearing – nearing with my thinking
>from distant cosmic soul-shores of my being. –

A heated battle nears – and my own thinking
must battle with the thoughts of Lucifer;
within another soul my thinking fights. –
Hot light is wafted – out of fierce dark coldness. –
It flashes lightnings, this hot light of soul –
the light of soul – in cosmic fields of ice –

LUCIFER    Perceive this light – hot cosmic light of mine –
Behold the lightnings which your thinking
strikes – from those domains where Lucifer holds
    sway.
Across the bounds of your horizon here
as you take in the cosmic midnight hour,
I bring the soul so closely bound to you.
In future you must change your searching's path
to come into communion with this soul.
And you, O soul, now following me, use here
the forces of the light rayed forth
by Saturn on her cosmic midnight hour. –

JOHANNES' SOUL (*An angelic figure, rose-red, without
    feet but with blue-red wings.*)

I can sense souls near by, but need more strength
to fortify their light in me to being.
However close they are, they generate
a thinking which only lights for me afar.
How can I raise them to my spirit sight?

PHILIA     You will behold them if you swiftly grasp
what they illumine in the cosmic light.
But when you look, use well the moment's flash;
the brightness quickly vanishes again.

JOHANNES' SOUL

> What yonder leader's soul speaks to his pupil,
> that pupil's soul so close and dear to me,
> shall shine upon the orbit of my soul.

BENEDICTUS' SOUL

> Create within this spirit midnight hour
> the power of will which you will feel again
> when forces of the earth renew your form.
> Your word will radiate into your friend's
> soul.

MARIA'S SOUL  So let in cosmic light my words grow strong
> which at this cosmic midnight I entrust
> unto the soul that Lucifer has brought.
> All that is dear to me in depths of soul,
> I will behold it and, beholding, speak
> and, speaking, form a tone within his soul
> that he, perceiving it again on earth,
> brings lovingly to life within his being.
> What do I see now in my inmost core?
> A holy, flaming script shines forth to
> me.
> My love is flaming out to that dear leader
> who guided me on earth, who guided me
> in spirit constantly from age to age,
> who always found me, when in earthly danger
> my ardent prayer besought his help, although
> he dwelt in spirit heights; in radiance
> this love appears to me; sound forth from me,
> you word of love unto the other soul.

> _ _ _ _ _ _ _ _ _ _ _ _ _ _ _
> _ _ _ _ _ _ _ _ _ _ _ _ _ _ _

What flames awaken with that word of love?
Gently they glow; their gentleness enkindles
a lofty earnestness. Lightnings of wisdom
are flashing – blessing us – through cosmic ether,
and blissfulness, joy weaving, gushes forth
to fill the wide horizon of my soul.
O everlasting time, I do entreat you,
pour out yourself into this blissfulness
and let the leader, let the other soul
abide with me within you, peace-imbued.

THE GUARDIAN

So shall the lightnings melt now into naught,
having shone dazzlingly on what must be
when wakeful souls live through the cosmic
        North.
Thunder shall lose its rumbling, rolling tone
of warning at the cosmic midnight hour. –
Astrid, to you I give a strict command:
safeguard the raging storm within this soul
until another cosmic midnight hour
finds her awakened in the flow of time.
She shall then face herself in ancient times
and know that in the flight to spirit heights
her wings gain strength as well by sudden
        falls.
The wish to fall should never tempt the soul,
but from each fall it must draw forth more
        wisdom.

ASTRID

The lightning's and the thunder's power I'll
        guard,
sustaining them within the cosmic life
till Saturn turns again unto her soul.

MARIA'S SOUL    Abiding, I feel blissfulness of stars
                and in the stream of time I enter it.
                Beneath its sway of grace I'll live and work
                in union with this ever-cherished soul.

LUNA            I'll guard your work in spirit here for you
                so that its fruits may ripen on the earth.

JOHANNES' SOUL
                Into my soul's horizon moves . . . this star . . .
                it shines forth blissfulness . . . it glows with
                    grace . . .
                a star of soul in cosmic ether . . . floating . . .
                _ _ _ _ _ _ _ _ _ _ _ _ _ _ _ _
                and there . . . in gentle light, a second star . . .
                though soft it sounds, I'll hear the words it
                    speaks.

                (With his last words, the Spirit of Johannes' Youth
                appears. An angelic figure; silvery sheen.)

SPIRIT OF JOHANNES' YOUTH
                I feed with living substance your desires.
                My breath will pour into your youthful aims
                illumining strength when worlds begin to tempt
                whereto I joyfully can be your guide.
                But should you lose me in yourself, I must
                fall victim to the shades, bereft of being.
                O blossom of my life . . . do not forsake me.

LUCIFER         Forsake you, he will not. I can perceive
                desires for light within his depths, desires
                which stray far from the other soul's pursuits.
                If these take root within his soul, with splendours
                they brilliantly create, they will bear fruit.

Nor will he be content to waste these fruits
within the realm where love holds sway
but love deprived of beauty.

(*The Curtain falls slowly.*)

## SCENE SEVEN

*A Temple somewhat in Egyptian style, the place of an initiation in the far-distant past. The third cultural epoch of the earth.*

*In order to identify each person with his or her later incarnation, the modern name is added in parenthesis.*

*At first only a conversation between the Hierophant, the Temple Warden and the Mystic.*

HIEROPHANT (Capesius)

        Are all the preparations duly made,
        my Temple Warden, in order that
        our holy rite may serve both gods and men?

TEMPLE WARDEN (Felix)

        As far as human forethought can provide
        they have been well prepared; the sacred incense
        has filled the temple now for many days.

HIEROPHANT    My Mystic, since this priest who will receive
        today the solemn rites of sacred wisdom
        is to become the counsellor of the king,
        have you, by testing him, assured yourself
        that he is not entirely given
        to wisdom which, neglecting earthly cares,
        lets his attention hang on spirit teaching?
        For such a counsellor would do us harm.

THE MYSTIC (Felicia)
                  The tests were given as the law requires.
                  The masters found them adequate; I think
                  our mystic has but little inclination
                  towards earthly cares; his soul is set upon
                  his spirit progress, the unfolding of his Self –
                  he often has been seen in spirit trance.
                  It's not too much to say he revels in
                  the union of the spirit with his soul.


HIEROPHANT        Has he been often seen in such a state?


THE MYSTIC        In truth he often shows himself like this.
                  He might be better suited to the service
                  of the temple than to be your counsellor.


HIEROPHANT        It is enough. Now go about your duty;
                  see that our holy rite is well performed.

                  (*Exit the* MYSTIC).

                  To you, my Temple Warden, I have more to say.
                  You know how much I prize your mystic gifts.
                  To me you stand much higher in your wisdom
                  Than well befits your grade within the temple.
                  How often have I taken recourse to your seership
                  to prove this spirit-sight of mine,
                  and so I ask what confidence you have
                  in this new mystic's spirit ripeness.


TEMPLE WARDEN
                  Why ask for my opinion?
                  My voice is never counted.

98

HIEROPHANT    For me it always counts.
Today you shall once more stand by my side;
we must together watch this holy rite
with probing eyes of soul; and should the mystic
show in smallest measure his unripeness
in spirit for the lofty meaning of our rites.
I shall refuse him rank as counsellor.

TEMPLE WARDEN

What could it be that might reveal itself
about this mystic at our holy rite?

HIEROPHANT    I know he is not worthy of the honour
the temple servants seek to give to him.
His human nature is well known to me.
His mystic aims have not that heartfelt urge
which stirs in men when light from spirit realms
draws souls in grace up to itself.
Strong passion surges still throughout his being;
the cravings of his senses are not curbed.
I do not, indeed, condemn the will of gods
which wisely also radiates its light
upon desire and passion in the stream of being.
But when the sensuous urge conceals itself
and revels mystically in veneration's mask,
it causes thought to lie, perverts the will.
The light that weaves the web of spirit-worlds
Can never penetrate into such souls
where passion spreads a mystic fog between.

TEMPLE WARDEN

My Hierophant, your judgment is severe
in dealing with a man who still is young

99

and inexperienced, who can not know
himself, nor take another course than that
which priestly guides and mystic leaders say
will reach the soul's true goal.

HIEROPHANT   I do not judge the man, I judge the deed
that will be wrought within this temple's solemn
          place.
The holy mystic ritual we perform
is of significance not only for us here.
Through word and deed of sacred priestly rites
there pours the fateful stream of world events.
What forms itself in symbols here will come
to everlasting life in spirit worlds. –
But now, good Warden, go about your task;
you will yourself discover
how best to help me in the holy rite.

(*Exit the Temple Warden*)

It will not be the fault of the young mystic
who dedicates himself today to wisdom
if, in the hours to come, a wrong emotion –
proceeding heedlessly out of his heart –
should throw its rays upon our sacred rites
and rise as image up to spirit spheres;
for from these spheres in consequence will flow
destructive forces into human life.
The guides and leaders are the guilty ones.
Do they still recognize the mystic force
which penetrates mysteriously with spirit
each word and gesture here within the temple? –
And still this force will work
when even elements of soul pour into it

which are injurious to world-becoming.
If only this young mystic consciously
would sacrifice himself unto the spirit!
Instead, his teachers drag him like a victim
into the holy place; here all unconscious
his soul is yielded up unto the spirit,
whereas he would indeed find other paths
if he could consciously sustain it in himself.
Within the circle of this temple's priesthood
the highest Hierophant alone knows clearly
the meaning of the ritual's mystic truths;
but he is mute as solitude itself.
Such silence his high dignity commands.
The others gaze uncomprehendingly
when of the ritual's true intent I speak.

— — — — — — — — — — — — — — — —

I am alone, therefore, with lonely care
which often weighs oppressively upon my heart
because I feel the import of this shrine.
Indeed, I've come to know in deepest measure
the solitude of this stern spirit shrine.
Why am I all alone here at this place ?
The soul must question – but the spirit –
when will it give the answer to my soul?

*Curtain*

# SCENE EIGHT

*The same set as in Scene Seven, at the beginning hidden by a curtain before which an Egyptian Woman has the following monologue:*

AN EGYPTIAN WOMAN (Johannes)
>This is the hour in which he dedicates himself
>to serve the ancient, holy mysteries,
>which tear him evermore away from me.
>From out those heights of light to which his soul
>has turned, the ray of death descends on mine. –
>Without him – there remains for me
>but sorrow on the earth –
>renunciation – suffering – and death.
>– – – – – – – – – – – – – – –
>But in this hour that he abandons me,
>I will remain yet near the place
>in which he gives himself unto the spirit.
>And if my eyes are not allowed to see
>how he will cut himself adrift from earth –
>perhaps the revelation of a dream,
>divining him, will bring me close in spirit.

*The curtain opens, disclosing everything and almost everyone in readiness for the initiation of the Neophyte. Deep silence is sustained for a while. Then the Temple Warden and the Mystic lead in the Neophyte*

102

*through a doorway on the left side. They place him in
the inner circle close behind the altar, and remain
standing near him.*

*The grouping for the ceremony* as seen from the audience:

TEMPLE WARDEN                  CHIEF HIEROPHANT

MYSTIC                                           HIEROPHANT

NEOPHYTE
*– altar –*

RECORDER                              KEEPER OF THE SEALS

AIR ELEMENT                          WATER ELEMENT

EARTH ELEMENT                    FIRE ELEMENT

AHRIMAN *as Sphinx*              LUCIFER *as Sphinx*
*with the Bull*                          *with the Cherubim*
*emphasized*                             *emphasized*

PHILIA     ASTRID     LUNA     THE OTHER PHILIA

TWO PRIESTS                                      TWO PRIESTS

TEMPLE WARDEN (Felix)

From out that web of unreality
which thou in error's darkness namest world,
the mystic has conducted thee to us.
From being and from naught the world was made
which to a semblance wove itself for thee.
Semblance is good when from reality beheld;
but thou didst dream it in the life of semblance;
and semblance known by semblance fades away.
O semblance of a semblance, learn now to know
thyself.

THE MYSTIC (Felicia)

> So speaks the one who guards the temple's
> threshold.
> Feel in thyself the full weight of his word.

THE REPRESENTATIVE OF
THE EARTH ELEMENT (Romanus)

> Within the weight of earth's existence, lay hold
> upon the semblance of thy being fearlessly
> that thou mayst sink into the cosmic depths.
> In cosmic depths search for reality in darkness.
> Bind to thy semblance that which thou dost find;
> its weighing down will grant to thee existence.

THE RECORDER (Hilary)

> Thou shalt perceive whereto we lead thee, sinking,
> as soon as thou hast carried out his word.
> We forge for thee the form of thine own being.
> Know thou our work; or thou must vanish
> as semblance in the cosmic nothingness.

THE MYSTIC

> So speaks the one who guards this temple's words.
> Feel in thyself the words' down-weighing might.

THE REPRESENTATIVE OF
THE AIR ELEMENT (Gairmanus-Bellicosus)

> Escape from heavy weight of earth existence
> which kills the being of thy self in sinking.
> Take flight from it with lightness of the air.
> In cosmic space search for reality in brightness.
> Bind to thy semblance that which thou dost find;
> in flying, it will grant to thee existence.

THE RECORDER
>Thou shalt perceive whereto we lead thee, flying,
as soon as thou hast carried out his word.
We light for thee the life of thine own being.
Know thou our work; or thou must vanish
as semblance in the cosmic weightiness.

THE MYSTIC   So speaks the one who guards the temple's words.
>Feel in thyself the words' uplifting force.

THE CHIEF HIEROPHANT (Benedictus)
>My son, thou shalt upon high wisdom's path
obey with right concern the mystic's words.
Thou canst not see the answer in thyself;
for error's darkness still doth weigh thee down.
Delusion strives in thee for distant heights.
Gaze, therefore, on this flame which is more close

>*(the sacred fire with bright tongues of flame flares up
on the altar in the center of the stage.)*

>to thee than is the life of thine own being, –
and read thine answer hidden in the fire.

THE MYSTIC   So speaks the one who leads this temple's rites.
>Feel in thyself the ritual's holy power.

THE REPRESENTATIVE OF
  THE FIRE ELEMENT (Strader)
>The error of thy sense of self be burned
in fire, enkindled in this rite for thee.
Burn thou thyself with substance of thine error.
In cosmic fire seek reality as flame;
bind to thy semblance that which thou dost find;
in burning, it will grant to thee existence.

THE KEEPER OF THE SEALS (Theodora)

> Thou shalt perceive why to a flame we form thee
> as soon as thou hast carried out his word.
> We cleanse for thee the form of thine own being!
> Know thou our work; or thou must lose thyself
> within the cosmic ocean formlessly.

THE MYSTIC  So speaks the one who guards the temple's seal;
> feel in thyself the brightening power of wisdom.

THE REPRESENTATIVE OF
  THE WATER ELEMENT (Theodosius-Torquatus)

> Prevent the world of fire's flaming power
> from robbing thee of self-sustaining might.
> Semblance will not arise into existence
> unless the wave-beat of the cosmic ocean
> can penetrate thee with its spheric tone.
> In cosmic ocean seek reality as wave;
> bind to thy semblance that which thou dost find;
> in surging, it will grant to thee existence.

THE KEEPER OF THE SEALS

> Thou shalt perceive why to a wave we form thee
> as soon as thou hast carried out his word.
> We shape for thee the form of thine own being.
> Know thou our work; or thou must lose thyself
> as formless being in the cosmic fire.

THE CHIEF HIEROPHANT

> My son, thou shalt by stalwart exercise of will
> obey with right concern these mystics' words.
> Thou canst not see the answer in thyself;

106

by cowardly fear thy power is frozen still;
thou canst not shape thy weakness to a wave
that lets thee sound throughout the spheres.
So listen to the forces of thy soul;
and recognize thy voice within their words.

PHILIA          In fire cleanse thyself; and lose thyself
as cosmic wave in tones of spirit spheres.

ASTRID          Form thou thyself in tones of spirit spheres;
in cosmic distances fly light as air.

LUNA          In cosmic depths sink heavily as earth;
Take courage as a self in weightiness.

THE OTHER PHILIA
Unloose thyself from out thy narrow selfhood;
unite with forces of the elements.

THE MYSTIC     So speaks within the temple thine own soul;
feel thou therein the guidance of its powers.

THE CHIEF HIEROPHANT (*to the Hierophant*)
My brother Hierophant, explore this soul,
which we must lead towards wisdom's path,
down to its depths. –
Proclaim to us
what thou beholdst within its present state.

THE HIEROPHANT (Capesius)
Fulfilled is what our ritual ordains.
The soul has now forgotten what it was.
Opposing elements have swept away

the web of semblance, spun on error's loom,
which still in elemental strife lives on.
The soul its inner core alone has rescued.
It must now read what lives within this core
as cosmic Word that speaks out of the flame.

THE CHIEF HIEROPHANT

O human soul, now read what through the flame
the cosmic Word proclaims within thyself.

(*A long pause occurs during which the stage becomes
completely dark, only the flame and the indistinct
outlines of the figures are visible. Then the Chief
Hierophant continues:*)

And now from out the cosmic vision wake!
Declare what can be read as cosmic Word.

--- --- --- --- --- --- --- --- ---

(*The Neophyte is silent. The Chief Hierophant, much
alarmed, continues:*)

He's silent. The vision has escaped you? Speak!

THE NEOPHYTE (Maria)

Obedient to your stern and sacred words
I sank into the being of this flame,
awaiting sounds of lofty cosmic words.

(*The assembled priests, with the exception of the
Hierophant, show an ever-increasing alarm during
the speech of the Neophyte.*)

I felt that I could liberate myself
from weight of earth and be as light as air.
I felt the loving tide of cosmic fire
receiving me as flowing spirit waves.

I saw the body that I wear on earth
as other being stand outside myself.
Though wrapt in bliss, and conscious of the light
of spirit round me, yet I could regard
my earthly sheath with longing and desire.
Spirits rayed light on it from lofty worlds;
like shining butterflies there hovered near
the beings tending, quickening its life.
The body in these beings' flickering light
reflected sparkling colours manifold;
they shone close by, grew fainter further off
and then were scattered and dispersed in space.
Within my spirit-soul existence rose the wish
that gravity of earth would plunge me down
into my sheath where I might feel
and hold the sense of joy in warmth of life.
Thus, gladly diving down into my sheath, –
I heeded your stern summons to awake.

THE CHIEF HIEROPHANT (*himself terrified to the terrified priests*):
This is no spirit vision; earth's desires –
wrung from the mystic – rose as offering
to radiant spirit heights.
O sacrilege, sacrilege!

THE RECORDER (*angrily to the Hierophant*)
It never could occur, had you performed
the duty granted you as hierophant
which ancient holy practice has ordained.

THE HIEROPHANT
I did the duty which from higher realms
was laid upon me in this solemn hour.

I barred myself from thinking of that word
which ritual customs have enjoined on me,
the word which, sent forth from my thinking,
should work in spirit on the neophyte.
And now the young man has declared to us
not thoughts of others but of his own being.
The truth has triumphed. –
                    You may punish me,
I had to do what shocks you into fright.
I feel the time approaching that will free
the single ego from a group-bound spirit
and liberate his individual thought.
What if the youth escapes your mystic path
at present? Later lives on earth will show
with clearest signs the kind of mystic way
which powers of destiny ordained for him.

THE MYSTICS    O sacrilege – – –

                  demand atonement! – – –

                          punish!

*(The sphinxes begin to speak; hitherto they have been*
*motionless statues; what they say is heard only by the*
HIEROPHANT, THE CHIEF HIEROPHANT *and the*
NEOPHYTE; – *the others are full of excitement over*
*the preceding events.)*

AHRIMAN as Sphinx

    For my domain, I want to capture
    what here unduly seeks the light,
    and I must further foster it in darkness.
    Thus will it form in spirit its own power
    to weave itself in future into human life
    as beneficial in its rightful time.

Yet till it gains this power, I will make
subservient to my work what here appeared
within this holy rite as weight of earth.

LUCIFER as Sphinx
I want to carry off into my realm
what here as spirit-wish has joy in semblance.
As semblance it should gladly shine in light
and so in spirit dedicate itself
to beauty. At present it is kept from this
by burden of earth-weightiness. In beauty
can semblance change itself into reality:
as light descending that escapes from here,
it shall in future be the light of earth.

THE CHIEF HIEROPHANT
The sphinxes speak – who were but images
since ancient sages first performed this rite.
It is the spirit that has seized on lifeless form.
O fate, through you resounds the cosmic Word!

*(The other priests, with the exception of the Hierophant
and the Neophyte are amazed at the words of the
Chief Hierophant.)*

THE HIEROPHANT *(to the Chief Hierophant)*
The holy mystic ritual we perform
is of significance not only here for us.
Through word and deed of sacred priestly rites
there pours the fateful stream of world events.

– – – – – – – – – – – – – – – – –

*(While the mood of excitement is at its height,
the curtain falls.)*

III

# SCENE NINE

*A small room in Hilary's house with a general atmosphere of seriousness, like a study. At first Maria alone in meditation, then Astrid appears, later Luna, The Guardian of the Threshold and Benedictus.*

MARIA      A star of soul . . . there . . . at the spirit shore . . .
it draws near . . . nears in spirit brightness . . .
my Self it brings . . . and nearing,
its light gains strength . . . gains calmness too.
You star within the circuit of my spirit . . . what,
approaching, shines on my beholding soul?

*(Astrid appears)*

ASTRID     Perceive what I can now bestow on you;
from cosmic strife of light with darknesses
I wrested thinking's power; faithfully
I bring it back into your earthly form
from out the cosmic midnight's wakening.

MARIA      O Astrid, until now you have appeared
as shining shadow only of my soul;
what forms you into this bright spirit star?

ASTRID     I kept the lightning's and the thunder's power
to hold them safe for you in soul existence

and now you can behold them knowingly,
recalling thus the cosmic midnight hour.

MARIA        The cosmic midnight hour – before the sheath
of body enclosed my Self on earth –
passed wakingly in Saturn's light-filled
    colour.
My earthly thinking has till now concealed
this spirit life in dullness of the soul.
It rises upwards now in clearest vision.

ASTRID      Within the cosmic light you spoke the word:
'O everlasting time, I do entreat you,
pour out yourself into this blissfulness
and let the leader, let the other soul
abide with me within you, peace-imbued.'

MARIA        Abide you too, O moment, you that could
create for me this spirit happening
as strength of self. Prepare and arm my soul
that you may not pass from me like a dream. – – –
Within the light that lights the cosmic midnight
which Astrid now creates out of my dullness,
my Ego joins that Self that for its service
created me within the universe.
But how, O moment, do I hold you fast
in order not to lose you when my senses
feel once again earth-clarity around me?
For mighty is their strength; and if they deaden
this spirit vision, dead it will remain
when the Self again in spirit finds itself.

(*Luna appears as if called by these last words.*)

LUNA      Preserve and heed, before your sense existence
brings you to dream again, the power of will
which now this moment could create for you.
Recall the words I spoke myself when you
beheld me at the cosmic midnight hour.

MARIA      My Luna, from the cosmic midnight hour
you brought me my own power of will, to be
a firm support within my earth existence.

LUNA      The Guardian's warning followed thus my words:
'You shall behold yourself quite differently
as image of yourself in ancient times,
and know that in the flight to spirit heights
your wings gain strength as well by sudden falls.
The wish to fall should never tempt the soul,
but from each fall it must draw forth more
         wisdom.'

MARIA      Whereto does your word's power carry me?
A spirit star, there at the shores of soul! –
It radiates ... draws near ... in spirit form;
my Self it brings and nears ... approaching,
nearing, its light now grows in density ... forms
         darken
within the light, they shape themselves to beings.
A youthful mystic and a sacred flame,
the Highest Hierophant's austere command
to tell the vision seen within the flame.

– – – – – – – – – – – – – – – –

The group of mystics overcome by fear,
because of the young mystic's self-confession!

(*The Guardian appears during her last lines.*)

THE GUARDIAN

In spirit listening fathom for yourself
the Highest Hierophant's austere command.


MARIA

'O human soul, now read what through the flame
the cosmic Word proclaims within itself!'
Who spoke these words which my own thinking,
recalling, lets emerge from tides of soul?

*(Benedictus appears after the first line.*


BENEDICTUS

With my own words you've called me here to you.
When in times past I gave you this command
you were not yet prepared to follow me.
My word then dwelt in evolution's womb.
The lengthy course of time gave it new strength
which flowed to it out of your inner life.
Thus it was active during later lives
on earth, in your soul depths, unconsciously.
Through it you found me as your guide again.
Now it transforms itself as conscious thought
into the mighty purpose of your life:
'The holy mystic ritual we perform
is of significance not only here for us;
through word and deed of sacred, priestly rites
there pours the fateful stream of world events.'


MARIA

It was not you who spoke those words – it was
the Hierophant who used to be your comrade
within that ancient mystic brotherhood.
He knew that by the power of destiny
its end was then already foreordained. –

Unconsciously, the Hierophant foresaw
the rosy dawn of beauty's shining semblance
announce a new sun rising over Hellas
within the spirit current of the earth.
So he forebore to send the power of thought
which he should have directed to my soul.
He was the cosmic spirit's instrument
there at the holy rite through which he heard
the whispering stream of cosmic evolution.
He spoke a word then from his inner depths:
'Indeed, I've come to know in deepest measure
the solitude of this stern spirit shrine.
Why am I all alone here at this place?'

BENEDICTUS    Into his soul the seed of solitude
was planted. Later it matured and grew
into a soul-fruit in the womb of time.
Capesius is tasting now this fruit
as mystic, driving him to follow Felix.

MARIA    But there is still that woman who was waiting
near by the temple, whom I see in ancient times –
and yet my sight can still not penetrate
to where she is today. How can I find her
when sense-life makes me dream again?

THE GUARDIAN
   You will discover her when in soul realms you see
that being which she feels as shade among the
      shades.
She strives for it with strongest power of soul.
She will not free it from the realm of shades

till in her present body, through your aid,
she will behold her long-past life on earth.

*(The Guardian and Benedictus disappear.)*

MARIA     There moves as star of soul the solemn Guardian,
in glowing light, unto my soul horizon . . .
his shining spreads forth calmness through
great spaces . . .
solemnity shines forth from him . . . his sternness
pours strength into my being's deepest core.
I will submerge myself in peacefulness. – –
I can divine that through it I will guide
myself to fullest spirit wakening.
I hold you fast, my messengers of soul,
forever fast, alive as radiant stars. – –
I call on you, O Astrid, when my thoughts
tend to withdraw from clarity of soul. –
And may my word find you, O Luna, when,
in soul depths, power of will is fast asleep.

*Curtain*

# SCENE TEN

*The same room. Johannes alone in meditation.*

JOHANNES
'This is the hour when he will dedicate
himself to serve the ancient, holy rites.
Perhaps the revelation of a dream
will let me linger close to him in spirit.'
The woman I behold as spirit image
spoke thus in ancient times, outside the temple.
Rememb'ring her, I feel how much I'm
    strengthened.
What does this picture rouse in me? What
holds me, on seeing it, so spellbound? Certainly
it is not sympathy to which this picture
compels me; for if I saw this scene
in sense existence, it would have for me
no meaning. What wants to speak to me from
    this?

(*As if from afar the voice of The Other Philia*)

THE OTHER PHILIA
Enchanted weaving
of your own being.

JOHANNES
And wakening dreaming
reveals to the souls

the enchanted weaving
of their own being.

(*While Johannes is speaking these lines, The Other
Philia approaches him.*)

Mysterious spirit, tell me who you are.
You brought true counsel to my soul –
and yet as to yourself, you have deceived me.

THE OTHER PHILIA

Johannes, you created from yourself
your being's second form. As shadow, too,
I must encircle you so long
till you yourself can liberate that shade
on which your guilt bestows a spellbound life.

JOHANNES      It is the third time that you speak these words.
I will obey. Direct for me the way.

THE OTHER PHILIA

Johannes, search for what within yourself
has been preserved alive in spirit light.
It will give light to you from its own light.
Thus you can look within yourself to see
how in your next life to erase your guilt.

JOHANNES      How shall I search for what has been preserved
within myself alive in spirit light?

THE OTHER PHILIA

So give me what you are yourself when thinking,
and lose yourself in me a little while,
but do not change into another self.

JOHANNES     How can I give myself to you until
I have beheld you in your truest being?

THE OTHER PHILIA

I am in you; I'm part of your own soul.
I am myself the power of love in you.
The heartfelt hopes that come to life in you,
the fruits of long past lives in earth
preserved for you within your present life,
O see them all through me . . . feel what I am,
and through my power in you behold yourself.
Search out the meaning of that picture, which
your vision, without feeling, formed for you.

(*The Other Philia disappears.*)

JOHANNES     O you mysterious spirit, I can feel
yourself in me, – but you I see no more.
You are alive for me – but where?

(*As if from afar the call of The Other Philia.*)

THE OTHER PHILIA

Enchanted weaving
of your own being.

JOHANNES     The enchanted weaving
of my own being.
O enchanted weaving of my own being,
search out the meaning of that picture, which
my vision, without feeling, formed for me.

– – – – – – – – – – – – – – – –

Whereto does this word's power carry me?
A spirit star on yonder shore of souls –

120

it glows, approaches – as a spirit form, –
comes nearer, growing brighter . . . forms take
    shape; –
Like beings are they, active and alive . . .
a youthful neophyte . . . a sacred flame,
the stern command of highest hierophant
to speak the inner meaning of the flame . . .
— — — — — — — — — — — — — — — —

The youthful neophyte seeks now the woman
whom imagelike my vision, without feeling,
    formed.

(*Maria appears as a thought-form of Johannes.*)

MARIA      Beholding the sacred flame, who thought of you?
Who felt you near the temple's holy rites?
— — — — — — — — — — — — — — — —

My friend, if you would wrench your spirit shade
away from worlds of soul-enchantment now,
give life to aims that shine on you from him!
The sign that you pursue will lead you on,
but you must rightly rediscover it.
The woman near the temple points it out
when she lives powerfully within your thoughts.
She strives, among enchanted shadow spirits,
to draw near to the other shadow-being who,
through you, does evil service to cruel shades.

(*The Spirit of Johannes' Youth appears.*)

THE SPIRIT OF JOHANNES' YOUTH
I will be bound to you and joined forever,
if lovingly you cultivate the powers

121

that youthful neophyte of ages past
kept faithfully for me in time's deep source,
that neophyte your soul sought at the temple.
And you must also see, in very truth,
the spirit at whose side I now appear.

MARIA         Maria, as you have desired to see her,
does not exist in worlds of radiant truth.
My holy, solemn vow rays forth new strength
to hold for you what you have gained.
You'll find me in bright fields of light,
where glowing beauty brings forth powers of life.
Seek me in grounds of worlds where souls
must struggle to achieve their feeling for the gods
through love, which in the All beholds the Self.

(*While Maria is speaking the last lines,
Lucifer appears.*)

LUCIFER      So work, compelling powers,
and feel, you elemental spirits,
the forces of your master;
then pave the way
that from the realms of earth
there can come forth
to Lucifer's domain what
my wish desires,
what shall obey my will.

(*Benedictus appears.*)

BENEDICTUS    Maria's holy, solemn vow creates
within this soul redeeming rays of light.
He will admire you but not succumb to you.

122

LUCIFER        I mean to fight.

BENEDICTUS     And fighting serve the gods.

               *Curtain*

## SCENE ELEVEN

*The same room. Benedictus and Strader enter.*

STRADER        You spoke grave words, Maria also, harsh ones,
when at my life's abyss you showed yourselves.

BENEDICTUS   You know, those pictures are not fully real;
their inner meaning tries to reach the soul
and thus reveals itself in picture form.

STRADER        And yet how harsh was what the picture spoke:
'Where is your light? You radiate fierce darkness –
you pour confusing darkness into light.'
So, in Maria's image, spoke the spirit.

BENEDICTUS   Because you have attained a higher stage
upon the spirit path, that spirit being
who led you to itself aloft, declared
that all that you had reached before was
            darkness.
It chose Maria's image, since your soul
has visualized this spirit in her form.
The spirit, my dear Strader, at this hour
works mightily within you and will lead
you on swift wings to lofty grades of soul.

STRADER        Yet terrifying still resound the words:
               'You are too cowardly to ray out light.'
               This, too, the spirit spoke in that same picture.

BENEDICTUS     The spirit had to call you cowardly,
               for cowardice indeed is for your soul
               what would be bravery in lesser souls.
               As we progress, what formerly was courage
               turns into cowardice that must be conquered.

STRADER        How deeply moving are these words to me!
               Romanus told me recently his plans:
               I was to carry out the work myself,
               apart from you, without your help,
               and then he was prepared to stand by Hilary
               with all his earthly means and influence.
               When I declared I could not separate
               my work from you and from your circle, he
               replied that then all further effort were
               in vain. Romanus backs the opposition
               of Hilary's assistant to my plans.
               Without these plans my life indeed seems
                       worthless.
               Since these two men have torn away from me
               my field of action, I see ahead of me
               a life bereft of air that can sustain it.
               In order that my spirit does not prove
               unwinged and lame, I need that bravery
               of which you spoke just now. If I shall have
               the strength for this, I cannot tell. For I
               can well perceive how much the force that I
               am trying to unchain, at that same time
               will turn with its destructive power on *me*.

BENEDICTUS     Maria and Johannes have recently
progressed in seership: from moving forward
from the life in spirit into the world of sense,
there's nothing holds them back. In course of time
goals will be found to join them both with you. –
Not as a guide but as creative source
of strength, these occult words indeed have value:
'All that will come that has to come about.'
Therefore in wakefulness must we await
the signs by which the spirit points the way.


STRADER     A picture lately formed itself which seemed
to be for me a hint of destiny:
I was aboard a ship; you gave the course;
I, hand on wheel, controlled the rudder's task.
Maria and Johannes we were taking
where they might start their work. Quite near to
    us
appeared another ship; we saw in it
Romanus with the friend of Hilary;
they lay athwart our course as enemies.
I battled with them; then into the fight
came Ahriman, strode forward at their side.
I saw myself in bitter fight with him;
but then my Theodora came to help me.
And now the picture faded from my sight.
I once was bold enough to tell Capesius
and Felix I could bear the opposition
which outwardly is threatening my work, –
yes, even if it breaks my power of will,
I still could hold erect my Selfhood. –
That picture, did it wish to let me know

that outer opposition only means
an inner battle . . . to battle Ahriman?
Am I then armed and strong enough to fight?

BENEDICTUS    My friend, I see within your soul this picture
has not as yet matured for you.
I feel that you can strengthen still the power
which showed the image to your spirit eyes. –
And I can also see, you will create
new forces for yourself and for your friends,
if only you will rightly strive for strength.
This I can sense. How it will come to pass
remains a secret hidden from my sight.

*Curtain*

# SCENE TWELVE

*The interior of the earth. Gigantic crystal formations, with streams like lava breaking through them. The whole scene is faintly luminous, transparent in some parts, and with the light shining through from behind in others. Above are red flames which appear to be pressed downward from the roof.*

AHRIMAN (*at first alone*)
>There falls essential stuff now, from above,
>of which I must make use. Demonic matter
>corrodes away in the domain of form. –
>A man is striving
>to extirpate completely from his being
>the spirit-substance he received from me.
>I have inspired him in the main quite well.
>But he's too close now to that crowd of mystics
>who by the wisdom-light of Benedictus
>could boldly dare effect awakening
>at the cosmic midnight hour. So Lucifer
>has lost them, and Maria and Johannes
>have well escaped from his domain of light.
>Henceforth I must tenaciously hold Strader.
>Once he is mine, I'll catch the others too.
>Johannes stunned and blunted himself badly
>against my shadow; – now he knows me well.
>I cannot get at him except through Strader.
>And in Maria's case it is the same.

Still, Strader may not yet look through the maze
of spirit that appears to men as Nature.
He'll not perceive in it my spirit baggage,
supposing rather that he sees blind weavings
of energy and matter there where I,
denying spirit, spiritually create.
The others, I admit, have talked a lot
to Strader of my being and my realm;
and yet, I don't regard him as quite lost.
He will forget that Benedictus sent him
to me in a half-conscious state, to rid him
of his belief that I am nothing but
a silly spectre of the human brain.
But I'll need earthly help should I abduct him
to my domain before it is too late.
So now I'll call me down a human soul
that thinks itself so clever that to it
I'm nothing but a stupid fraud for fools.
He serves me, now and then, when I can use him.

*(Ahriman goes off and returns with the Soul of
Ferdinand Fox, whose figure is a sort of copy of his
own. Entering, he removes a bandage from the eyes of
the individual who is playing the soul.)*

AHRIMAN His earth-intelligence he'll leave behind him.
He must not understand all that he hears
from me; for he is honest still and would
not do my work for me if he could grasp
the aims with which I plan now to inspire him.
He also must forget them later on.

- - - - - - - - - - - - - - - -

Do you know Doctor Strader, he who serves me?

He roves about upon the earthly star,
trying to bring to life his learned drivel.
Each windy puff of life will knock it down.
He listens greedily to mystic snobs,
and by their fumes already is half choked.
And now he tries befogging Hilary
whose friend, however, keeps him well in check
because that bragging bunch of crooks would soon
destroy the firm with spirit-blubberings.

AHRIMAN
With such a line of talk I am not served.
It's Strader that I need . . . as long as he
can still have perfect faith within himself,
will Benedictus easily succeed
in forcing all his teaching on mankind.
The friend of Hilary might be of service
to Lucifer, but I must otherwise proceed.
Through Strader I must damage Benedictus.
Should he lose Strader, he'll accomplish nothing
with all his other pupils, here and now.
It's true, my enemies are still most potent;
and Strader, after death, will then be theirs.
If I perplex and lead his soul astray
on earth, my gain would be that Benedictus
makes use of him no further as outrider.
Already, in the book of fate, I've read
that Strader's course of life will soon be run.
This Benedictus surely cannot see . . .
My loyal knave, you're almost supercunning,
you take me for a stupid fool's invention.
Men listen to your clever reasoning.
So go at once to Strader and explain,

his mechanism actually is faulty;
not just because of unpropitious times
it's failed, but in itself it's thought out badly.

THE SOUL OF FERDINAND FOX
For that, I think, I'm well prepared. For long
my pondering is aimed at proving clearly
beyond the shadow of a doubt to Strader
that he has gone astray, misled by errors.
If someone racked his brain for many a night
about such stuff, he well can think
the failure does not lie in his own thinking,
but that it's really due to outer causes.
In Strader's case it's truly pitiful.
If he'd stayed out of all that mystic fog
and used his intellect and common sense,
mankind would certainly have profited
immensely from his great potential gifts.

AHRIMAN
See to it now that you are armed with shrewdness.
Your task shall be to undermine the trust
that Strader up to now has in himself;
no longer then will he desire to hold
to Benedictus, who must soon rely
upon himself alone and his own plans.
But these are not so pleasing to the people.
His aims will all the more on earth be hated,
the more their inmost nature is revealed.

THE SOUL OF FERDINAND FOX
I see already how to demonstrate
to Strader where his thinking's error lies.
His new machine embodies a mistake,

but he is unaware of it, because
the mystic darkness keeps him from this fact.
I, with my down-to-earth mentality,
can be of so much better help to him.
I've wanted this already for some time
but did not know how to accomplish it.
Now finally I feel myself *inspired*.
I'll concentrate on all the arguments
which must for sure convince him of the truth.

(*Ahriman leads out the Soul of Ferdinand Fox and
again blindfolds the individual playing the soul, before
he is allowed to depart.*)

AHRIMAN (*alone*)

He will be able to give expert service.
The mystic light on earth is burning me.
I must press onward, but without permitting
the mystics to reveal my work to men.

(*The Soul of Theodora appears.*)

THE SOUL OF THEODORA

However much you force yourself on Strader,
I shall stay at his side, for he has found me
upon bright paths of soul, and is united
with me, wherever he must lead his life,
in spirit land or in the earthly realm.

AHRIMAN

If she, indeed, will not forsake him now,
as long as he is dwelling still on earth,
the battle will be lost for me. But there
is hope that he can finally forget her.

*Curtain*

132

## SCENE THIRTEEN

*A large reception room in the house of Hilary. When the curtain opens, Hilary and Romanus in conversation; later Capesius, Felix Balde, The Secretary, Philia.*

HILARY

It pains me to confess to you, my friend:
the knot of destiny which forms itself
here in our circle nearly crushes me.
What can we build upon with nothing firm?
The friends of Benedictus keep aloof,
through you, from all our aims; and Strader's
    burdened
and torn by bitter agonies of doubt. –
A man who often shrewdly and with . . . hatred
has been opposed to all our occult strivings,
was able to point out to him that he
has been quite wrong about his mechanism
and that it in itself will be unworkable,
not just because of outer hindrances. –
Life has not favored me with any fruits.
I wished for deeds. – Yet thoughts which could
have brought them to fruition never came to me.
Soul emptiness has tortured me most sharply.
Only my spirit vision has upheld me,
and yet – in Strader's case – I was deceived.

ROMANUS

I often felt as if a dreadful nightmare
were pressing painfully upon my soul

when, through the current of events, your words
could gravely show themselves in error,
and thus your spirit vision seem delusion.
The nightmare grew to be my inner guide.
Through it a feeling was released in me
that now can well illuminate my judgment.
You trusted spirit vision much too blindly
and so as error it appears to you
when none the less, it leads you toward the truth.
In Strader's case you were correct, despite
the things that super-clever man thought up.

HILARY

Your faith still does not waver; you hold fast
to the opinion which you had of Strader?

ROMANUS

I came to it for reasons unrelated
to Strader's friends. They are still valid, whether
his mechanism may prove true or faulty.
Supposing he has made mistakes with it, –
well, man through error finds the way to truth.

HILARY

The failure does not disconcert you – you,
whom life has offered nothing but success?

ROMANUS

Success comes if you're not afraid of failure.
We have to understand the occult view
in its true meaning for our special case.
It shows us clearly how to think of Strader.
He certainly will prove victorious
in battles that lay open spirit portals;
undaunted, he will stride to pass the threshold
where stands the Guardian of the spirit land.

I've taken deeply to my heart the word
which this stern Guardian at the threshold spoke.
I sense his presence now at Strader's side.
If Strader *sees* him or unconsciously
comes near him – that, in truth, I cannot fathom.
But I believe to know him well enough.
With courage he will come to the conviction
that self-enlightenment must come through pain. –
The Will becomes companion to the one
who bravely goes to meet what is to come
and, fortified by Hope's strength-giving stream,
will boldly face the pain which knowledge brings.

HILARY      My friend, I thank you for these occult words.
I've heard them often; for the first time now
I feel the secret meaning they contain.
The cosmic ways are hard to penetrate.
And I, dear friend, am called upon to wait
until the spirit shows me the direction
which is in keeping with my spirit sight.

*(Both exeunt right. Capesius and Felix Balde enter
from the left; the Secretary shows them into the
room.)*

SECRETARY    I thought that Benedictus would return
today; however, he is not yet back
from his long journey. If you will try again
tomorrow, you will surely find him here.

FELIX BALDE    Then may we speak with our friend Hilary?

SECRETARY    I'll go and tell him that you're waiting here.

135

*(Exit Secretary).*

FELIX BALDE     Your vision is indeed significant.
Could you repeat to me what you have said?
One can't evaluate these things correctly
unless they're grasped exactly in the spirit.

CAPESIUS     It was this morning: I could feel myself
quite close to a true mystic's solemn mood,
the senses silent, memory silent, too,
expecting only spirit happenings.
At first appeared what I'm familiar with. –
But then the soul of Strader stood, distinct,
before my spirit sight. He did not speak;
it gave me time to measure my alertness.
And soon I heard his words, completely clear:
'Stray not from the true mystic's solemn mood,'
as if from his soul depths the words resounded.
Then he continued, with great emphasis:
'To strive for nothing . . . wait in peaceful stillness,
one's inmost being filled with expectation –:
that is the mystic mood – and of itself
it wakes – unsought amid the stream of life
and when the soul has strengthened itself rightly, –
in spirit search, imbued with powers of thought.
This mood comes often in our quiet hours,
in heat of action, too, but then it wants
the soul not to withdraw in thoughtlessness
from gently viewing spirit happenings.'

FELIX BALDE     This speech sounds almost like an echoing
of my own words – yet not quite what I meant.

CAPESIUS     On close consideration one might find
a meaning in full contrast to your words;

and this interpretation is confirmed
on pondering what he went on to say:
'Whoever wakes with artifice the mystic mood
diverts his Self only into himself.
He weaves indeed before the realm of light
the darkness of his self-indulgence.
Whoever strives for this through mysticism
destroys his spirit sight through mystic fancy.'

FELIX BALDE    This can be nothing else than my own words,
reversed by Strader's spirit views, and then
re-echoing in you as harmful error.

CAPESIUS    Moreover Strader's final words were these:
'A man will never find the spirit world
by wanting to unlock it through his seeking.
Truth does not sound within the soul of him
who through the years has only sought a mood.'

*(Philia appears, perceptible only to Capesius;
Felix Balde shows by his attitude that he does
not comprehend what follows.)*

PHILIA    Capesius, if you will soon pay heed
to what, unsought, in seeking shows itself,
the multi-coloured light will strengthen you
and permeate you with its pictured essence
because the forces of your soul reveal it.
What then your sun-filled self can radiate
will be subdued by Saturn's ripened wisdom,
and to your inner sight will be revealed
what you can comprehend as earthly man.
Then I myself shall lead you to the Guardian
who at the spirit threshold keeps his watch.

| | |
|---|---|
| FELIX BALDE | Out of spheres strange to me are sounding words<br>whose tones do not create enlightening life<br>and so they are not fully real to me. |
| CAPESIUS | The admonition Philia gives to me<br>shall lead me on, so that in coming times<br>may be revealed to me as well in spirit<br>what I as earthly man already find<br>in my life's circle understandable. |

*Curtain*

# SCENE FOURTEEN

*The same room as in Scene Thirteen. At the beginning, the Wife of*
*Hilary in conversation with the Business Manager.*

HILARY'S WIFE   Destiny itself did not desire
          the deed my husband thought imperative.
          It almost seems so, – noticing the threads
          which fate has spun and now entangled here
          into a knot that binds our lives so firmly.

MANAGER       Into a knot of destiny which seems
          insoluble indeed to human sense.
          – – – – – – – – – – – – – – – –
          And so, I take it, it must needs be cut.
          – – – – – – – – – – – – – – – –
          I see no other possibility
          than that a severance be made between
          your husband's work and my own sphere of life.

HILARY'S WIFE   To separate himself from you . . . he never will.
          It contradicts the spirit of the firm,
          that spirit, carried on from his dear father,
          and faithfully continued by his son.

MANAGER       This trust . . . has it not been already broken?
          The aims that Hilary envisions surely

must deviate from those his father's spirit
had always wanted to pursue.

HILARY'S WIFE  My husband's happiness entirely
depends on the success of these new goals.
I saw how he was utterly transformed
since they had sprung to life like lightning flashes
within his mind. His life had brought him only
a dreary, inner emptiness which he
hid carefully from even closest friends,
but which consumed his own life-force the more.
He thought himself a mere nonentity
because there did not germinate in him
ideas worth the bringing into life. –
But when the plan for these activities
was brought to him, he was rejuvenated,
another man, and full of joy. These aims
gave to his life new values, made it worthy.
That you could set yourself against him
did not occur to him . . . until he saw it.
He felt the blow more heavy than any other
that in his life has yet befallen him.
If you could only realize the pain
you caused him, you would surely be less harsh.

MANAGER  To act against my own conviction seems
to me like losing my own dignity. –
To see myself put at the side of Strader
oppresses me; however, I decided
to bear this burden for Romanus' sake.
He spoke to me of Strader, and I know
that what he said to me is a beginning
of my development in spirit striving.

Out of his words was flaming forth a power
that entered actively into my soul.
Such power I had never felt before. –
His counsel carries weight for me, although
I cannot follow yet with understanding. –
Romanus intercedes for Strader only.
The others' share in the activities
appear to him as hindrance to the work,
and also as a danger to themselves.
So much I value what Romanus thinks
that I believe if Strader cannot find
a way to act without his friends, it would
become for him a sign of destiny, –
a sign that he remain now with these friends
and later on, through his own occult striving,
create new impulses for outer deeds.
The fact that recently he's come much closer
than before to all his friends, despite
a slight estrangement from them for a while,
makes me believe that he will find a place
within this state of things, though it involves
a failure, for the present, of his aims.

HILARY'S WIFE   You're seeing Strader only from that viewpoint
which by Romanus was disclosed to you.
You should regard him more impartially.
He can so steep himself in spirit life
that he appears removed from earth-existence.
The spirit is then full reality
to him, and Theodora still alive.
In speaking to him it appears as if
she too were present. Many mystics can
express the spirit message in such words

as bring conviction after careful thought.
What Strader speaks has its effect within
the spoken word itself. One sees how little
he values the inner spirit life that finds
sufficient satisfaction in the feelings.
The urge for spirit research is his guide.
With mysticism he will not obscure
his scientific mind, that proves in life
both practical and useful. – Try to see
this quality in him, and learn through him
how he has formed a judgment of his friends
that should then seem to you of greater weight
than the opinion that Romanus has.

MANAGER        In such a situation, far removed
from what my thinking is accustomed to,
Romanus' judgment seems like solid ground
to stand on. If I should step into those realms
which bring me close to mysticism, I
would need the guidance of a man who's won
my fullest confidence because I've come
to understand his character completely.

(*The Secretary enters.*)

MANAGER        You look upset, my friend, what has occurred?

SECRETARY (*hesitantly.*)
A few hours ago . . . our Doctor Strader died.

MANAGER        Died? . . . Strader?

HILARY'S WIFE  Strader dead! O, where is Hilary?

142

SECRETARY   He's in his room . . .
it seems, quite stricken by the news
just brought to him from Strader's home.

(*Exit The Wife of Hilary; The Secretary
follows.*)

MANAGER (*alone*)
Died . . . Strader . . . is this reality?

— — — — — — — — — — — — — —

Am I affected by the spirit sleep of which
I've heard so much? . . . The power of destiny
that guides the threads of life shows a stern face.
O little soul of mine, what mighty power
has now laid hold upon your thread of fate
and given it a part within this knot?

— — — — — — — — — — — — —

Yes, that will come which has to come about.

— — — — — — — — — — — —

Why is it that these words have never left
my mind since Strader spoke them long ago
to Hilary and to myself? As if
they reached him from another world, they
          sounded . . . spoken
by one transported into spirit regions . . .
What has to come about? . . . I feel,
the spirit world laid hands upon me then.
Within these words . . . there sounds its language
. . . sternly
it sounds . . . How do I learn to comprehend it?

*Curtain*

143

## SCENE FIFTEEN

*The same as in Scene Fourteen. Strader's Nurse sits, waiting. The Secretary enters. Later Benedictus, Ahriman.*

SECRETARY    Soon Benedictus will be here himself
to take the message safely from your hands.
He was away, and has returned just now.
Our Doctor Strader . . . what a man he
      was!
At first I did not have much confidence
in Hilary's ambitious plan of work.
But often in my presence Strader spoke,
describing everything the work required,
then my objections quickly lost their
      force.
Ardent and full of spirit, sensing strongly
the possible and what was purposeful,
he ever strove to reach the final goal
by keeping always clearly in his mind
the facts themselves, while presupposing nothing
in form of idealistic thought. He worked
as any mystic should, – as men must do
who wish to see the beauty of a view
from highest mountain peaks. And yet they wait
till they have reached the heights, and do not try
to form in mind the picture in advance.

| | |
|---|---|
| NURSE | You saw him in the midst of active work: |
| | a man of special gifts, unbending spirit. |
| | And in the weeks I was allowed to give him |
| | last services on earth, I could admire |
| | his loftiness of soul. This gentle soul – |
| | except for seven years of rarest bliss, – |
| | passed through his earthly life in loneliness. |
| | The mystics offered him their wisdom: *he*, |
| | however, needed love, and his desire |
| | for deeds was love, indeed, . . . a love which seeks |
| | to show itself in life in many forms. |
| | And what this soul sought on the mystic path |
| | was needful to his being's noble fire, |
| | as sleep is to the body after toil. |
| | |
| SECRETARY | For him, the spirit wisdom was the source |
| | of what he thought, and everything he did |
| | was always fully charged with its ideals. |
| | |
| NURSE | – – Because it was his nature to give himself |
| | and love unswervingly with all his soul |
| | what life could offer as its sum and substance. |
| | His last thoughts, too, were still about his work, |
| | to which he was devoted with the deepest love. |
| | As men depart from beings whom they love, |
| | the soul of Strader took its leave of all |
| | the earthly work to which his love belonged. |
| | |
| SECRETARY | He lived with all his being in the spirit |
| | and Theodora always stood beside him |
| | as living – all true mystics feel like this. |
| | |
| NURSE | – Because his loneliness joined him to her. |
| | At death she was still with him, and by her |

he felt that he was called to spirit worlds
to finish there his uncompleted task.
Not long before he died, for Benedictus
he wrote the words which now I want to put
into our spirit leader's hands myself.

_ _ _ _ _ _ _ _ _ _ _ _ _ _ _

And so upon the earth this life of ours
must take its course, replete with riddles, – yet
illumined by sun-beings such as he,
from whom the others, just as planets do,
receive the light rays which awaken life.

(*Benedictus enters; exit the Secretary.*)

NURSE  These are the lines that Strader wrote for you
before his strength had ebbed away from him.
I've come to bring them to his spirit friend.

BENEDICTUS  And after he had written down these words,
where did his soul abide, in those last hours?

NURSE  At first the latest of his plans in life
still lived within his thoughts; then Theodora
was joined with him in spirit. Feeling this,
his soul rose gently from his body's sheath.

BENEDICTUS  My faithful friend, I thank you for the love
and service which you gave him still on earth.

(*Exit Nurse.*)

BENEDICTUS (*reading Strader's last words*)
  'My friend, when I felt close to being crushed,
  and knew that opposition to my work

did not arise alone from outward sources,
but that the inner flaws of my own thought
were obstacles to check my plan's success,
I saw again that picture I described
to you not long ago. Its outcome, though,
was not the same. Not Ahriman arose
as my opponent. A spirit messenger
appeared where he had been, whose form I felt
distinctly as my own erroneous thinking.
Then I recalled those words that you had spoken
about the strengthening of my own soul powers.
And thereupon the spirit disappeared.'
There are a few more words . . . I cannot read
    them . . .
a chaos covers them for me and weaves
and works its all-enshrouding veils of thought.

(*Ahriman appears, Benedictus sees him.*
 Who are you, you who come to shadow-life
from out the chaos of my soul-horizon?

AHRIMAN (*aside*)

He sees, but yet he does not recognize me
and so he will not cause me painful terror
when at his side I try to use my power.

(*to Benedictus*)

I can reveal to you what Strader still
wants further to confide for your own good
and also for your pupils' mystic path.

BENEDICTUS    My mystic group will always know itself
to be in touch with Strader's soul, although
the life of sense no longer forms a bridge.

But when a spirit messenger draws near
who manifests himself from his own worlds,
he must gain first of all our confidence.
To do this he must show himself to be
well recognizable to spirit sight.

AHRIMAN     Self-knowledge surely is what you are seeking;
so any stranger spirit-entity
that wants to do you service is compelled
to yield itself as part of your own self,
if you accept its presence so far only
as it is recognizable to you.

BENEDICTUS     Whoever you may be, you only serve
the good, when for yourself you will not strive,
or when you lose yourself in human thinking,
to rise anew in cosmic evolution.

AHRIMAN     It is high time for me to turn away
in haste from his horizon, for when his sight
can think me as in truth I really am,
there will arise and grow within his thinking
part of the power that slowly will destroy me.

(*Ahriman disappears.*)

BENEDICTUS     I recognize now, it is Ahriman
who flees from here, creating in myself
the knowledge of his being in thought form.
His aim is to confuse our human thinking,
for, through an error long since handed down,
he seeks in it the source of all his woe.
As yet he does not know that he will find
redemption in the future, if he only

can find his Self reflected in this thinking.
And so he shows himself to men, but not
as in reality he feels himself.
Himself revealing and concealing, too,
he tries to utilize in Strader's case
in his own way the moment's chance, –
to strike, he thought, through Strader all his
    friends.
He can, from now on, not conceal his nature
from those devoted to my spirit work. –
In wakefulness their thinking shall create him
when he holds sway within their inner sight. – –
His many shapes and forms they will decipher,
with which he'd like to hide when in disguise
he must reveal himself to human souls. – – –
But you, O soul of Strader, sun-imbued,
who through the strengthening of your spirit
    powers
have driven Error's Envoy into flight,
you shall as spirit-star shine on your friends.
Your light shall in the future penetrate
into Maria's and Johannes' lives.
Through you they will be able to prepare
themselves with greater strength for spirit deeds,
and by revealing inner light will prove
endowed with power of thought, at such times,
    too,
when, over full-awakened spirit sight,
the fierce, dark Ahriman, suppressing wisdom,
attempts to spread Chaos' gloomy night.

*Curtain*

CPSIA information can be obtained at www.ICGtesting.com
Printed in the USA
LVOW041848150812

294487LV00003B/19/A